The Guinness Book of
FOOTBALL BLUNDERS

CRIS FREDDI

GUINNESS PUBLISHING

This publication © Guinness Publishing Limited (1996),
338 Euston Road, London NW1 3BD
Reprint 10 9 8 7 6 5 4 3 2

Quotes courtesy of *Private Eye*'s Colemanballs

Text design and layout by Moondisks Ltd, Cambridge

Cover design by Dryden Design.

Cover illustrations courtesy of Allsport UK Ltd.
Clockwise from top: Paul Gascoigne 'books' the referee
(Mark Pain), Graham Taylor & FIFA official *(Chris Cole)*,
Gary McAllister penalty miss in Euro 96 *(Shaun Botterill)*

Printed and bound in Great Britain by The Bath Press, Bath

A catalogue record for this book is available from the British
Library

ISBN 0-85112-625-1

CONTENTS

Introduction & Acknowledgments

Naturally, many of the best football clangers went straight into the original *Guinness Book of Sporting Blunders* – but there were always going to be plenty left over for a separate book. If a well-known error isn't in this one, there's every chance of finding it in the original (shamelessly signposted BLUNDERS VOL.1).

As before, we've generally kept to mistakes that mattered (own goals and penalty misses in internationals, refereeing decisions that decided cup finals, etc) while leaving space for the more harmlessly humorous. Anyone spotting a deliberate mistake should of course blame it on the author and not on the following folk, who were kind enough to help out, some not for the first time.

Private Eye, for permission to dip into their famous Colemanballs postbag.

Andy Lyons and Phil Cornwall at *When Saturday Comes*, still very much the best mag of its kind, for allowing us free access to their remarkable collection of newspaper howlers.

The usual suspects, much appreciated yet again: Brian Mellowship, Steven Lynch, Roger Titford, George 'Poyser' Church, Neil Glenn, Dave Smith, Mervyn Baker, Ron Templeton, Albert Sanders.

Above all, as always, Charles Richards, my editor at Guinness, not only for keeping some linguistic flights of fancy in check but for his encyclopaedic football knowledge, vital in correcting examples of received wisdom. Supports the right football team, too.

About the author

Cris Freddi was the natural choice to write this, his fourth book for Guinness. His knowledge of the game has served him on TV sports quizzes and in his work for national newspapers, football magazines, and *A Question of Sport*. And he's one of that select band who've conceded three penalties and missed another in the same cup tie.

Passing: the buck stops here

It didn't take David Ginola long to become a firm favourite in Newcastle, showing the speed and flair which had been wowing them at Paris St Germain for several years.

Despite all the obvious talent, however, it's possible that the rest of France will remember him as the man who cost them a place in the 1994 World Cup finals.

Needing only a draw at home to Bulgaria to get to the USA, France took the lead through Eric Cantona's sixth goal of the competition, were level at 1–1 in the very last minute, and had possession deep in the left-hand corner of the Bulgarian defence. When the referee awarded them a free-kick, that seemed to be that.

Ginola had been on the pitch for only 22 minutes, brought on in place of Jean-Pierre Papin partly for his ability to hold on to the ball. Now, at the very death, he did the opposite, suddenly hitting a long square ball across the penalty area. Bulgaria took possession, worked it along their right wing, and found Emil Kostadinov, whose second goal of the night won a place in the finals at the expense of France, who haven't reached them since 1986.

It wasn't all Ginola's fault. In their previous

David Ginola contemplates having to leave the country

qualifier, also at home, France had led 2–1 until the last five minutes, then conceded two goals to lowly Israel – and they'd also given away a last-minute equaliser in Sweden. But it was still a costly little aberration, and not altogether out of character...

In 1952 Northern Ireland were leading 1–0 in the last few seconds of the match at Hampden Park when their left-winger Charlie Tully was given the ball out on the left wing. Tully was a controversial character but a tricky, skilful ball player, and he was given the ball now because he was the most likely player in the team to be able to hold it while the seconds ticked by. Instead, unpredictable as ever, he tried to chip it over the head of giant George Young, mishit it badly, and had to watch as Young banged it upfield for Laurie Reilly to head the equaliser that cost the Irish any chance of the Home Championship. They didn't win in Scotland between 1934 and 1971.

Real possession football, this. And Zico's lost it.

JOHN HELM

Five seasons later, the Irish went to Cardiff needing to win to take the title outright for the first time since before the First World War. Again they led 1–0 with time running out, again a skilful player had the ball out on the wing, again he should have held on to it...

Jimmy McIlroy was actually up against the Welsh corner flag. Had he been playing for his club, he said, he'd have tried to keep possession, 'but this was an international occasion, hardly the ideal setting for time-wasting.' He crossed the ball, Wales moved it upfield, Ron Hewitt scored.

'Even now I blame myself for the failure to win that Home Championship.'

It's part of Goodison Park folklore that all the success of the mid 1980s – two League titles, an FA Cup, a Cup-Winners Cup – started with a bad back-pass.

Everton were 1–0 down ten minutes from the end of a League Cup fourth round match at the Manor Ground when Oxford United's talented midfielder Kevin Brock, under pressure from Peter Reid, hit a loose back-pass which was intercepted by Adrian Heath for the equaliser. If Everton had lost, it would surely have meant the end of Howard Kendall as manager: they were 18th in the First Division at the time.

Instead, Brock threw him this lifeline, he stayed, Everton won the replay 4–1 and didn't look back, reaching the final, where they lost unluckily to Liverpool (see BRITISH REFEREES), which in turn gave them the confidence to win the FA Cup later in the season, the springboard to all the rest.

Stanley Matthews had the 1953 FA Cup final named after him because a) he was 38 and the whole country wanted him to win the thing at last, and b) his pass made the winning goal. Mind you, he owed Blackpool one.

Five minutes into the second half of the 1951 final they were level with Newcastle when the great one beat Bobby Corbett five minutes after half-time and tried to find Stan Mortensen, but admits to hitting his pass too hard. It was intercepted by Jorge Robledo, who put Jackie Milburn in for his first goal of the game. Blackpool, who'd also lost the 1948 final, went down 2–0.

Halfway through the first half of an FA Cup match in 1939, there was no score between Second Division rivals Manchester City and Norwich City when a throw-in reached Norwich right-winger Jack Friar on the halfway line. Instead of looking to pass short or hit a long ball forward, he suddenly and unaccountably turned round and banged the ball towards his own goal fifty yards away – straight into the path of Man City centre-forward Jack Milsom, who rolled it in at his leisure. A demoralised Norwich conceded another soon afterwards and lost 5–0.

Len Shackleton was the great entertainer of the 1940s and '50s, a regular Clown Prince with all the ball skills. That he won only five England caps (despite scoring a skilful goal in his last match) is still the subject of discussion. From 1948 till injury ended his career in 1957, he played in a Sunderland team which was expensively assembled (the £20,000 fee for Shack was a British record) but didn't win a major trophy – and didn't get past the fourth round of the FA Cup in 1949, even though they were drawn against a non-League club.

When people read who their opponents were, it doesn't sound quite so surprising. Yeovil Town have struck apprehension into the hearts of League opposition before and since – and were at home in this match. But they were sixth from bottom of the Southern League, and Sunderland brought three England internationals with them: Shackleton, Jackie Robinson, Willie Watson. Surely…

As it happened, if the game had been played in later years, it would have been drawn 1–1 and replayed at Roker Park. But, so soon after the war, extra time was played to limit the amount of travelling and save money on petrol, an arrangement that Sunderland fell victims to at the end of the first half of extra time.

A loose ball went over Shackleton's head near halfway, leaving him facing his own goal. The sensible course in this situation would have been a simple lay-off to the nearest team-mate. But this was the Shack, and he didn't do things that way. Perhaps some playing to the reputation was involved. Or maybe he simply believed an overhead kick was the best option. Whatever, he tried it, caught the ball with his toe, and sent it

straight to the Yeovil inside-left Wright, whose cross was turned in by Eric Bryant for the winner.

Yeovil lost 8–0 at Manchester United in the next round and Sunderland had to wait till 1973 to reach the final again.

> *The Spaniards have been reduced to aiming aimless balls into the box.*
>
> **RON ATKINSON**

A similar thing happened in a bigger match some years later. Real Madrid, in their seventh European Cup final (1964), fell 2–0 behind to Inter, in their first, but pulled a goal back and were pressing for the equaliser when Luis Suárez, the Spaniard playing for Inter, chipped a long but inaccurate pass towards Sandro Mazzola, who chased it willingly but without much expectation, given that it was covered by José Santamaría, once one of the great central defenders.

Not this time, though. Facing his own goal, with Mazzola close behind him, Santamaría's best option was a pass back to his goalkeeper. Instead, like Shackleton, he went for an overhead kick, hit Mazzola with it, and couldn't recover in time to stop the striker from running on and shooting in off the far post. It was Mazzola's second goal in Inter's 3–1 win.

Back in 1938, much the same thing. Against Scotland at Wembley, England left-back and captain Eddie Hapgood tried an overhead kick 'that went the wrong way', sending it to Jackie Milne, who found Frank O'Donnell, who in turn put Tommy Walker clear for the only goal of the game. England didn't beat Scotland at Wembley again till 1955.

After twelve minutes of the 1922 Scottish Cup final, Billy McCandless, one of Rangers' two Irish full-backs, was too short with a back pass, forcing keeper Willie Robb to pick the ball up outside the area. From the free kick, Morton half-back Jimmy Gourlay scored the only goal of the game. It was Morton's first ever win in a cup tie against Rangers, who'd also lost the previous year's final by the same score. Neither McCandless nor Robb ever picked up a winners' medal.

After Nottingham Forest and Bury had drawn in the 1900 FA Cup semi-final, Forest took a 2–0 lead in the replay, only for Bury to pull a goal back – then save the match thanks to one of the monumental back-pass howlers of all time, by Forest centre-forward Beveridge. From almost on the halfway line, he banged it back towards his own goal, but so far wide of his keeper that it went out for a corner, from which Jimmy McLuckie headed the equaliser. Bury's 3–2 win put them in the final, where they won the Cup for the first time. Forest didn't reach the final again till 1959.

England's final group match in the 1988 European Championship finals was largely academic – they were already almost certainly eliminated – so there was only pride at stake, and not much of that left after a terrible performance in a 3–1 defeat, which was started as early as the third minute when Glenn Hoddle tried either to nutmeg Sergei Aleinikov or pass round him. Aleinikov intercepted the ball and ran on to score. Hoddle never played for England again.

When Norway won the women's World Cup in 1995, they were relieved as well as triumphant, none more so than defender Tina Svenssen. Four years earlier, in the final of the first ever women's World Cup, Norway were level with the USA until 13 minutes from time, predictably unlucky for someone, in this case Svenssen, who tried to pass back to goalkeeper Reidun Seth, only to mishit it into the path of Michelle Akers-Stahl, who went round the keeper to score her second goal of the game. Norway – and Svenssen – were glad to beat the USA on the way to that win in 1995.

A home win against Germany at the end of 1990–91 put Wales on top of their European Championship qualifying group, leaving them needing only a draw in the return in Nuremberg to virtually guarantee a place in the finals.

They held out for 34 minutes, and even at 1–0 down there was still a chance – which was wiped out within ten minutes by two more German goals. The first, the killer, was the result of a back pass by stand-in right-back Gavin Maguire, who set up Rüdi Völler for a stooping header past Neville Southall. Wales lost 4–1 and failed to qualify.

Werder Bremen and Monaco have reached one European final each, and they did it together, contesting the 1992 Cup-Winners Cup decider, which was sealed by a mistake ten minutes after half-time, Monaco defender Emmanuel Petit giving the ball away while under no pressure on the halfway line. The rest of the defence, up in support, couldn't get back in time to stop Wynton Rufer scoring Bremen's second goal.

Penalties of fame

When Scotland reached the European Championship finals for the first time (1992), they owed it in the end, and paradoxically, to the brilliant Gheorghe Hagi. After the Scots failed to score enough goals against San Marino at home, they left Romania needing to win at home against Bulgaria, and score at least twice, to pip them for the one qualifying place.

They took the lead after half an hour, but Adrian Popescu's goal should have been the clincher: earlier, Hagi had hit a penalty straight at Borislav Mihailov. If he'd scored, Romania would have won 2–1 and reached the finals. Instead, the eventual 1–1 draw sent Scotland through.

Irony here, because when the Scots were sailing through the group they were pulled up by a 1–0 defeat in Romania, whose goal was scored by Hagi – from the penalty spot.

Those who believe England has one domestic cup too many can use the 1985 League Cup final as ammunition, a throwback to the early days when the leading sides didn't enter and the Rochdales and Rotherhams reached the final. In this case, for the only time, two of the top division's relegated teams, Norwich and Sunderland, contested the final.

The match, which had no trouble living down to its billing, turned on two incidents. First, Asa Hartford's low shot from the left hit Gordon Chisholm and went in at the near post. Then, only a minute later, Dennis Van Wijk handled in the area and Clive Walker, a flashy winger who'd scored against his old club in the semi-final at Stamford Bridge, hit the base of a post, the first penalty miss in a major Wembley final. Norwich, having lost two League Cup deciders by a single goal, won by the same margin. Sunderland have never won the trophy.

In the 1929 Scottish Cup final, holders Rangers were awarded a penalty in the first half. The previous year, their first goal in a 4–0 win (the first time they'd won the Cup since 1903) had been scored from the penalty spot by Davie Meiklejohn. This time he left the kick to Tom 'Tully' Craig.

He shot too close to goalkeeper Sam Clemie and Kilmarnock went on to win the Cup for the last time. If Rangers had won, they'd have taken the Cup three years in a row (1928–30). Craig's miss, as far as records show, was the first in any Scottish Cup final. Of the first six misses in a final, five were by Rangers players. Only Craig's affected the result.

After a disastrous first appearance in the World Cup finals (they lost 7–0 to Uruguay in 1954), Scotland didn't make much more of an impression four years later, a draw with Yugoslavia and defeat by Paraguay leaving them needing to beat France (Kopa, Fontaine and all) to reach the quarter-finals. They lost 2–1 but only after John Hewie, the tall South African full-back, had hit a post from the penalty spot. Scotland have never qualified for the second stage of any World Cup finals.

For all the brilliance of the Dutch, West Germany were the most successful national team of the 1970s, beating Holland in the 1974 World Cup final, reaching three European Championship finals in a row. But by 1976 they were on the wane (no Netzer, Overath, Breitner, Grabowski or Gerd Müller) and probably not favourites to win the final. Czechoslovakia, who'd reached it by beating more difficult teams – England (yes they were), the USSR, Holland – led 2–0 in the first half.

However, West Germans have dined out on their history of footballing recoveries: against Hungary in 1954, England 1966, Holland 1974, Argentina 1986. They added to that roll here, Bernd Hölzenbein heading in a last-minute corner to force extra-time, which came and went without incident. Penalties would decide a major international championship for the first time.

The first seven went in (Masny, Nehoda, Ondrus & Jurkemik for Czechoslovakia, matched by Bonhof, Flohe & Bongartz). Uli Hoeness took West Germany's fourth.

Not usually mentioned in the same breath as Beckenbauer and Müller, Hoeness was nevertheless one of the most important players in the successful Bayern and West German teams, a dynamic blond runner from midfield who scored twice in the 1974 European Cup final and in 1972 against England at Wembley.

As a penalty taker he was less successful, missing one in the 1974 World Cup. He says he didn't fancy taking one in this final against Czechoslovakia but was persuaded by Beckenbauer. His own view of the kick: 'I decided to give him a heavy shot, to try to put it in one corner. The ball was over the wall and I think they found him now a year ago. They had a war and the stadium was destroyed and they found the ball.'

He shot over the bar, you understand. Antonin Panenka, producing a strange little chip, won the Championship for Czechoslovakia with the last penalty, and Hoeness didn't play for West Germany again.

A number of players who missed penalties in important shoot-outs were featured in BLUNDERS VOL.1 (Pearce, Waddle, Brady, Rix, etc). A full list would be too long to be reproduced here – but some deserve a special mention.

Chris Waddle's post-penalty photo was used, with our apologies, for the front cover of BLUNDERS VOL.1. After that miss in the 1990 World Cup, he didn't take another spot kick until an FA Cup fourth round replay in 1994–95. He surprised few people by missing it, and Sheffield Wednesday lost the shoot-out to Wolves.

A number of European club finals have been decided by shoot-outs, but only the Barcelona team of 1986 missed every kick they took, four in all (their opponents Steaua missed two; all six were saved), taken by Marcos (Alonso), captain José Ramón Alexanko,, and two fallen Angels, Pedraza and 'Pichi' Alonso. Surprising, that – because they'd won their semi-final on penalties.

In 1978 Poland played their first World Cup second round group match against the hosts Argentina, who'd had their share of luck in scraping through: two Hungarians sent off, a penalty wrongly awarded against France, defeat by Italy. Poland, no longer the dashing team that finished third in 1974, had been just as unimpressive.

Still, they had a great chance of equalising against Argentina. Their captain Kaziu Deyna took a free kick, a scramble followed, and Mario Kempes (whose goal was dividing the teams) made another major contribution by handling on the line. Deyna, whose lame spot kick was easily saved by Ubaldo Fillol, was the only player to miss a penalty in his 100th international. He wasn't capped again after the tournament, which Argentina went on to win.

When Michel Platini appeared at the far post five minutes from half-time, it was the first goal Brazil had conceded in the 1986 World Cup finals, and this (the quarter-final) was their fifth match. With a stern midfield, Julio César and Edinho superb in central defence and Careca scoring up front, things looked set fair, especially when the latter's fifth goal of the tournament put them ahead against France.

Then Platini equalised with his last goal for France and it was anyone's game, though Brazil had chances to win it, first when Careca hit the bar, then when Branco was brought down by goalkeeper Joël Bats: penalty.

Zico, touted as one of the white Pelés since the mid '70s, had been on the field for less than two minutes. Back in the 1978 finals he'd come on as substitute against Peru, insisted on taking a penalty within two minutes, and scored, to his inordinate joy. Now, in an eerily exact repetition, he took the kick that would probably send Brazil into the semi-finals.

He hit it too close to Bats, France went on to win the penalty shoot-out, and Zico didn't play for Brazil again.

The battle for the 1985–86 Bundesliga title went to the wire. With two matches left, Werder Bremen led the table by two points but had to play their nearest challengers Bayern Munich in the penultimate round. A win for Werder would give them the title, a draw would leave them two points clear (but with an inferior goal difference) with one match to play.

There was no score with only two minutes left when they were awarded a penalty, which was taken by their central defender Michael Kutzop, who'd already converted seven spot kicks that season. This time he hit the post. Bayern escaped with a draw

then won their last match 6–0, while Werder lost theirs 2–1 and missed the title on goal difference.

At one stage of the 1993–94 season, Deportivo La Coruña led the Spanish first division by seven points, but went into their last two games needing maximum points to win the title. A sturdy 2–0 away win over Logroñes set them up for the decider at home to Valencia.

On this final day, while nearest challengers Barcelona were recovering from 1–2 down to beat Sevilla 5–2, La Coruña were being held goalless in their Riazor stadium. Then, inside the last two minutes, they were awarded a penalty.

The regular taker, Donato Gama da Silva, had been substituted, which left the responsibility to the Serbian sweeper Miroslav Djukic, one of the stars of their season. In front of 30,000 success-starved fans, his weak shot was easily saved by José Luis González, he fell on his knees in despair, for the third season in a row Barcelona won the title thanks to a blunder by their closest rivals, and Deportivo La Coruña have never won the Spanish league.

The previous year, they'd finished third after topping the table for much of the season. In the game that turned the tide, away to Real Madrid, they lost 2–1 after leading 1–0 at half-time – and missing a penalty!

In 1912 Manchester City missed three penalties in the same League match (Eli Fletcher two, Irvine Thornley one) which cost them a win against Newcastle, who drew 1–1.

Coincidentally and far worse, City went into the last match of the 1925–26 season needing a draw at Newcastle to stay in the First Division, and were leading 2–1 when their England winger Billy Austin missed a penalty that would have kept them up. They lost 3–2 and were relegated by a single point.

It really wasn't their year. They were the highest scoring club ever to go down (89 goals) and they lost 1–0 in the FA Cup final.

In the first leg of the 1994–95 First Division play-offs, Stuart Lovell scored twice in Reading's 3–1 win at Tranmere, effectively ensuring a place in the play-off final against Bolton.

But at Wembley he missed the penalty that would have put Reading 3–0 ahead and almost certainly into the top division for the first time in their history. Later in the same match, he missed an easy chance, then lost the ball to let Bolton in for the equaliser with only seven minutes left. Reading lost 4–3 in extra-time.

Forgiveness is divine, and sometimes Redingensian. Lovell was given a two-year contract, and the Elm Park fans called for him to take the next penalty at home the following season. He scored.

After each team had won the home leg of the 1974 Libertadores Cup (South American equivalent of the European Cup), São Paulo of Brazil fought out a tense play-off with Independiente of Argentina, a match decided by two penalties, one scored by Independiente's Uruguayan defender Ricardo Pavoni, the other (which would have brought the equaliser) taken by Zé Carlos and saved by Carlos Alfredo Gay. São Paulo had to wait eighteen years to win the Cup for the first time.

Welsh fans look back on the relative golden years of 1974–76, when the national team reached the European Championship quarter-finals and came close to doing even better. But at Ninian Park, Josip Katalinski scored from a penalty, Terry Yorath missed another, and the 1–1 draw sent Yugoslavia through to the last four.

Ajax won the European Cup three times in a row (1971–73) and might have challenged Bayern Munich in 1974 if they'd survived a tough opening tie against CSKA Sofia. In the first leg, the Dutch unveiled their new striker, the sharp and dangerous Jan Mulder, who'd scored twice and hit a post for Anderlecht in the 1970 Fairs Cup final

Stuart Lovell spares Reading a season of propping up the Premier League

against Arsenal. He scored another here – but also missed a penalty, and the 1–0 win wasn't quite enough. Ajax lost the return 2–0 after extra time.

Despite losing the first leg of the 1973 European Cup semi-final 3–1 in Turin, Derby County had every chance of winning the tie at home, especially when 17-year-old Steve Powell put Alan Hinton clear in the second half. The winger ran into the penalty area, was brought down, and got up to take the kick himself. Normally a fierce and reliable penalty expert, he shot wide, the 0–0 draw sent Juventus through to the final, and Derby never went so far in Europe again.

The machinations of Italian clubs in European competition have been the subject of much speculation, to say the least. Ask Liverpool (1965), Derby & Leeds (1973) among others. A big subject, which has filled a book of its own.

Space here for a couple of examples. When Juventus reached the 1965 Fairs Cup final, they managed to have it played over a single leg – and have it held in their own stadium! They lost 1–0 to Ferencváros.

In 1973, after they'd lost in the European Cup final and Ajax refused to play in the World Club Cup, Juve were up to the same tricks, persuading Independiente to play just a single match for the title – in Rome.

Again Juventus lost 1–0, but only after Antonello Cuccureddu, their nuggety defensive midfielder, had missed a penalty when the score was 0–0. A second helping of just desserts.

Although a bad knee injury prevented Len Thompson from staking a regular place in the strong Arsenal team of the late 1920s, he did become the club's leading penalty taker. Indeed, before a game against Sheffield United, Highbury was festooned with placards announcing 'How I take penalty kicks, by Len Thompson', and action pictures of his technique.

No prizes for guessing. Midway through the first half, Arsenal were awarded a penalty, the photographers lined up behind the United goal, and Thompson's kick nearly hit the corner flag.

Jupp Heynckes scored a record five goals in UEFA Cup finals, including the last hat-trick in any European final (1975). Two years earlier, in the decider against Liverpool, he scored both goals in the 2–0 win in the second leg – but if he'd converted a penalty in the first leg at Anfield, Moenchengladbach would have won on away goals. As it was, they lost 3–2 on aggregate.

Hard to think of Tommy Hutchison's long legs as the most natural tools for taking penalties, and so it proved in the European Championship match against Spain at Hampden in 1974.

Scotland were leading 1–0 when the big Spanish stopper Migueli handled in the area. Encouraged by Hutchison's missed kick, Spain won 2–1, and Scotland didn't qualify for the finals until 1992.

The penalty missed by John Mackin against Charlton Athletic in September 1972 didn't affect promotion or relegation at the end of the season, but it cost York City the match – and set up a neat little coincidence.

The kick was awarded for handball by Charlton's Vince O'Kane. Later in the game, O'Kane scored the only goal of the match, from a penalty given for handball – by Mackin!

In 1959, after winning the first three European Cups, Real Madrid faced a stiff challenge in the semi-final from the club on their own doorstep, Atlético Madrid, who were only 2–1 down in the away leg when they were awarded a penalty, which was taken by Eduardo Isidio Netto, better known as Vavá, who'd scored twice for Brazil in the World Cup final the previous year. He missed it (Ferenc Puskás had scored with one for Real), Atlético were beaten in a play-off and didn't reach the final till 1974.

In their very first European Cup match, in Belgium in 1956, Manchester United conceded an early penalty taken by the Anderlecht captain, the classy striker Jef Mermans. He hit the post and was beaten to the rebound by Bill Foulkes, who cleared downfield for Dennis Viollet to score. United won this first leg 2–0 – and the second 10–0!

One purely for the statisticians, this. Well, alright, two. They're important people.

Before the match against Wales in 1902, England had scored in each of 52 consecutive internationals going back to 1884. Ernest Needham (see DEFENDANT DEFENDERS) missed a penalty and the game was drawn 0–0, whereupon England scored in their next 32 matches – but for the Nudger's miss, this would have added up to a remarkable 85 in a row. As it was, that 52 was the world record before Hungary overhauled it in 1955. It was Needham's last penalty kick for England. He was the first to take three, and miss with two, in international football.

When Carmel Busuttil had his penalty pushed onto the post in an international match in 1995, the earth didn't move.

Clashes between Malta and Luxembourg don't register on the Richter scale. Still, it mattered to both of them, and not just because European Championship points were at stake.

To the Maltese, it meant that Busuttil didn't add to his national record of 20 goals in internationals (14 ahead of the next on the list!). To the good burghers of Lux, Paul Koch's save, made in the last minute too, showed an appropriate sense of occasion. It preserved a 1–0 win, which ended a run of exactly 80 internationals without a win, far and away the world record. It was Luxembourg's first victory against anyone since 1980, their first against a European side since 1973, and their first away from home since 1963!

After that, like waiting for a bus, two more victories came along in brisk succession, against Malta again and the Czech Republic, no less. Follow San Marino's progress to see if the record's ever broken.

Roger Byrne was unlucky that the goalkeepers who faced the two penalties he took for England were among the best in the world: Gylmar dos Santos of Brazil and Vladimir Beara of Yugoslavia. Both saved his kicks, which didn't affect the results (England won 4–2 and 3–0) but made Byrne the only player to never score for England despite taking two penalties.

Against Belgium in 1982, Kenny Dalglish had one of his few commanding games for Scotland, scoring two goals in Brussels: one breathtaking, the other merely marvellous. They put the Scots 2–1 up and seemed to have given them two European Championship points. Then, in the 78th minute, after Belgium had recovered to take the lead, Scotland were awarded a penalty for a trip by Jan Ceulemans on Graeme Souness.

John Robertson, who took these kicks for Scotland and Nottingham Forest, was on the

The captain loses out to the able Seaman: Gary McAllister's penalty miss in Euro 96

substitutes' bench, leaving the responsibility to left-back Frank Gray, whose confidence probably wasn't helped by the ball rolling off the spot. Jean-Marie Pfaff saved his shot, the 3–2 scoreline stood, and Scotland yet again didn't reach the finals.

Towards the end of the 1992–93 season, Crystal Palace were awarded a penalty in the last minute of their vital Premier League relegation match at Ipswich. The young player who stepped up had never taken one before at this level. He put it against the post, the match was drawn 2–2, and Ipswich survived while Palace were relegated on goal difference. The young player didn't take another penalty until the semi-final of Euro 96.

Widespread sympathy for Gareth Southgate – but his mother did say, after his second kick had been saved by Andreas Köpke, 'Why didn't you just belt it?'

Two penalties were missed in the course of actual play in Euro 96. The first, by Scotland's captain Gary McAllister (the ball rolling off the spot again!), was the turning point of the match against England, who scored their second goal a minute later. The other, Gianfranco Zola's weak attempt against Germany, cost Italy not only a place in the quarter-finals, but (in view of how far the Czech Republic went) even greater things.

Four years earlier, McAllister had scored for Scotland in their only win of the 1992 finals – from the penalty spot.

How fitting that the 1994 World Cup finals should end with a missed penalty; they'd also started with one.

At the opening ceremony in Chicago, a ball was placed for a spot kick only a few yards from goal. Unmissable? Not for singer Diana Ross, whose links with football were proved to be as tenuous as we thought when she hooked the ball wide to the left. After that, the only way for the tournament was up.

The following year, Ross opened another World Cup, this time the rugby league version at Wembley. She wasn't asked to take a kick at goal.

Needing to win their last qualifying match, in Vienna, to reach the 1990 World Cup finals, East Germany saw their best chance disappear when Rico Steinmann missed a penalty – this after Austria had scored their second goal from the spot. It was East Germany's last competitive match as a separate nation.

A number of FA Amateur Cup finals were decided by penalty misses. Alan Bermingham's for Skelmersdale in 1967, for instance, and Kenny Kent's for Chesham in 1968 [BLUNDERS VOL.1].

Back in 1915, centre-forward Hopper missed an early spot kick for the holders Bishop Auckland, just before Clapton scored the only goal of the game.

In 1922, Bishop Auckland again, and again as holders – but this time the boot was on the other foot, their goalkeeper Potts saving a penalty by South Bank right-back Thompson which would have given the outsiders a 3–2 lead. The Bishops won 5–2 after extra time.

In 1929, a penalty miss by Leyton centre-half Wright halted their recovery against Ilford, who won 3–1.

Oh, and a player called Steward missed the penalty which would have equalised for Crook Town in the 1958 semi-final – after

Ilford's Whittall had scored the only goal of the game from the spot.

In the Home Championship match against England at Goodison Park in 1935, Northern Ireland went a goal down in the first half, equalised in the second, then had a golden chance to go ahead only a few minutes later when they were awarded a penalty for handball by the England captain Eddie Hapgood. But Jackie Coulter's kick hit the bar, the Irish lost 2–1, and didn't beat England in England between 1914 and 1957.

And some that made little difference

In 1908, in the first match for either country, Sweden conceded a goal to Norway after only 45 seconds – then, with the score still 1–0, became the first team to miss two penalties in a single international, through Karl Gustafsson (saved by Sverre Lie) and Erik Börjesson (shot wide). Gustafsson went on to score twice, Börjesson four times, as Sweden won 11–3!

Gary Bailey saved three spot kicks for Manchester United at Ipswich in March 1980, from Kevin Beattie (twice taken) and Frans Thijssen. United still lost 6–0!

Jimmy Crabtree took (and missed) England's first ever penalty, against Ireland in 1899. It didn't exactly affect the result (England won 13–2) but if he'd converted it they would have scored more goals than in any game before or since – and it made a difference to Crabtree's international goalscoring record. If he'd put away the penalty, he'd have had one!

Chances are a fine thing...

Andy Cole practises some straight shooting at West Ham in 1995

The chances Andy Cole missed in the last game of the 1994–95 League season weren't exactly glaring, but one in particular, from the corner of the six-yard box with only the keeper to beat, looked the kind of thing he'd been putting away all season. Ludek Miklosko made a good save, one of several in that match, but even so...

If Cole had scored even once, he'd have gone a long way to paying off that British record transfer fee of £7 million – and made Manchester United only the fourth club to win the title three years in a row.

In the last match of the following season, Cole seemed to have reversed things in dramatic fashion, scoring in the win that sealed the title – but it was purely cosmetic by then. He'd missed countless chances all season, and was substituted in the FA Cup final. It's not too harsh to say that United won the Double despite him.

That's the kind he normally knocks in in his sleep with his eyes closed.

ARCHIE McPHERSON

After taking a fourth-minute lead against Sweden in their deciding group match at the 1992 European Championship finals, England had chances to make the game safe in the first half, two in particular falling to right-winger Tony Daley, controversially preferred to Chris Waddle by Graham Taylor. Daley missed them both and hasn't been capped again, England lost 2–1 and were eliminated.

One of the most glaring misses in any match was committed in the European Championship qualifier at Hampden Park in 1968. England, needing a draw to reach the quarter-finals, took the lead through Martin Peters. Scotland, needing to win, equalised through the big Celtic striker John 'Yogi' Hughes, who won't remember the game for that header.

When Charlie Cooke swung over a corner, Gordon Banks palmed it onto the bar, from where it dropped right in front of Hughes. A photograph shows him standing no more than four feet from the line, with the ball coming down, Banks still getting up, and Peters, Moore and Newton unable to do anything but watch.

That same year, Hughes' club captain Billy McNeill wrote that 'John has on many occasions aroused the fans' wrath by working himself into a scoring position, then making a poor job of his finishing effort. Changed days now.'

From little more than a yard, Hughes put the rebound wide and England escaped with the draw. He didn't score for Scotland again, and they didn't qualify from a European group till 1992.

When Arsenal signed Peter Marinello in 1970, it looked a genuine attempt to polish up their rather dull image (*plus ça change*, eh?). A slim, baby-faced, orthodox Scottish winger of Italian extraction, he came with a reputation for outstanding dribbling skills and great potential.

For whatever reason – inexperience (he was only 19), physical fragility, London nightlife – he didn't make it, playing only 32 League matches in three years while Arsenal were winning the Double. He did have one golden opportunity, but it's worth remembering that he scored only five times in those 32 games...

Having lost only 2–1 in the first leg of the 1972 European Cup quarter-final, Arsenal needed only a 1–0 win at Highbury to knock out the holders, Cruyff's brilliant Ajax. Almost immediately, their excellent German sweeper Horst Blankenburg failed to control a throw-out from keeper Heinz Stuy, letting Marinello in through the inside-right channel with only the latter to beat.

This was probably the last thing he wanted in the first minute of his first senior game in six months. He shot against Stuy's right leg and was transferred to Portsmouth the following year. Ajax went on to retain the Cup, which Arsenal didn't compete in for another twenty years.

If it's any consolation to Marinello, more famous strikers have missed their share. In European Cups too – and from closer range.

After winning 5–1 away to Benfica, Manchester United were heavy favourites to beat unfashionable Partizan Belgrade in the 1966 semi-final, and would surely have done so if Denis Law, of all people, he who scored 217 League goals in England, as well as 28 in European club competitions, including five hat-tricks, plus a record 30 for Scotland – if *the* Denis Law hadn't missed from close in with the score still 0–0.

'Close in' doesn't do it justice. Law himself remembered it being about two yards out, after George Best had pulled the ball back from the goal line, and called it 'that dreadful miss'. He missed with his foot, connected with his thigh, and hit the bar. Partizan scored soon afterwards, won 2–0, and held on at Old Trafford to reach the final. By the time United got there two years later, Law was out with an injury.

Against Leeds in the 1970 FA Cup semi-final replay enlivened by Best and partner [see PREPARING FOR TROUBLE], Law headed wide in front of an open goal. United drew 0–0 and lost the second replay.

The great Denis also missed an easy chance in the 1965 Fairs Cup semi-final – which could have been included in the goalkeeping or refereeing sections but finds its way into this one by the sheer number of chances missed.

United were leading Ferencváros 3–1 at home in the first leg when centre-half Bill Foulkes remembered a long ball into the area being 'hopelessly misjudged' by goalkeeper Pat Dunne, who 'drops the odd centre in practically every game' and let it 'bounce gently into our goal'. Then the Hungarians won the second leg 1–0 from a penalty awarded when a fierce shot hit Nobby Stiles on the shoulder.

The missed chances came in the play-off, also in Budapest, the first after only five minutes, 'a complete sitter' by Law, who was robbed when he hesitated. Bobby Charlton shot over the bar 'in front of an open goal', David Herd missed another in the dying minutes – and Best crowned everything at the end of a wonderful, typical dribble. Estimates vary as to how many players he beat (one says six!) but whatever the number he tried to go past one too many – and fell over goalkeeper István Geczi!

Sándor Mátrai cleared and Ferencváros won 2–1 to reach the final and become the only Hungarian club to win a European trophy. It's the one European competition United have never won.

Karl Zischek was one of the stars of the Austrian *Wunderteam* of the early 1930s, a fast, skinny young winger who scored twice against England at Stamford Bridge in 1932. Equally effective in the 1934 World Cup, he scored the winner in the quarter-final against Hungary to set up a semi against Italy in Milan.

Austria had won 4–2 in Turin earlier that year – but now, against a rugged defence, on a heavy pitch, they didn't manage a shot at goal till the 42nd minute. Only seconds from the final whistle, they were 1–0 down when goalkeeper Peter Platzer's punt upfield was picked up by Zischek, who outpaced the defence, had virtually the whole goal to shoot at (it was an era when goalkeepers didn't come off their line), and shot wide.

It was the closest Austria have ever come to the World Cup final. Italy went on to win the tournament for the first time.

The scoreboard in Vienna after the match with the Republic of Ireland in 1952 didn't tell the whole story. In the first attack of the match, Arthur Fitzsimons shot wide when unmarked from close range. Within minutes, he laid on an open goal for Tommy Eglington, who missed the ball completely. Then Eglington went round the keeper and set up Reg Ryan: another opportunity gone.

While the Republic were dominating entire periods of play and missing chances, Adolf Huber was scoring a hat-trick in four minutes: Austria won 6–0, Ireland's record defeat until 1982!

> *Charlie Redmond's penalty miss will cause him nightmares for many sleepless nights.*
>
> **MICK DUNNE**

The fourth round of the 1974–75 FA Cup was enlivened by the pre-match comments of Leatherhead's centre-forward Chris 'The Lip' Kelly, who forecast all kinds of derring-do against First Division Leicester City, even though the non-Leaguers had opted for a larger gate by switching the game to Filbert Street after being drawn at home.

In the event, he was as good as his word, or very nearly, his sharp back-header putting Leatherhead 2–0 ahead at half-time. Only a few minutes after the interval, Leicester midfielder Graham Cross stumbled to give Kelly a clear run on goal. The Lip went round goalkeeper Mark Wallington – then The Brain got in the way, delaying the obvious shot into the open goal so long that Malcolm Munro had time to come across and clear. Leatherhead lost 3–2.

In the same competition the following season, Kelly – back after a very brief and unsuccessful stay at Millwall – made both goals as Leatherhead beat another League

side, Cambridge United. In 1978–79 he scored the goal that drew the Cup match with Third Division Colchester United.

Scotland went into their last group match at the 1986 World Cup finals needing to beat Uruguay to reach the second round – and had every chance, because a) Uruguay had just lost 6–1 to Denmark, and b) they were a man down almost immediately, José Batista being sent off after only 55 seconds, a World Cup record, for a reckless foul on Gordon Strachan.

Even against ten men, however, Scotland struggled. They'd scored only one goal in their previous two matches, and rarely looked like doubling that here, especially with Enzo Francescoli keeping possession so magisterially up front. But they did have one golden chance, after only 18 minutes, when Roy Aitken put Strachan clear on the right and the little man's low cross reached Steve Nicol unmarked only six yards out.

Nicol had missed the first kick in the penalty shoot-out that decided the 1984 European Cup final, but it hadn't mattered in the end. Now, from half the distance, with half an empty goal to aim at, he contrived to prod the ball back towards goalkeeper Fernando Alvez, who was dashing across his line but must have thought it was in a lost cause. He scooped the ball away, the goalless draw was enough to send the Uruguayans through, and Scotland have never qualified for the knockout stages of any World Cup finals.

Czechoslovakia put up spirited resistance to the favourites Brazil in their first group match of the 1970 World Cup finals, taking a spectacular lead through Ladislav Petras, staying level till just after the hour. Even after Pelé had put Brazil ahead, they came back almost immediately, Jozef Adamec's short corner on the left finding Vladimir Hagara, whose cross reached veteran substitute

Andrej Kvasnák unmarked five yards out with only the goalkeeper to beat (and those who remember Félix will know it wasn't much). Kvasnák scored 13 goals in 47 internationals. He put the ball over the bar.

Within two minutes, Brazil had scored again on the way to a 4–1 win that set them up for their eventual lifting of the Cup. Czechoslovakia were eliminated after losing all three matches.

It was the second time Brazil had deflated Kvasnák in the World Cup. Eight years earlier he'd played well in the final itself, but Czechoslovakia lost 3–1. This 1970 match was his last chance for revenge; he wasn't capped again after the tournament.

Holland, World Cup runners-up in 1974 and 1978, needed to win in Paris to qualify for the 1982 finals. After a goalless first half, they had a marvellous chance to take the lead three minutes into the second, when substitute Simon Tahamata found Arnold Mühren in front of goal.

Mühren, one of the two Dutch players who transformed Bobby Robson's muscular Ipswich Town into a skilful and successful side, had an excellent left foot but was no great goalscorer (three in 23 matches for Holland, one every eight games in England, several of those from penalties), which he proved here by missing the chance. France went ahead almost immediately, won 2–0, and qualified at Holland's expense.

Six seasons later, at 37, Mühren was an important part of Holland's splendid European Championship winning team, but he never played in the World Cup finals.

Julio Salinas was (still is) a big orthodox striker who was regularly out of favour at Barcelona but scored for Spain in the finals of three World Cups. With only a few minutes left in their 1994 quarter-final against Italy, the Spanish were level at 1–1 and bossing the match, so much so that it was no surprise when Salinas was put clear

in front of goal with only the goalkeeper to beat from close range.

Remarkably, he hadn't started a league game all season – but scored 9 times in 13 internationals, despite playing less than an hour in almost every one. Now, presented with the best chance of the match, he prodded the ball against Gianluca Pagliuca and Spain's last chance was gone. Within two minutes, Italy had scored the winner and were on their way to the final. Spain haven't reached the last four since 1950.

Two years later in Euro 96, Salinas did much better with a chance against England at Wembley but was still thwarted [see FOREIGN REFEREES].

Spain and Bulgaria drew 1–0 in Group B.

MOIRA STUART

England were also helped in Euro 96 by Swiss striker Marco Grassi hitting the bar from inside the six-yard area and Spanish winger Jávier Manjarín getting it all wrong with only David Seaman to beat.

Elsewhere, Goran Vlaovic of Croatia also missed with only the keeper to beat and the score still 0–0 against Germany, while Liuboslav Penev, Bulgaria's lumbering centre-forward and the manager's nephew, put the seal on his woeful tournament by missing from very close in against France then heading the own goal that eliminated the Bulgarians from the competition.

Ally McCoist's marvellous long-range shot gave Scotland their 1–0 win over the Swiss, but ultimately didn't compensate for the chance he hit against the keeper after bringing the ball under control a few yards out – and Italy's Pierluigi Casiraghi chested the ball past the last Czech defender before shooting over from eight yards. If either of these (or the missed penalties by McAllister and Zola) had gone in, Scotland and Italy would have reached the quarter-finals.

Final chances

And Bailey must save. Gordon Smith misses his great chance in the Cup Final

Although the 1983 FA Cup final was the first in Brighton's history, Gordon Smith wasn't likely to be affected by big match nerves. Before his move to England, he'd played in six cup finals with Rangers.

His experience showed at Wembley after only a quarter of an hour, his fine header giving the Seagulls a half-time lead against heavy favourites Manchester United. 'I remember going off at half-time and seeing my name on the scoreboard and thinking it would have to stay like that. Underdogs only win 1–0 in finals.'

Prophetic words they seemed too, when United went 2–1 ahead – then Gary Stevens equalised with only three minutes left and Brighton held their own through extra-time; so much so that in the very last minute, the limited but persistent Michael Robinson battered his way into the United penalty area to set up Smith, who had only the goalkeeper to beat. In the 1978 Scottish League Cup final he'd scored the winner against Celtic in the last minute of extra-time.

Now, from very close range, he made one of the most famous misses in Cup Final history, shooting straight at Gary Bailey. United won the replay 4–0, Brighton were relegated from the First Division, and a club fanzine was named *And Smith Must Score*.

Good to see Gianluca Vialli back at the top in the last few years, helping Juventus win the domestic Double and the European Cup – because there was a time when it looked as if his career was on the way down, mainly through injury but also as a result of some loss of form in front of goal.

To be fair to him, he's never been an out-and-out striker, more an all-round forward (he started as a winger) who made chances as well as taking them. Still, he scored both goals when Sampdoria won the 1990 Cup-Winners Cup final, so a lot was expected of him in the World Cup finals in Italy later that year. In the event, he didn't score, missed a penalty, and was replaced as a national hero by Toto Schillaci. Two years later, in the European Cup final at Wembley, things were even worse.

Three times he was put clean through on goal. First he shot over the bar, then straight at Zubizarreta, then – the worst of all – just wide of the far post. Substituted in extra-time, he had to watch while Ronald Koeman's free kick gave Barcelona the Cup (which Samp have never won) for the first time.

Four years later, Vialli lifted the trophy as captain of Juventus – but was grateful for Angelo Peruzzi's saves in the penalty shoot-out: he'd missed a chance to win it near the end of normal time, going round the keeper and hitting the side netting.

Five minutes from the end of the 1968 FA Cup final, Howard Kendall's cross was deflected out to Johnny Morrissey, whose lob found Jimmy Husband completely unmarked close in. He headed over the bar, West Brom won 1–0 in extra time, and Everton had to wait till 1984 before winning the Cup again.

Barcelona, under manager Terry Venables, were expected to win the 1986 European Cup final held in Seville, but were kept out by a disciplined Steaua team. Then, five minutes into extra time, the Romanians' goalkeeper Helmut Ducadam came out for a free kick and punched it feebly straight to substitute José Moratalla, who couldn't miss but did, volleying wide. A reprieved Ducadam saved four penalties in the shoot-out as Steaua became the first Eastern European club to win the Cup. It was the beginning of the end for Venables – and Moratalla – at Barça. By the time they won the European Cup for the first time, six years later, neither was involved with the team.

Benfica, trying to win the European Cup for the third consecutive year, were 1–0 up in the 1963 final against Milan when their giant new centre-forward José Torres, later a star of the 1966 World Cup, for once got past Milan's smooth sweeper and captain Cesare Maldini (Paolo's father) and found himself with only the keeper to beat. He shot wide, Benfica lost 2–1 and never won the Cup again.

> *He's perfectly fit – apart, that is, from his physical fitness.*
>
> **MIKE ENGLAND**

Three years later, almost exactly the same thing. Milan Galic was one of the top goalscorers of his time: 37 in 51 games for Yugoslavia, including at least one in each of ten successive games, equalling a world record that still stands. In 1960 he scored in the finals of the European Nations Cup and the Olympics.

By 1966 he was still a class striker, scoring important goals early in Partizan Belgrade's European Cup run before injury kept him out of the semi-final against Manchester United. He was back for the final against Real Madrid.

Partizan, playing the game of their lives, took the lead after 56 minutes and had a great chance to seal the match soon afterwards, putting Galic clear with only the keeper to beat. As defenders closed in, he hit his shot firmly – but too high. Hit by a tackle, he had to go off for five minutes. Partizan, in their only European final, lost 2–1.

Eusébio da Silva Ferreira was one of the most famous and prolific strikers of all time

(57 goals in European competitions, a record 41 for Portugal, top scorer in the 1966 World Cup finals) despite having all kinds of trouble with the English (losing in a World Cup qualifier, a World Cup semi-final and a friendly, three times to Manchester United in the European Cup) and an English stadium: he hit the bar twice against England in 1961, scored but was on the losing side in the 1963 European Cup final, and hit the bar again with the score still 0–0 in the final of 1968, all three at Wembley.

In the 1968 match, he had a great chance to win the final before it went into its famous extra time. In the last few minutes, with Benfica having just equalised and Man United in disarray, a through ball from little António Simoes sent Eusébio charging into the United penalty area with Tony Dunne and Bill Foulkes unable to converge on him before he got in his shot.

Goalkeeper Alex Stepney prepared himself for a chip or a placed shot, then saw Eusébio nudge the ball ahead, which meant he'd decided on a full-blooded shot. What made him change his mind? The thought of winning the big event with a spectacular finish? Whatever, that little nudge gave Stepney time to make the save, which he did, even clinging on to prevent the rebound, then waving Eusébio away when he tried to shake hands.

John Motson remembers it as 'an expensive miss: with hindsight, the turning point of the match.' Stepney wasn't just being modest when he said, 'It was a bad mistake by Eusébio rather than brilliant goalkeeping.' Benfica lost 4–1 in extra time and haven't won the Cup since 1962.

In a defensive, very disappointing 1967 Cup-Winners Cup final, Rangers had the best chance before extra time, their 18-year-old winger Willie Johnston reaching the Bayern Munich goal line before turning the ball back for Roger Hynd, clear in front of goal with only the keeper to beat. He didn't – and while Celtic won the European Cup that year, Rangers lost 1–0 and had to wait five

years to take the Cup-Winners Cup, their only European trophy, by which time Hynd was no longer in the team.

When Milan left that dynamic and prolific striker Jean-Pierre Papin out of their starting line-up for the 1993 European Cup final, it looked a dangerous gamble, especially as it left the responsibility for goals to Daniele Massaro, who'd scored a mere five of them in Serie A that season, and only one more in the Champions Cup.

He didn't add to that total here. After only five minutes, he put a header over the bar. After twelve, put clear in the penalty area, he dithered before passing unnecessarily to Marco van Basten. After seventeen, he found space, only to shoot straight at the Marseille keeper. Papin was brought on for the last 35 minutes of the match: too late; the feel of the contest had changed. Seven minutes from time, Massaro couldn't quite reach Van Basten's chip, and Milan lost 1–0, the first time a French club had ever won the Cup.

Massaro, to his credit, redeemed himself with two goals in the final the following year – but in the World Cup final that followed it, his was the crucial miss in the penalty shoot-out, after Italy and Brazil had scored two apiece.

Johnny Rep was a classic '70s star. Blond, arrogant, skilful, and Dutch. His entry at the highest level was impressive (the two goals that won Ajax the 1972 World Club Cup), he scored the only goal of the 1973 European Cup final, and a record 7 for Holland in the World Cup finals. And yet it's just possible – not fair, but possible – that he'll be remembered for two misses in the biggest matches of all.

The score was 1–1 in the first half of the 1974 World Cup final when the Dutch captain Johan Cruyff burst through the middle and descended on his opposite number Franz Beckenbauer with Rep free on his left. Cruyff drew Beckenbauer and passed, giving the golden boy a clear run in on Sepp Maier. With space, time, and a good angle, he hit the ball straight at the keeper. Minutes later, Gerd Müller put away a more difficult chance to win the Cup for West Germany.

Four years later, again in the final, again against the hosts, again with the scores level, Arie Haan hit a free-kick high into the box, exploiting Argentina's vulnerability in the air (which led to Dirk Nanninga's goal later in the match). Rep beat Daniel Passarella and Luis Galván easily (one photo shows him getting in the header while they're still grounded) – and missed from close range. Again the Dutch lost, this time agonisingly in extra-time after Rob Rensenbrink had hit the post in the last minute.

Manchester City were the better team in the 1969 FA Cup final, and Neil Young's goal was worthy of winning any match – but underdogs Leicester City had their chances, especially two before half-time. First their Welsh international Peter Rodrigues, only a few yards out, missed the ball completely. One national paper thought 'It looked easier to score.' Rodrigues was a full-back, so perhaps there was some excuse – but when centre-forward Andy Lochhead 'missed a sitter' from Allan Clarke's knockdown, Leicester must have known it wasn't their day.

It's never been their day at Wembley, at least in FA Cup finals: they've famously appeared in four without winning any. A few weeks after losing to Man City, they were relegated to the Second Division.

In the very first minute of the 1936 final, Arsenal goalkeeper Alex Wilson went up for a high cross and dropped it right at the feet of Sheffield United's goalscoring winger Bobby Barclay, who hit it straight back to him from close range. United lost 1–0, haven't reached the final since, and haven't won the Cup since 1925.

Bristol City were a goal down in the 1909 final when their left-winger Frank Hilton missed from the same close range as Sandy Turnbull had scored for Manchester United. City, in their only appearance in the final, lost by that goal to nil.

The following year, Barnsley also missed a 'glorious chance of equalising' in the final, Wilf Bartrop shooting wide in front of 'an open goal and close in'. Newcastle immediately went downfield and scored their second from a penalty to win 2–0.

> *I think if they hadn't scored, we might have got a better result.*
>
> **HOWARD WILKINSON**

These FA Cup final equalisers can be maddeningly elusive when the score's 1–0. In 1914, in the last few minutes, Liverpool's classy Irish inside-forward Billy Lacey headed a clear chance against the post. Burnley won 1–0 to take the Cup for the first and only time. Liverpool didn't win it till 1965.

In 1992, having won the European Cup at last, Barcelona met São Paulo for the World Club Cup, took the lead through Christo Stoichkov, lost it after 26 minutes, and were still level at that score as the first half drew to a close. Then Stoichkov released Aitor Beguiristain on the left, the winger drew goalkeeper Zetti to set up a great chance – and hit the ball straight at Ronaldo Luíz, the covering defender on the line. It was the best chance of the match; Barça lost 2–1.

Chequebook Charlies

Transfer troubles

In May 1979, Liverpool paid a hefty £300,000 for the lean St Mirren striker Frank McGarvey. In pre-season training, they seem to have discovered that the leanness had something to do with lack of conditioning. Whatever, the Boot Room boys decided he wasn't 'a Liverpool player'. A year later, he was sold to Celtic (at a £10,000 loss) without having made a single first-team appearance.

After Willie Crilley had scored 49 of Alloa's 81 goals to help them win the Division Two title in 1921–22, League champions Celtic hoped his striking power would help them retain the Championship. He played in only three league matches, scoring a single goal, before being transferred back to Alloa, who were immediately relegated. Celtic lost the title to Rangers.

> ## *The boys all handled the ball well.*
>
> **DAVE MERRINGTON**

The tug-of-war between Derby and Manchester United for the services of Ian Storey-Moore seemed to have been settled when Brian Clough paraded the Nottingham Forest winger on the pitch before a match at the Baseball Ground in 1972. Storey-Moore had, after all, according to Peter Taylor, signed not once but seven times (!), trusting the Derby managers so completely that he left the documents blank for them to fill in.

It turns out that things weren't that simple. Forest unearthed a technicality (the forms hadn't been signed by their secretary) which allowed United to sign Storey-Moore for £200,000 – this while the League were fining Derby a swingeing £5,000 for showing the double-barrelled one to the crowd while he was still officially a Forest player.

A bad mix-up – but the blunder wasn't so much Clough's as United's and especially Storey-Moore's. He joined a club in turmoil (manager Frank O'Farrell resigned soon afterwards and they were relegated in 1974) and missed the chance of playing for a skilful Derby team that won the League title without him that same season. He appeared in only 39 League matches for United.

Another who may have regretted his choice of club was Sheffield Wednesday full-back Wilf Smith, who turned down a move to Chelsea at the beginning of the 1970–71 season because he thought housing in London was too expensive. He went to Coventry City instead.

He could probably have been able to afford a modest little pied-à-terre in the capital if he'd joined the club which won the Cup-Winners Cup that year. He won nothing with Coventry.

Dennis Bergkamp finished the 1992–93 season as top scorer in the Dutch First Division for the third consecutive year, and one of his four goals for Holland was that clever volleyed lob which helped save a vital World Cup point at Wembley.

Then the inevitable move to Italy – and

Inter fans enjoyed seeing the back of Dennis Bergkamp

problems all round. Actually, by the end, the 1993–94 season seemed to have gone well for him on paper, Inter winning the UEFA Cup, Holland doing well in the World Cup finals thanks to his three goals and all-round performances.

But the £8 million Inter had paid for him was supposed to help them challenge Milan for the Serie A title. Instead they finished a point above the relegation zone – and Bergkamp not only scored just 8 goals in 30 league matches, but five of those were from penalties, and his general play was disappointing to say the very least. His goals in the UEFA Cup weren't enough of a return on a reported annual salary of £650,000.

When his second season didn't improve (and this time Inter won nothing), he was sold to Arsenal, where things have generally gone better for a potentially great player.

So far Villa have troubled Bradshaw twice with shots that did not trouble him.

LARRY CANNING

Bergkamp can take some consolation from the experience of other players who failed after moving to Inter: Wim Jonk, who went with him from Ajax for £4 million and wasn't much more of a success, Russian playmaker Igor Shalimov, who had his moments but not enough of them for someone who cost £8 million – and the remarkable Darko Pancev, once the most feared striker in Europe.

Less skilful than Yugoslav team-mates like Savicevic, Prosinecki and Boban, Pancev had nevertheless been good enough to win his first cap at 18 – and his strike rate in 1990–91 was simply freakish: winner of the Golden Boot as the highest scorer in any European first division, goals in every round of the European Cup before the final (where he put away Red Star's winning penalty in the shoot-out), ten for Yugoslavia in the

European Championship qualifiers. The following season, he scored in the World Club Cup and a hat-trick in the European Cup. A phenomenon in front of goal.

Then a move to Inter in 1992 – and oblivion. Whether because the Italian league exposed his lack of a really good first touch, or because he couldn't get on with Rubén Sosa up front, or whatever, he played only nine league matches, scoring just once, and didn't appear in Serie A at all the following season. Meanwhile the break-up of Yugoslavia had deprived him of at least an international stage. Definitely a sense of waste.

Before the 1979–80 season Nottingham Forest spent the sizeable sum of £450,000 on Manchester City's competitive Scottish international midfielder Asa Hartford – and regretted it almost at once. Hartford's passing was accurate but too short for the Forest style.

There were two, typical ways of looking at it. Peter Taylor: 'Hartford is one hell of a player and will fit in very well for someone, but Forest are too big a club to change their play pattern for one player.' And undiluted Clough: 'Asa is running about all over the place without any discipline in his play. He has never played disciplined football in his life. If he is no good, he will go.'

After only three League appearances, Hartford was sold to Everton, at a loss (which must be how he felt).

In 1965 Sunderland paid £72,500 for the Rangers wing-half Jim Baxter, one of the best playmakers in Britain – then sold him to Nottingham Forest for £100,000. Two risky buys, which surprised people even at the time: it was widely believed that Slim Jim, once one of the genuine greats, hadn't been quite the same player since breaking a leg in 1964 (see PRIDE COMETH...). Forest were happy to let him go back to

Rangers on a free transfer the following season.

In 1981, Sunderland paid St Johnstone £400,000 for Ally McCoist, gave him little support up front, then in 1983 sold him for only £180,000 to Rangers, where he's had enormous goalscoring success.

But Sunderland's most costly appointment, in every sense, was made at the end of 1984–85.

Along with Norwich, they'd reached the League Cup final that season. Along with Norwich, they were relegated to the Second Division. Unlike Norwich, who stuck by their manager, the genial Ken Brown, and came straight back up, they opted for what looked like a dream ticket, bringing in Lawrie McMenemy from Southampton – and went in the opposite direction.

It looked like the ideal homecoming. The Geordie boy made good (Southampton had won the 1976 FA Cup) coming back to awaken the sleeping giant. The word 'messianic' could have been invented for precisely this move. It's said Margaret Thatcher used his salary as evidence that football clubs didn't need any financial assistance from the government!

The exact figure was apparently never confirmed, certainly not by McMenemy himself, who protested that his appointment had brought lucrative deals to the club – 'So I paid my way.' Anyway, said Sunderland chairman Tom Cowie, 'He's a handsome man who does a handsome job and deserves a handsome salary.'

The results he brought in didn't look too pretty. In his first season, Sunderland finished just above the relegation zone. A month before the end of his second, he left the club while they were on their way down into the Third Division for the first time in their history.

When McMenemy was manager of Bishop Auckland, they drew 0–0 at home with Halifax in the 1966–67 FA Cup, which made the big man confident enough to claim that 'We're alright now, boys. We'll beat them down there. It's a better pitch and it'll suit our football.' They lost 7–0!

Not that this abashed the Bishops players too much. After the defeat, they told their conquerors that 'You lot will never get to Wembley, but we'll be there in the Amateur Cup.'

The following week they lost in the next round, 3–0 to Skelmersdale.

> *I don't know if that result's enough to lift Birmingham off the bottom of the table, but it'll certainly take them above Sunderland.*
>
> **MIKE INGHAM**

Few managerial moves came more expensive than Brian Clough's to Leeds United in 1974. It had to be doomed from the start when the likes of Billy Bremner, Leeds' captain, were later saying, 'It was a complete mystery why they appointed Clough in the first place, but you know what directors are like.'

The very first team-talk didn't help matters. Clough seemed to misjudge every player in the room. When he told Norman Hunter, for instance, that he had a dreadful reputation but deep down wanted to be loved, the leg-biter, one of the most popular players in the team, replied that he didn't give a fig, or a word to that effect. Johnny Giles said much the same thing. When Clough tried the opposite approach, telling Allan Clarke and Gordon McQueen how good they were, the others rolled their eyes: they'd spent years trying to bring those two egos into line, and now the new man was undoing all the good work.

Things didn't improve. Clough brought in two of his Derby County players, John O'Hare and John McGovern (who could only have become reserves in that strong Leeds side), and the ball-juggling Duncan McKenzie, who would surely struggle to bed down in a passing team, this while planning to sell the fans' hero Terry Cooper. But it was the poor results that finally undermined Clough: four points from the first six League games. Not that 'finally' is exactly the right word; he lasted only a famous 44 days before going into temporary retirement.

That month or so cost Leeds £100,000, a huge daily rate at the time – but they lost more than that. While Clough went on to all that success with Nottingham Forest, Leeds reached the European Cup final that season but were relegated in 1982 and didn't win a major trophy till 1992.

> *Don't tell those coming in now the result of that fantastic match. Now let's have another look at Italy's winning goal.*
>
> **DAVID COLEMAN**

There once was a boy who loved the blue giants in his home town. His father had been taking him to their home, a fortress called Ibrox, since he was five, and the giants knew all about his magic with the leather ball. From time to time, their chief scout Jimmy Smith would tell people about this small boy who would one day play for the big club.

But the big club never came to fetch the small boy, even though he didn't live very far away. His home was in a multi-storey block near Ibrox and his window overlooked the club's training ground. Instead, the giants from the other side, the ones in green and white, came to find him. When they arrived, the boy was rushing around his home taking down pictures of the blue giants from the walls. That's how much they had meant to him. If only they had come to take him away.

The boy grew up and helped the green-and-white giants to win four league titles in his country, four cups and a league cup, before moving south to the land of the red giants, where he won everything there was to win, in that country and on the continent.

And that's the story of how Rangers failed to sign Kenneth Mathieson Dalglish.

There once was also a boy – well actually there was a full-grown man called Alfredo Di Stéfano, who even in the early '50s was suspected of being the best player in the world. Certainly he became the greatest in the history of the European Cup, scoring in each of the first five finals as Real Madrid won them all.

But it might all have been very different. It was a complicated situation. Di Stéfano had moved from River Plate, his club in Argentina, to Los Millonários in Colombia, who were promising El Dorado to a number of well-known players (Neil Franklin's career disappeared there, for instance). When a tug-of-war began for Di Stéfano's signature, Real Madrid signed an agreement with Millonários, Barcelona with River Plate. The Spanish FA decreed, bizarrely, that he should spend alternate years with each club, starting at Real.

The situation was never put to the test. Barcelona offered to give up their option on the player if Real would give them the fee they'd paid to River Plate. It was the most disastrous abdication in football history. In his first season, Di Stéfano's 27 goals in 30 games (including four in one match against Barcelona!) won Real the championship. While they were accumulating those five European Cups, plus an assortment of Spanish titles, Barça had to wait till 1992 to win it for the first time.

Real's domination of those early European Cups was built on the sheer quality of the foreign stars they imported, most of whom were successful, often very: Di Stéfano of course, Puskás, Santamaría, Kopa. One who didn't join this pantheon, through no fault of his own, was Waldir Pereyra, the fabulous Didí, playmaker of the great Brazilian team which had just won the 1958 World Cup.

When he arrived in Madrid soon after the tournament, he was met by Di Stéfano, who brooked no rivals at the club. 'So you're here to take my place? Well, you're not good enough and you're too old.' Not much would have been lost in translation. Didí would certainly have been good enough, given the chance – and as for being old, he was three years younger than Di Stéfano!

In the face of Don Alfredo's hostility, Real couldn't find a regular place for Didí, eventually using him only in exhibition matches and loaning him to Valencia. He asked for his contract to be revoked and returned to Brazil in 1960, one of the few times the club lost big money on a transfer.

Revenge would certainly have been his in 1962 – he led Brazil to a second successive World Cup win – but for the injury that kept Di Stéfano out of the tournament. For all his enormous fame and success at club level, Di Stéfano didn't play in a single World Cup finals match.

Diego Maradona's £6.9 million transfer to Napoli was one of the most successful in history, leading to the club's first two Serie A titles, the Double in 1987, and the UEFA Cup success of 1989 (Maradona scored in the first leg of the final). Few eras (it included the 1986 World Cup) have been so dominated by a single player

Before that, however, his £4.8 million move from Boca Juniors to Barcelona in 1982 had been something of a personal disaster – and Barça didn't get much value for money either – as another great Argentinian, Alfredo Di Stéfano, had foreseen.

'Maradona will have a lot of problems in Spanish football…You only have to turn your back for a moment and your legs are whipped away. The defenders always go for the ball, but if there's something else in the way, like a leg, they take that as well. Nothing gets past them, and the referees just shout "Play on, play on." Maradona will have to change his style of play – if he can.'

He wasn't really given the chance. The foul by Andoni Goikoetxea that put him out of action for weeks was so bad that the Butcher of Bilbao was banned for 18 matches, Maradona didn't recover his form, and Barcelona were glad to off-load him to Napoli, who weren't the losers in that arrangement.

The advantage of being at home is very much with the home side.

DENIS LAW

Maradona's a famous name in the game, of course. It seems to have persuasive powers on its own, even when Diego's not attached to the front of it. Napoli once bought his brother Hugo, then in 1987 loaned him out to Ascoli, who bought him after Pescara had turned him down. Later he was voted Bad Buy of the Year by a Swiss newspaper after playing so infrequently for his club that he was costing them £4,000 a game, a huge sum at the time.

Even though Peter Taylor had made mistakes in the transfer market before – he once turned down Kevin Keegan, for example (BLUNDERS VOL.1) – it was still surprising to see him make a string of unsuccessful buys towards the end of his association with Clough at Forest: Raimondo Ponte, Jürgen Rober, Einar Jan Aas, etc – and especially Ian Wallace and Justin Fashanu.

To be fair to Wallace, who cost a whopping £1.25 million in 1980 and was

Justin Fashanu leaves the football behind

sold abroad for only £100,000 four years later, in each of his first three seasons he finished as Forest's leading scorer in the League – and if his total of 36 in 128 First Division games isn't overly impressive, he'd been prolific enough at Coventry to be capped by Scotland, so his reputation holds up better than some. Than Justin Fashanu's, for instance.

Big Justin was John's twin brother, but they weren't identical. Even after scoring that spectacular Goal of the Season for Norwich against Liverpool, he looked almost apologetic (Fash the Bashful?) – and his stay at Forest was most definitely not a success: three goals in 32 League games in his first season, none in none in the next before being loaned to Southampton (on his return, he went straight into Forest's third team!) and sold to Notts County for only £150,000 – this after he'd refused to go on loan to Derby and Clough had called the police to ban him from the ground. Then a drift out of the first-class game, followed by sporadic comebacks that never looked particularly long-term.

So what prompted Forest to spend £1 million on the gentle giant? Because he was an England Under-21 player and no doubt Clough thought he of all people could bring the best out of him. It didn't happen, partly because our Brian had to admit, years later, to discovering that 'Justin Fashanu didn't want to play football.'

A decade later, as Forest slipped towards relegation from the Premier League, Clough decided against buying Stan Collymore (at a time when Forest's overriding concern was the scoring of goals) and instead saved money in the short term by bringing in Robert Rosario from Norwich – even though the tall front man had an appalling strike record.

'If he's a success,' joked Clough, 'he'll be one of my signings. If he blows it, he's one of Ronnie Fenton's [his assistant].'

He was one of Ronnie Fenton's, definitely. Rosario scored only one goal in ten League games, Forest went down and Clough retired. Collymore later joined Forest for an increased fee.

You'd think Ossie Ardiles and Glenn Hoddle would know a good player when they see one, but...

At the beginning of 1993–94, Ardiles paid Ipswich Town £1.9 million for the all-purpose Jason Dozzell, who'd once been very promising (nine England Under–21 caps). It hasn't worked out for him at Tottenham.

And in July 1996, Chelsea made an £800,000 loss when they sold Hoddle's record signing Paul Furlong to Birmingham City after he'd scored 4 goals in his last 38 matches.

A sudden rush of goals in 1987–88 transformed Paul Stewart from a rather heavy, workaday striker into some seriously hot property. In 1988 Terry Venables paid Man City £1.7 million for him, then moved him into midfield (more by luck than judgment, it's said) the way Liverpool had done so successfully with Ray Kennedy. Stewart was no Kennedy, but he had a good game in the 1991 FA Cup final, scoring Tottenham's equaliser, and in 1992 Graeme Souness paid £2.5 million to take him to Liverpool.

If his stay at Tottenham was a partial success, this was totally something else. The intention was that he'd replace Steve McMahon in midfield, but there was simply no comparison. No great passer or tackler, Stewart often seemed at a loss as to what exactly his role was meant to be. At the start of 1993–94 he was in the reserves, then – with no other club desperate to sign him – he was loaned out to Crystal Palace, Wolves and Burnley before joining Sunderland on a free transfer in 1996.

Souness made some good buys for Rangers, enough to pay their way to pre-eminence in Scotland – but he made so *many* buys (spending more than any other British manager in history) that some of them, by the law of averages if nothing else, were bound to raise a few eyebrows, even those who'd done well elsewhere. Paul Stewart simply took his place alongside Rangers misfits like Colin West, Avi Cohen and Mark Falco, and the likes of István Kozma, Julian Dicks (ouch) and Torben Piechnik at Liverpool. Oh, and Souness sold Peter Beardsley.

> *He came on a free transfer and has been giving good value for money.*
>
> **CLIVE ALLEN**

One of the briefest signings of its type took place at the very end of May 1984, when Gordon Jago was hired as general manager at QPR, whose chairman Jim Gregory sacked him a week later, apparently because the appointment of a general manager made it hard for the club to attract leading candidates as team manager. 'I made a mistake,' was an unusual admission from the bullish Jim.

In January 1979 West Bromwich Albion paid Middlesbrough £512,000, the first half-a-million transfer fee between two British clubs, for David Mills, who was a competent all-round midfielder but never any more than that. In his five seasons with Albion, they twice finished in the top four of Division 1 – but he didn't have a great deal to do with that, playing a total of only 59 League games and scoring just 6 goals.

The move went through at almost exactly the same time as Malcolm Allison, who'd been managing Boro, returned to Man City. Bet he was annoyed at missing that one.

Big Mal, big spender

No doubts about Malcolm Allison's abilities as a coach. Three examples from all the evidence: his Manchester City team won a major trophy in each of three successive years (1968–69–70) with some of the best attacking football seen in the League. When he was a player at West Ham he told Bobby Moore to keep asking himself in a match: 'If I get the ball now, who will I give it to,' Di Stéfano's secret at Real Madrid. 'So simple,' said Mooro. 'So real. I've carried that with me into every great stadium in the world.' And he turned Joe Corrigan into one of the best goalkeepers in the world. He always did like a challenge.

Allison's biggest successes were achieved with Joe Mercer as general manager, but he wasn't going to be satisfied with being No.2 forever. When Uncle Joe was moved upstairs in the early '70s, Allison had all the reins at last – and for

Supermal – Honestly, some of the transfer fees were this big

a time at least, held them straight. At one point in the 1971–72 season, City were several points clear in the First Division with games in hand. Francis Lee was having his best season, and the use of a target man, big Wyn Davies, unusual in an Allison team, was working like clockwork.

But the big man was always fascinated by flair, not least when it came accompanied by a touch of glamour, a bit of flash (it was there in the Allison lifestyle we've all heard quite enough about: the champagne and girls, the heavy gambling, the preposterous fedora). Lee and Mike Summerbee had it; so did Freddie Hill, even when Allison brought him to City in his thirties. Don Rogers and Peter Taylor had it under Allison at Crystal Palace. So when the chance came to add some more of it to the championship leaders in 1972, Big Mal took it. It was a mistake. He bought Rodney Marsh.

A star since his Third Division days (two goals in the 1967 League Cup final), Marsh was a huge, flashy fish in the QPR pool. Allison's club record £200,000 was paid in the belief that the player's 'touch of theatre, his marvellous skill,' could make certain of the title.

However, as soon as Marsh made his debut, at home against Chelsea on 18 March, Big Mal saw the problem. City won 1–0 'but the game was a disaster for Rodney' and he had to be taken off ten minutes from time. His lack of fitness was suddenly obvious to everyone and it's arguable whether he ever matched up to City's standards. Allison remembered him being physically sick in training.

Two defeats, against Stoke and Southampton, stalled the title rush. The team, surely disorientated by the change in

Rodney over-reaching himself against the eventual champions – Marsh and Derby's keeper Colin Boulton, 1972

territory that demands a big paddle.

Almost as soon as his feet were under the table, he paid Wolves a British record fee of £1,437,500 for Steve Daley. The million pound spiral had already been started by Trevor Francis' move to Nottingham Forest – but Francis was the most talented forward of his generation, and Steve Daley was – well, Steve Daley. The price tag was to remain his only claim to fame, he made just 48 League appearances for City in two seasons, and – like Marsh before him – moved to the USA.

style, began to struggle. Within weeks of buying Marsh, Allison dropped him for the Manchester derby – then brought him on to score the goal that clinched the match 3–1, but the momentum was gone. City lost their penultimate game at Ipswich, and by the time Marsh scored a fine televised goal against Derby in the last match, it was too late. Derby won the title for the first time, with City only a point behind.

The Manchester City players have spent years denying that this single acquisition cost them the Championship – and of course there had to be other factors, including other players' loss of form – but it's hard to believe that if Allison hadn't bought the expensive thoroughbred in midstream, City wouldn't have found that extra point or two. Instead they haven't won the title since 1968.

It was the end of the road for Big Mal at City (at least the first road). By 1973–74 he was at Crystal Palace, who were relegated from the Second Division in his first season. After taking them to an FA Cup semi-final, he went back to City as an advisor – and soon advised the club into that financial

Allison's spending didn't stop there. One of his last acts as City manager was to give Norwich City £1.25 million for striker Kevin Reeves, who converted a penalty in the 1981 FA Cup final but was otherwise a disappointment, scoring only 30 goals in 130 League games. He did win two England caps, but the best thing that could said about him at international level was that he made his debut in the same match as Glenn Hoddle. Allison left Maine Road poorer but wiser (him as well as the club?) in 1980, was sacked by Middlesbrough in 1984, then had short stays on stages that weren't big enough for him (no offence to Fisher Athletic and Bristol Rovers). Fitting, in a way, that he should lose money in the BCCI crash, the biggest of its kind.

None of this should detract from that tremendous ability as a coach – but it probably will. Even though he only wore the wretched thing during Palace's Cup run in 1975–76, the first thing he was asked in a BBC interview years later wasn't 'How many great players have you developed over the years?' but 'Where's the fedora?'

Chequebook Charlies (2)

The British abroad (and the abroad in Britain)

When Juventus paid a British record fee of £3.2 million for Ian Rush in 1986 (he didn't play for them till 1987), they were buying one of the greatest British goalscorers of all time – but try telling them that now. After a promising start (four goals in a cup match), he eventually scored only seven times in 29 league games – not terrible by Italian standards, but not what was expected. Plus, unlike Keegan, Lineker & Co, he never came to terms with life abroad. When he was sold back to Liverpool after just a single season, he was regarded as merely another foreigner who failed in Serie A.

But the blunder in this case was mainly of Juventus' making. They bought Rush just as Michel Platini retired – and didn't sign a comparable playmaker to replace the Frenchman, which meant there was no-one to supply the bullets for Rush, or Michael Laudrup, to fire.

Ironically, the only thing Juve won that season was a place in the UEFA Cup, thanks to Rush scoring the deciding penalty in a shoot-out – and when a very unfancied Wales team played Italy in Brescia, he scored the only goal of the game.

Milan have generally done exceptionally well with their foreign players, winning any number of league titles and European Cups thanks to the likes of the Grenoli trio (Gren-Nordahl-Liedholm), Schiaffino, Hamrin, Schnellinger, the Dutch axis of Gullit, Van Basten and Rijkaard, and latterly Savicevic and Desailly.

Like any club, though, it hasn't been a case of success every time. In fact they made one of strangest purchases in Serie A history. Not Jimmy Greaves, who stayed for

Luther Blissett in Milan, a year spent looking over his shoulder

only a few games in 1961 – or Joe Jordan, who didn't win any prizes in 1981 – but the one and only Luther Blissett.

Although he regularly got himself into goalscoring positions, he missed a high percentage of chances ('Luther Missit') – and his ball control was never likely to survive in Italy – so what did Milan see in him to pay Watford a staggering £1 million in 1983? Don't expect answers here. It's been said, mischievously, that the Italian scouts sent back reports on the wrong player. Blissett scored just five league goals in his only season in Italy.

When Real Madrid bought Laurie Cunningham from West Brom for £995,000 in 1979, you hoped it would work out. A talented ball player whose career in England (and for England) hadn't reached the heights once promised, he must have expected better things in Spain, where they put more of a premium on pure skill.

Things started out brightly enough (he scored twice and made another in his first league match, scored three and made others in Real's run to the 1980 European Cup semi-final) then went rapidly downhill, the whole stay summed up by the hefty fine imposed on him for being found dancing in a nightclub while supposed to be resting a long-term foot injury. He scored against Kevin Keegan's Hamburg in the European Cup semi-final, but various bouts of surgery and a sending-off in Europe put paid to anything else, and Real were glad to loan him out to Manchester United in 1983.

After that, nobody seemed to want him for long. Marseille, Leicester City on loan, Sporting Gijon, Charleroi – finally Wimbledon, about as far from Real as it's possible to get, but at least a club that brought him a little success before his death at only 33: he came on as substitute in the 1988 FA Cup final.

Dave Watson won 65 England caps as an old-fashioned but effective central defender, the first when he was already 27, the last at 35. A classic late developer – too late, really, for a move abroad.

Manchester City sold him to Werder Bremen for £200,000 in June 1979, but he didn't adapt, was fined, dropped, and playing for Southampton by October. He was particularly miffed at having been sent off for pushing an opponent away with his hands, acceptable practice back home.

> *Hoddle hasn't been the Hoddle we know. Neither has Robson.*
>
> **RON GREENWOOD**

When Sampdoria bought Des Walker from Nottingham Forest in 1992, they seemed to be getting a bargain, paying only £1.5 million for one of the best and fastest central defenders in world football – and apparently doing it just in time, now that Pietro Vierchowod was surely coming to the end of his career. Another British success story for Samp, after Trevor Francis, Liam Brady and Graeme Souness.

But they'd reckoned without Vierchowod himself. No slowcoach in his own right, he'd been one of the most astringent defenders in Italy for more than a decade, first capped in 1981. Now 33, he must have seen Walker's arrival as a challenge – and promptly played so well that he couldn't be budged from central defence. (He was still good enough in 1996 to win the European Cup with Juventus.)

This status quo was neither here nor there as far as the club's league prospects went – they finished a moderate 7th – but ruined Walker's career at the top level. He played 27 league matches that season (Vierchowod 29) but many of those were at full-back, where his speed couldn't compensate for his inexperience. He was sold to Sheffield Wednesday the following season.

Worse, his England form suddenly dipped horribly and he began to make mistakes, an unheard-of phenomenon only a year earlier. The foul on Marc Overmars when beaten for speed, the hesitation in Poland and lapse in concentration in Norway cost four World Cup points and England didn't reach the finals. From being virtually ever-present almost since his debut in 1988, he hasn't been capped since Graham Taylor's last match in charge, in 1993.

The season after Barcelona's defeat in the 1986 European Cup final, manager Terry Venables bolstered his forward line with a double signing worth about £4 million: Gary Lineker from Everton and Mark Hughes from Manchester United.

The plan, presumably, was for Lineker to score goals by feeding off Hughes, but it never looked like happening. Whereas Lineker adapted immediately to the style of play, the language and lifestyle, and scored 21 goals in his first season, Hughes struggled with the lingo, was lonely off the pitch and too physical on it for the liking of Spanish referees. After a frustrating year, during which he scored only four goals in 28 league games and was sent off in a UEFA Cup match, Venables sent him on his way back to United via Bayern Munich.

> *Ian Rush, ready ten times out of ten – but that wasn't one of them.*
>
> **PETER JONES**

In 1979 Sunderland paid a club record £450,000 for Argentinian forward Claudio Marangoni, who played only 20 matches for them, scoring just three goals, before having his contract cancelled a year later, which meant that they received no transfer fee for him. Four years later he was playing in the Independiente team which beat Liverpool to become world club champions.

November 1982. Shock horror. Charlton Athletic buy Allan Simonsen for £324,000.

Now, this isn't a vast sum by today's standards, but it was twice as much as Barcelona had paid for him – and rather more than Charlton could afford, of which more anon.

Simonsen, forerunner of the new wave of world-class Danes, was one of the greatest forwards of all time: short, sharp, bristling with flair, European Footballer of the Year in 1977, the only player to score in the final of all three European club competitions, the latest only a few months before joining Athletic – who'd just finished 13th in the Second Division.

What made them think they could afford such a player? Well, it's said the size of the Valley had something to do with it. Its old capacity of around 70,000 was the largest of any club ground in England. Give the supporters a quality player and they might fill the old place. The receipts would more than pay off Simonsen's transfer fee.

Well, maybe. But that's not taking into account the little man's wages, which were astronomical by Division Two standards – and even before he arrived, there were signs that all wasn't well on Charlton's financial front: Barcelona delayed the sale for several weeks until they received a banker's guarantee.

After that, at least for a while, things didn't go too badly. The publicity machine was well oiled, a big crowd turned up for Simonsen's first reserve-team game, he scored on his League debut, and it's said that 60% of the Danish population watched Athletic's match against Newcastle on television.

It couldn't last. The highest home crowd while he was there was only 13,306, and although the player did his bit (9 goals in 16 League matches), he was gone by March, a stay of only five months – which cost the club dear (they admitted in February that the whole thing had been 'an expensive mistake'). A transfer embargo was imposed on them when it turned out that their total income for the season was £269,000 (less

Allan Simonsen at The Valley – the empty spaces in the stand say it all

than the cost of buying Simonsen!) – and his contract had stipulated that if things didn't work out, they'd have to let him go on a free transfer. So Vejle, his old club in Denmark, picked up a great player for nothing while Charlton, who finished five places lower than the previous season, were left with nothing but bills for their dabble.

Pick of the weak

(and other selectorial gaffes)

Remember the joke about the silent order of monks who entertain each other by reading out numbers? Each number corresponds to a well-known joke. Let's try that here. Ally McLeod. Yup, works every time. The very name raises a smile.

Scotland went to the 1978 World Cup finals as one of the favourites, respected by leading coaches like Miljan Miljanic and Rinus Michels, especially after the strong-arm qualifying win over Czechoslovakia. But once out there in Argentina, they were undermined by the team selections of their talkative manager. In the first match of the finals, he got just about everything wrong.

It was widely known that Peru had weaknesses, but also two excellent wingers in Juan José Muñante and Juan Carlos Oblitas. Indeed, Muñante was so important that they'd paid his Mexican club a large insurance premium to secure his services. Michels made it clear: 'They must watch Peru's wingers, who are two of the fastest and most dangerous in the tournament.'

'My name is Ally McLeod and I am a winner.'

What did McLeod do? Well, first, what didn't he do? He didn't have Peru watched except on video, so perhaps he didn't fully anticipate the danger. With Willie Donachie suspended, he picked the inexperienced Stuart Kennedy at right-back instead of Sandy Jardine, and paired him with Martin Buchan, a world-class central defender but too slow for a full-back. Muñante and Oblitas couldn't believe their luck.

Nor could the midfield of César Cueto and the 'elderly and rounded' (he was 29!) Teofilo Cubillas, star of the 1970 finals: McLeod persevered with the Derby County midfield pair of Bruce Rioch and Don Masson, who'd been impressive against the Czechs but were now clearly in decline (as well as both being older than Cubillas).

The result we all know. The full-backs and midfield were overrun, Masson missed a penalty and didn't play for Scotland again [BLUNDERS VOL.1], Cubillas scored twice, Peru won 3–1. Whatever changes were made at half-time didn't seem to work, and McLeod didn't substitute Masson and Rioch until Scotland had fallen behind.

It got worse before it got better. Scotland drew humiliatingly with Iran – then, when McLeod at last picked the obvious midfield of Souness-Hartford-Gemmill, beat eventual finalists Holland; too little, too late. McLeod kept his job by a single casting vote but left it four months later. It was the last time anything was expected of Scotland in the World Cup.

Arthur Berry won a full England cap in 1909 and scored in the 1912 Olympic final to help Britain win the gold medal. A brisk winger, he was an important part of the Oxford City team that almost won the 1913 FA Amateur Cup.

So important that he played when he shouldn't have. Injury kept him out of the final, but after a 1–1 draw with South Bank he was brought in for the replay, broke down completely, had to leave the pitch for several minutes in the first half and didn't come out for the second, leaving City with only ten

men. They lost 1–0 and didn't reach the final again.

Derby County shouldn't have picked goalkeeper Jack Fryer for the 1903 FA Cup final. Nothing to do with his record in previous finals (a decisive mistake in 1898 [BLUNDERS VOL.1], four goals conceded in 1899); it's just that he'd been badly injured just before the match. The *Bury Guardian* was understating things when it remarked that 'Fryer's breakdown affected the result.' And what a result. Derby lost 6–0, still the record for any FA Cup final. Mercifully, big Jack didn't play in any more.

Thank you for evoking memories, particularly of days gone by.

MIKE INGHAM

On the eve of the 1961 FA Cup final, Leicester City manager Matt Gillies sprang a major surprise (Gordon Banks, the Leicester keeper, called it 'a baffling decision') by leaving out Welsh international striker Ken Leek, who'd scored in every round so far and had caused problems for Tottenham's centre-half Maurice Norman because he was so hard to mark.

Although Gillies later claimed that Leek's replacement Hugh McIlmoyle 'justified himself at centre-forward. I was quite happy,' neither of these is easy to believe. Leicester rarely looked like scoring, lost 2–0, and have never won the FA Cup. Tottenham's win gave them the Double.

Looking for a playmaker to replace the great Alex James, Arsenal paid £14,000 for Brynmor Jones in August 1938, a new British record transfer fee that topped the previous highest by £3,000 and itself lasted nearly nine years. It didn't work out.

Jones, a class act with Wolves and Wales, didn't fit the Arsenal style. His game was based on quick bursts through the opposition defence, whereas the Gunners wanted a pure schemer in the James mould. On top of that, there's little doubt that the price tag weighed heavily on Bryn Jones, a retiring personality never at ease in the limelight. Before the war arrived to muddy the waters of opinion, his form had fallen away, and he was playing in the reserves, at his own request, before the end of the season.

> *Some of those players never dreamed they'd be playing in a cup final – but here they are today, fulfilling those dreams.*
>
> **LAWRIE McMENEMY**

The worst omission in all international football, arguably the most bizarre piece of selection ever, was committed by Brazil's manager Adhemar Pimenta just before the 1938 World Cup semi-final.

One of the most distinctive figures in the competition – short, black, moustachioed, playing part of one match without boots – Leônidas da Silva was also one of the greatest strikers of all time. First capped in 1932, he scored in each of his first ten internationals (16 goals), equalling a world record that still stands, finishing with 21 in 19 matches spread over 14 years.

Having scored Brazil's only goal in the 1934 World Cup, he was almost immediately left out until the next tournament – then returned with a bang. Three bangs, in fact, a hat-trick in the remarkable 6–5 win over Poland in the first round (all sources said four goals until Brazilian statisticians did some recent digging), followed by goals in both matches against Czechoslovakia in the

quarter-finals. Although the champions Italy were waiting in the semis, Brazil had a real puncher's chance.

Then, amazingly, they dropped their big right hand, a decision Pimenta explained by saying that he was saving Leônidas for the final! Against the holders and favourites with their formidable defence, this seemed complete lunacy. And sure enough.

Brazil lost only 2–1 (Italy's second goal was a penalty) and had to wait another twenty years to win the World Cup for the first time. Leônidas, restored for the third-place final, scored twice against Sweden to make himself the tournament's top scorer. Pimenta, sacked immediately after the finals, was recalled in 1942 – and again left the great man out.

In their qualifying group for the 1970 World Cup, Scotland were left with the worst till last, away matches in Hamburg and Vienna – and needing a win and a draw to reach the finals. Tough, very – especially when manager Bobby Brown decided that the West Germany game would be the easier to win (which raised a few eyebrows) and set out to attack.

Nothing very wrong with that. At least it was positive – and Scotland led 1–0 for most of the first half. But they were hampered by Brown's selections at full-back.

Nothing wrong with the players in question (John Greig and Tommy Gemmell both had international-class qualities), the position they played in (Greig in his normal place on the right, Gemmell as usual on the left) or even the fact that they were in the same team together. What, then? Well, nothing wrong in any normal circumstances – but the Germans had picked no left-winger (so Greig had no-one to mark) and installed Reinhard Libuda on the right.

A slim, snaky winger (nicknamed Stan after the great Matthews), Libuda had been one of Borussia Dortmund's stars in the 1966 Cup-Winners Cup final against Liverpool [see WITH FRIENDS LIKE THESE] and generally tormented full-backs through-out Europe for more than a decade.

It took him a while to affect things in Hamburg, where Scotland took the lead after only three minutes and were level at half-time. The strain, however, was beginning to show at the back: Greig and Gemmell had both been booked.

In the second half, more bad news for Gemmell when he (and Billy Bremner) hit the bar, after which Gerd Müller put the Germans ahead, only for Alan Gilzean to equalise almost at once. There was half an hour to play.

By now, Libuda had begun threatening the danger his manager had expected. Helmut Schön had picked him specifically once he heard who would be Scotland's left-back, 'because I knew he would exploit Gemmell's attacking inclinations.' These brought big Tommy goals for Celtic in two European Cup finals, and he had one of the hardest shots in the game – but as a defender he lacked Greig's ability to cover and tackle. Brown's mistake wasn't in picking Gemmell on the left but in not switching him with Greig during the match.

Sure enough, with only six minutes left, Stan Libuda found a blind spot over Gemmell's shoulder and raced away on his own to score the winner which sent West Germany through to the finals at Scotland's expense. Gemmell's misery was completed by his sending-off near the end.

Brown wasn't sacked as manager till the following season, which turned out to be too long a wait. Disastrous results in Belgium and Portugal, which knocked the Scots out of the European Championship, were followed by a dismal performance at Wembley. Scotland won only 9 out of 27 matches under him.

Whose idea was it to choose John Lewis to referee the 1920 Olympic Games final? Once one of Britain's leading officials, he'd been in retirement for some time (his last FA Cup final was back in 1898) and anyway his authoritarian attitudes hadn't always gone down well. Now he became one of the chief villains in the folklore of Czechoslo-vakian soccer.

The final was only their fourth match since becoming an independent country after the war. They'd won the first three, all in this Olympic tournament, 7–0, 4–0 and 4–1, and were favourites against the hosts Belgium.

Lewis, however, bewildered them with some of his decisions, including a controversial penalty after only six minutes. When he sent one of them off before half-time, the rest of the team went too, handing Belgium the gold medal. Czechoslovakia, banned from receiving the silver, had to wait another 56 years before winning the Olympic title for the first time.

They haven't forgiven John Lewis to this day, believing that he simply hadn't been able to keep up with the play. No great surprise in that, and FIFA should have expected it. After all, he was 69 years old!

> *With the benefit of hindsight, are we going to get goals in the second half?*
>
> **ELTON WELSBY**

Scotland's early forays into the World Cup were always something of a shambles, especially their very first, in 1954, when 'an inexplicable blunder was made in the manner of selecting the team for the qualifying matches and the finals.' Before the match against England, 18 players were picked – with no room for any additions.

When the team reached the finals, it was obvious that there was no natural captain. The usual skipper, big George Young, had been left out of the original squad through injury – and, although he was fully fit by now, the selection committee refused to bring him in. With manager Andy Beattie not allowed to pick the team, a leaderless

Scotland lost both their matches, the second 7–0 to Uruguay.

In 1958 the Scots did well to draw 1–1 with a Yugoslavian side that had beaten England 5–0. Before the second match, two of the players, Archie Robertson and Tommy Docherty, were sent to watch the team's next opponents, Paraguay.

They came back with the news that although the Paraguayans had lost 7–3 to France, they had some clever footballers (Silvio Parodi perhaps the best) and above all were a physical, rather rough side, especially at the back.

With this information in the bank, what did Scotland do but leave out the combative likes of Dave Mackay and Sammy Baird, and field a forward line made up entirely of the slim and small: Robertson, Jackie Mudie, Willie Fernie, Graham Leggat and Bobby Collins. They lost 3–2 (Paraguay's only win in the tournament) and didn't reach the quarter-finals.

And there'll be more football in a moment, but first we've got highlights of the Scottish League Cup final.

GARY NEWBON

Lothar Emmerich was a powerful goalscoring winger with limited technique but a hammer of a left foot, which brought him most of the 115 goals he scored in 183 league matches. In 1966, his big season, his goals for Borussia Dortmund were the talking point of the Cup-Winners Cup: six in one game (equalling a record that still stands), a vital one in the away leg of the quarter-final, two in each leg to knock the holders West Ham out of the semi-final. He was a major force in the final too, making the winner against Liverpool. Sheer weight of goals forced his way into West Germany's

team for the match against Holland. He scored in a 4–2 win, only to be left out again until the World Cup finals, in which he was a decisive figure…

The third group match was his first of the tournament, and only his second cap in all. Again he scored, a typical thunderbolt from an impossible angle – really almost on the goal line – a vital equaliser in a match West Germany needed to draw to reach the quarter-finals (they won 2–1).

After that, manager Helmut Schön couldn't leave him out of the team, even when he did nothing in the quarters and semis. It's now widely believed that Schön wanted to drop him from the final, but retained him either through fear (of public opinion) or hope (that one of those ferocious shots was all it would take). It didn't work.

With the big winger in the team, Schön had to use Franz Beckenbauer to mark Bobby Charlton – which robbed him of the Kaiser's creative input: he'd scored four goals in the tournament (and two when Emmerich scored one against Holland) and was already, at 20, the best attacking half-back in the world. Schön could have brought in a natural man-marker like Klaus-Dieter Sieloff to look after Charlton. Instead, Beckenbauer did well enough but was wasted, West Germany lost, and big Lothar, apart from the free-kick which led to the last-minute equaliser (and that took several deflections), was rarely seen at all.

Of the 22 players in the final, he was the most inexperienced as far as international matches were concerned (this was only his fifth) and the only one never to be capped again.

Four years later, Schön's use of substitutes in the semi-final led to the headline in an Italian paper: *Danke, Schön*. He won the World Cup at last in 1974.

Although Switzerland's English manager Roy Hodgson knew that his star player Alain Sutter had a badly injured toe, he picked him for the third group match in the 1994 World Cup finals, even though Switzerland didn't need a result from it to go through. Indeed, they lost it – and lost Sutter too, when his broken toe predictably didn't recover in time for the knockout stage. Without his midfield promptings, the Swiss rarely looked like scoring and lost 3–0 to Spain.

It's far too simplistic to say that buying Faustino Asprilla cost Kevin Keegan the Premiership in 1996, of course it is, but it must have had *something* to do with it. At one point before the Colombian's arrival, Newcastle United were 12 points clear at the top, with Les Ferdinand scoring almost at will, feeding on crosses from left (David Ginola) and right (Keith Gillespie). Although Asprilla himself didn't play at all badly, his inclusion had a domino effect.

Gillespie was left out and Peter Beardsley moved over to the right, which cost Newcastle the crosses of a natural winger and Beardsley's subleties in the middle. So when Ginola lost form, the service dried up from both flanks and Ferdinand scored far less freely.

When Gillespie was recalled, he immediately scored the only goal of the game at Leeds – but there were only two League matches left after that and the momentum had been lost to Manchester United. Newcastle could only draw the last two games and finished four points behind.

Pick of the weak (2)

The England story

Why did Brian Clough win only two England caps even when he was one of the most prolific goalscorers in the country? Partly because the manager did him no favours.

For the first two matches of the 1959–60 season, against Wales and Sweden, Walter Winterbottom chose a central front three of Jimmy Greaves, Clough, and Bobby Charlton. A dream team within a team, surely? The highest scorers in England's history alongside a man who was doing it every week in the League. There was just one problem: Winterbottom hadn't picked a playmaker, someone to load the bullets. No Johnny Haynes, no Peter Broadbent, nobody. Instead, a forward line of three strikers and two wingers. Balance wasn't the word for it.

England drew 1–1 in Wales then Clough did his best at Wembley against Sweden, making a goal for John Connelly, hitting a post. But the Swedes, who'd reached the previous year's World Cup final and were too good for this makeshift collection, became only the second foreign country to win in England. Like Clough, the three-striker plan wasn't tried again.

And now an international soccer special: Manchester United v Southampton.

DAVID COLEMAN

The England team picked by Don Revie for the crucial World Cup qualifier in Rome in 1976 had its share of good players but somehow didn't look quite right. Actually, according to Kevin Keegan, it represented 'the worst technical error of Revie's life', 'the worst team ever picked by Don Revie'. The Italian captain Giacinto Facchetti agreed: 'The worst England team I have ever seen. Disorganised, confused, of only modest ability.'

The fault line ran through every department. The recall of Emlyn Hughes ('Why are you including me now after leaving me out for fifteen games?') wasn't necessarily a bad thing in itself – but he hadn't partnered Roy McFarland before and this was the tenth central defensive pairing in Revie's 21 England matches so far. Of the full-backs, Mick Mills was played on the wrong side yet again, and Dave Clement wasn't quite international class. Midfield consisted of two ball winners – Brian Greenhoff & Trevor Cherry – with Trevor Brooking, still lacking confidence at this level, as the only playmaker, easily marked out of the game by the fearsome Romeo Benetti and Marco Tardelli. A front line of Keegan, Mick Channon and Stan Bowles looked good on paper, but Bowles hadn't been capped for two years and anyway all three tended to play in much the same way. No wingers, said Keegan, nobody going wide.

In the match, virtually the only shots Dino Zoff had to face came from Greenhoff and Cherry, and if the former seemed to be having his best game for England, a) that wasn't saying much, and b) the Italians were quite happy to let him have so much of the ball. Channon had scored twice against Italy in the summer, but that had been an experimental Italian team. Here he was finding a world-class side too good for him and was booked in his frustration. Cuccureddu was booked for seeing to Keegan, who wasn't yet the product finished at Hamburg. Brooking? What Brooking?

England lost 2–0 (Keegan: 'a very fair result') and faced an impossible task in the remaining qualifying games. Revie seemed to think so too: he resigned with two still left to play.

Before that, in fact in the very next match after Rome, he surpassed even that fiasco. When McFarland went down with yet another injury (he wasn't capped again), Revie called up an even more aerial stopper of the old school in Dave Watson, pairing him with the equally physical Mick Doyle – and again used two ball winners in midfield. In all, there were six back-four players in the team – this against Johan Cruyff's brilliant Dutch side, who hadn't fielded an orthodox centre-forward for years!

After only ten minutes on the pitch, Johnny Rep was telling Kevin Keegan that this was the worst England team he'd ever seen ('You have problems here'). Holland scored twice in the first half and contented themselves with a stroll through the second.

Graham Taylor stands back and thinks of Watford

Not entirely through any fault of their own, Doyle, Clement, Bowles and Paul Madeley didn't play for England again.

Revie, who made a series of other strange selections (giving Alan Hudson only two caps, Charlie George only 65 minutes, Brian Talbot any caps at all, etc), picked only one unchanged England team, against Uruguay in 1977 – his last match in charge!

> *If history is going to repeat itself, I should think we can expect the same thing again.*
>
> **TERRY VENABLES**

In many ways, Graham Taylor's reign as England manager paralleled big Don's, not least in the fact that it was short – and that he never seemed to be quite sure what he wanted.

Did he plan to embrace the idea of wing-backs like the rest of the world? Then why drop Rocastle and Sinton after only one match in that position? He said the sweeper system couldn't work in an England team. So why use it for a vital World Cup match? Um, he discarded it immediately afterwards. So that's alright then.

There were other oddball decisions along the way. Dropping Gazza for a game in Dublin and replacing him with the even frailer Gordon Cowans, who wasn't capped again. Dropping two World Cup points in Norway by picking 'a pig's arse of a team' (his words, everyone's opinion) just to counter Jostein Flo. Keeping Tony Daley in the team while Chris Waddle was being voted Footballer of the Year. Leaving out Robson and Beardsley, recalling Hateley and Mabbutt for just one match, substituting Lineker in his last international.

Meanwhile some of his other selections – Brian Deane, Andy Gray, Carlton Palmer, Paul Stewart, Geoff Thomas – haven't survived the test of time, or at least the test of Venables. The kind of list that makes us all glad Graham Taylor went back to doing what he does (or did before Wolves) best.

Hungary came to Wembley in 1953 with 24 unbeaten matches and the Olympic title under their belts, but most of the sterling was on another home win. Indeed, when Hungary were held 2–2 at home by a weakened Swedish team, an English scribe opined that 'if Sweden can draw with these much-vaunted Hungarians, England can beat them handsomely.'

However, someone should have looked harder at that 2–2 draw. Admittedly the visitors looked weak on paper: success at the 1948 & 1952 Olympics and 1950 World Cup had led to literally dozens of Swedish players moving abroad – and, since their FA refused to include professionals in the national team, rebuilding had become an ongoing state of affairs.

So yes, Hungary had just drawn with a weakened side – but there was more to it than that. Sweden's shrewd English manager George Raynor had pinpointed the deep-lying centre-forward Nándor Hidegkuti as the hub of the attack, and laid his traps accordingly. Hidegkuti was marked wherever he wandered (but not by the same player), the supply lines to Puskás and Kocsis were cut off: just enough to avoid defeat.

After the match, Raynor offered his solution to a member of the English FA, who ignored it. Against the best team in the world, the English selectors not only put together one of their traditional hotpotches but surpassed themselves. They could hardly have picked a team less likely to withstand what was coming.

To mark Hidegkuti: 34-year-old Harry Johnston, who was a reluctant stopper at the best of times (he preferred to captain Blackpool from wing-half). To make the play: fragile little Ernie Taylor, winning his first cap. On the left wing, in place of the great Finney: another debutant, the Finchley schoolteacher and Tottenham amateur George Robb. Stan Mortensen was slightly

out of position at centre-forward, Billy Wright had been in the wrong position for years. On top of all this, it was the oldest England team so far (an average of nearly 31).

Within a minute, it aged further still, Hidegkuti swerving to the right-hand corner of the penalty area before smashing in a cross-shot high beyond Gil Merrick: 1–0 within a minute, and at least one foreigner who could shoot as well as pussyfoot. Soon afterwards he had a goal disallowed. Hungary won 6–3 easing up, the first national team from outside the British Isles to win in England. The home truth alright.

Wembley 1953 – only Billy Wright seems to think he's got the right team to play Hungary

Johnston, Taylor, Robb, Mortensen, Bill Eckersley and Alf Ramsey weren't capped again.

After this historic humiliation, England travelled to Budapest for the return match. Asked how he thought it might go this time, Stanley Rous, later president of FIFA, said simply, 'We will win.' We didn't. England suffered their heaviest ever defeat: 7–1.

Sam Barkas was one of the best left-backs in the country just before World War II – but the England selectors picked him at inside-left for his first international, against Belgium in 1936. England scored twice but never got going, the other four forwards weren't capped again, and Belgium won 3–2, their only win against England in 18 attempts.

One-cap wonder blunders

After the fiasco of the 1992 European Championship finals, Graham Taylor picked three new caps for the first game of the following season, in Spain: Paul Ince, substitute David Bardsley – and the Manchester City wide player David White, who had one of the most promising starts to any international career. Sort of.

With less than two minutes gone, he was put clear on goal in the inside-left channel. With no defenders in close pursuit, and all the time he needed to draw the keeper, he went instead for an early shot, hitting it too softly and too close to Andoni Zubizarreta. Substituted in the second half, he hasn't played for England since.

> *John Lyall, very much a claret-and-blue man, from his stocking feet to his hair.*
>
> **PETER JONES**

Tony Brown scored more League goals for West Brom than anyone else (218), which earned him a call-up for England against Wales in 1971. After 74 minutes, Sir Alf had seen enough (or rather he hadn't) and put Allan Clarke on in his place. It's said that the main contribution of 'Bomber' Brown ('who looked totally out of his class') was to get himself offside when Francis Lee scored what should have been the only goal of the game.

When their opponents Bohemia scratched from the 1908 Olympics, France found themselves in the semi-finals without playing a match – and facing Denmark, the strongest team in continental Europe, who'd just beaten a French 'B' side 9–0 in the previous round.

For some reason, the French selectors made five changes to this team which hadn't actually played together yet, bringing in six new caps, including the entire back four (they weren't called back fours in those days, but you get the drift).

Within six minutes, this hastily-assembled defence had let Sophus Nielsen in for a hat-trick. Both his final total of 10 and the 17–1 scoreline (young Vilhelm Wolffhagen scored four on his debut) are still records for any *bona fide* international. Not one of that team ever played for France again!

By 1878 England's individualistic dribbling had proved itself inferior to Scotland's short-passing game. They'd lost 3–0 in 1876, 3–1 in 1877.

Now, however, their 'tall athletic forms' were expected to lord it over the 'diminutive bulk' of the Scots. In fact, 'it was generally admitted that the English possessed a stronger team than their rivals'; indeed it was thought 'the strongest ever chosen to do battle in an international match' – even though it included seven new caps, among them goalkeeper Conrad Warner, whose performance for London against Sheffield earlier in the season had been described as 'capital' (not sure if pun intended).

At Hampden, although 'the play of the English was very good', Warner blundered in the second and third Scottish goals, had a hand in at least two more, and wasn't picked again after being on the receiving end of a 7–2 defeat (Scotland led 6–0 till the last few minutes despite finishing with ten men), England's record defeat until 1954.

By 1897, England had gone 20 matches without defeat (still the national record) spread over seven years, beating Wales 9–1 in the 20th. Then, just before the match with Scotland at Celtic Park, two vital players, Ernest Needham and the great Steve Bloomer, dropped out injured – and the selectors made important mistakes in replacing them with Harry Wood, who'd once been international class but was now past his best, and especially Cuthbert James Burnup, a 20-year-old winger with Cambridge University and Old Malvernians, credentials that didn't prepare him for the pressure cooker match against the Scots, who fielded players with English clubs for the very first time.

There was universal surprise and condemnation at CJ's selection. Evidence of southern bias, it was said, amateurs favoured ahead of professionals, 'a smart little fellow but not up to international standard.'

Seems he rather lived down to it all. In front of a restless, aggressive crowd, 'the amateur was painfully weak, almost everything he did ending in utter failure.' England lost that unbeaten run 2–1 and Burnup wasn't capped again. In 1900, playing cricket for the MCC, he bowled a ball that was hit for ten runs, a record in first-class cricket.

John Arnold was a talented all-rounder who played for England in two sports – but there were reasons why he won only a single cap in each.

In cricket, he was out for a duck in his first Test innings, against the lowly New Zealanders in 1931 – and at football he was thrown in at the deep end, at Hampden Park two years later.

Unlucky in being part of a very inexperienced forward line (four new caps, and Joe Hulme recalled after four years), he nevertheless should have done better with the goalscoring chances he was given. Twice put through with only goalkeeper Jakey Jackson to beat, he shot wide each time. The *Daily Mail* wrote of its 'infinite regret' in describing him as a failure ('the responsibility of those who chose him is greater than his own'), and England's 2–1 defeat handed the Home Championship to Wales.

Is he speaking to you yet?

IAN ST JOHN

No, but I hope to be incommunicado with him shortly.

JIMMY GREAVES

One of the reasons early FA officials arranged international matches was surely to give themselves a cap or two. Actually, sometimes they deserved their place – Charles Alcock in England, Bob Gardner & Co in Scotland, Llewelyn Kenrick in Wales – but poor John McAlery was in the Ireland team that lost its first ever international 13–0 – and Alex Hunter appears to have been the worst of the lot.

When the respected half-back Humphrey Jones dropped out of Wales' match in Belfast in 1887, Alexander Hunter Hunter (no misprint) was called in at the last minute – even though he had no credentials at all as a player. Worse, he was put in at centre-half, the hub of the team in those days. Oh, and being the Welsh FA secretary, he presumably helped pick himself.

'It is needless to say that the team was neither strengthened nor stabilised by his presence. He must have thought it a good joke to get playing international or he would never have donned the jersey, for whatever his knowledge of the theory, he was glaringly deficient in practice.' Wales lost 4–1.

When he won his first England cap, against Ireland in 1928, Jimmy Barrett was carrying an old leg injury. He kept it quiet and played – but not for long, having to come off after only eight minutes, the shortest international career of any England player. His weight (he was almost 15 stone), and presumably his little deception, prevented any more caps.

> *History, as John Bond would agree, is all about todays and not about yesterdays.*
>
> **BRIAN MOORE**

In the 1920s, the England selectors were fond of picking amateurs to play against Continental countries while leaving the real thing of the Home Championship to the professionals. Some of these unpaid chaps weren't especially good players, but such jolly decent fellows that they were chosen to captain the team.

One such was Claude Thesiger Ashton, no less, who played against Ireland in the 1925–26 Home Championship. With his brothers Hubert and Gilbert, he made up an amateur footballing family of some repute, but this was a different proposition.

About the only thing he did right was win the toss. A slim centre-forward, 'he failed in giving cohesion to the line, and his shooting was weak,' so much so that England could only draw 0–0. He never came close to winning another cap.

In the 48 matches they played from 1919–20 to 1928–29, England picked no fewer than 60 one-cap wonders. Nothing so unsporting as team-building in those days. Small wonder that they didn't win the Home Championship outright between 1913 and 1930.

When Austria came to Wembley in late 1951, the English press presented them as the best team in Europe. This wasn't strictly true – Puskas' Hungarians were approaching their peak – but the threat to England's unbeaten home record against Continental opposition was clear: Ocwirk & Co were a serious test.

It should have been passed in the first few minutes. The ball was moved quickly to the England right wing, where Arthur Milton, the young Arsenal outside-right who later played Test cricket, drew his man and pushed the ball inside to set up a good chance for his inside-forward partner Ivan Broadis, who missed it. Three minutes later, much the same thing, Milton making the inside pass, Broadis making nothing of it.

If either of those chances had gone in, Austria would have been on the back foot. Instead they took the lead, and England were hard pressed to draw 2–2. As soon as the Austrians' superior ground passing found its rhythm, Broadis had to drop back to help his defence, leaving Milton isolated and underfed on the wing. It was his only game for England.

He did better in his first Test, scoring a century at Headingley. He was the last man to be capped by England at both sports.

When Wales picked their team to play Ireland in 1898, they seem to have taken the match rather lightly, staging it at Llandudno (no disrespect, but even then it wasn't a hotbed of the international game), and picking new caps in three key positions: goalkeeper Jack Morris, centre-half Jack

Edwards and inside-forward Albert Lockley. None of them was ever capped again.

Morris did nothing very wrong, but Wales had better keepers to choose from (Jimmy Trainer and Dickie Roose) and Edwards was a full-back in club football. Meanwhile, Lockley was criticised for 'a lack of energy and pluck'.

This mattered. Wales not only lost 1–0 but became the first team ever to fail to score against the Irish! This in Ireland's 46th international since their first in 1882, a world record that still stands. So, when Edwards was left out of the record books for years (his sole appearance being lumped in with those of Jim Edwards), he may have been glad of the anonymity!

John Toshack has been a successful club manager for many years, notably with Swansea, whom he took from the Fourth Division to the First, and in Spain. So it looked a reasonable choice by the Welsh FA to appoint him the new national team manager after the failure to qualify for the 1994 World Cup finals.

There were two objections. One, that his sacked predecessor Terry Yorath had been popular with the players and public. Two, that Toshack would be doing the job on a part-time basis while keeping his post at Real Sociedad. In the event, he didn't do it for long. Whatever the Tosh saw during his first game in charge (substandard players perhaps, internal politics, a crowd that didn't want him), it was enough to make it his last as well. He resigned after just that one match, a 3–1 home defeat by Norway, leaving egg on some faces and a bad taste in everyone's mouth.

Drop-outs

(who stayed out)

Although Finn Laudrup was an international in his own right – he scored the only goal of the game for Denmark against Scotland in 1970 – he's much better known as the father of Michael and Brian, two of the most talented players of their generation. Both won their first caps at 18 (Michael on his 18th birthday), both have had considerable success at club level, Michael with Juventus and Barcelona, Brian with Rangers.

They've had their moments at international level too – Michael scored a marvellous goal in the 1986 World Cup finals – but these seemed to have dried up at the end of 1990. After a 2–0 home defeat by Yugoslavia in a critical European Championship qualifier, team manager Richard Møller Nielsen found fault with the brothers' contribution. *Dared* to find fault might be more exact: they were national icons, virtually beyond criticism. In their own opinion, at least.

Both immediately refused to play any more matches for Denmark while Møller Nielsen stayed in charge. Many thought he'd either have to back down or be sacked: he didn't have the stature of his predecessor Sepp Piontek, and they were after all still the Laudrups.

But Møller Nielsen stayed – and then things began to happen, especially in Bosnia, so that although Yugoslavia won their qualifying group, they weren't allowed to take part in the finals and were replaced by the country which finished second behind them...

That was enough for Brian Laudrup. He made his peace with the manager and was back in the team by April 1992, in time to take part in Denmark's amazing run to the European title.

Big brother, however, stayed out – thereby missing out on a winner's medal. When he finally deigned to return, at the beginning of

1993–94, he couldn't help Denmark to reach the World Cup finals, and was very disappointing in Euro 96.

When you walk out of an England squad, you're gambling on how highly you think the boss rates you. Kevin Keegan, for example, went AWOL before the match against Wales in 1975 because the manager wasn't talking to him. Luckily for him, Don Revie took him back – which was more than Bobby Robson did in 1982 when Keegan vowed never to play for England again because Robson hadn't told him he was being left out of the squad. He wasn't recalled.

Paul Madeley turned down a place in the 1970 World Cup party but Alf Ramsey didn't hold it against him: he was too versatile. Big Gordon West did the same, with the same squad – and Alf didn't pick him again. It had always looked a risky decision with alternatives like Banks, Bonetti and Shilton around.

It takes a rare player to reject a European Cup winner's medal, but then Stan Bowles was an unusual man.

Even an expert judge of talent like Peter Taylor didn't always get it right: 'Maybe I made a mistake by refusing to pay £90,000 to Carlisle United for Stan Bowles.' Eight years later, Taylor had to spend £250,000 to get him, whereupon a spate of injuries at Nottingham Forest meant that Bowles had every chance of playing in the 1980 European Cup final.

But he'd been growing restless, annoyed that Brian Clough wasn't picking him for away matches. Being left out of a testimo-

Stan Bowles doing what Peter Taylor wanted him to

nial game was the straw that broke him. Just before the kick-off, he told Taylor he wanted a transfer. Taylor told him to wait, but the famous last words sealed it: 'I can't stick it here, I'm off.' He walked out of the ground and didn't turn up for the trip to the final, which Forest won 1–0. After just 19 League matches for Forest, Stan Bowles drifted down to Orient and Brentford, leaving behind memories of a classy talent, and a sense of what might have been

The fact that Bowles liked the odd flutter wasn't exactly a secret ('If only Stan could pass a betting shop the way he passes the ball'). He once put £6,000, a very hefty sum at the time, on his club QPR to win the 1975–76 League title at 16–1. They finished runners-up by a single point. When he joined Gamblers Anonymous, a friend of his, trying to help, bet him he wouldn't last the week!

> *Ibrox is filling up slowly but rapidly.*
>
> **JAMES SANDERSON**

Forest, always looking for skill under Clough and Taylor ('You win nothing without it'), signed the very gifted but by now rather neglected Charlie George in January 1980. Like Stan Bowles above, this gave George a chance for some renewed success almost a decade after the famous goal which won Arsenal the Double in 1971. Like Stan Bowles, he blew it.

He was initially signed from Southampton on a month's loan, with a view to a £500,000 transfer if he proved his fitness. By the end of the month, he'd been restricted to only three matches, so Forest asked him to stay for another four weeks, which seemed fair enough. Instead, Charlie was impatient: 'I've been here long enough. Make your mind up.' When Forest said in that case the answer's no, he asked for another chance and was picked the following day.

'It was a mistake,' said Taylor, 'because he didn't have a kick. If he'd stayed when we first asked…' The transfer didn't go through and Forest retained the European Cup without him.

Plus one who was dropped

Andrés Mazali was one of the best-known, and best, goalkeepers of the 1920s. No great handler of the ball perhaps, but a fine shot-stopper in the fashion of the times – and definitely a star of the Uruguayan teams which won the Olympic title in 1924 & 1928. Still only 27 in 1930, he was undisputed No.1 choice for the first World Cup, held in Montevideo.

Like so many South American teams, Uruguay were closeted away in a training camp for several weeks before the tournament. When Mazali broke the curfew (it's said that he was caught creeping back in with his shoes in his hand) he was summarily dropped from the team and replaced by Enrique Ballestrero, who looks downright immobile in films of the tournament.

It was the biggest mistake of Mazali's career. Instead of keeping goal in the first ever World Cup final, which Uruguay won, he didn't play international football again.

Many unhappy returns

Comeback trials

Larry Lloyd, a big straightforward central defender, won three caps for England in 1971–72 before his reputation as something of a handful began to count against him: Liverpool let him go to Coventry, and neither of the next two England managers included him in their plans.

International rescue came with a move to Nottingham Forest, where Peter Taylor knew how to recognise a good player and Brian Clough how to handle one who fancied himself. Big Larry won a League Championship medal, two in the League Cup and two in the European Cup, plus an England recall against Wales in 1980.

Talk about a great comeback. If only we could. Instead, needing only to stay on his feet to go to the European Championships, he had the worst comeback of any England player: booked, injured, substituted, generally run ragged, as well as scoring what looked like (but wasn't listed as) an own goal. He wasn't capped again after Wales came from a goal down to win 4–1, the last team to score four, or win by three, against England.

For his first match as England manager, Ron Greenwood included six Liverpool players in the team against Switzerland at Wembley in 1977, plus Kevin Keegan, who'd moved from Liverpool to Hamburg only a few months earlier. Part of this Anfield six-pack was Ian Callaghan, who'd won his last cap as a winger in the 1966 World Cup – a gap of 11 years 59 days.

It didn't work. England muddled through a 0–0 draw with the Swiss, then kept Callaghan for the World Cup match in Luxembourg, where a miserable 2–0 win virtually confirmed England's absence from the finals. He wasn't picked again.

Several other players have had long gaps in their international careers, including Otto Kaller, brought back for Austria's first match after the Second World War, a purely sentimental gesture (his last cap had been back in 1933). Austria lost 5–2 to Hungary and Kaller wasn't capped again.

Ernest Gravier was recalled by France against Norway in 1923, almost twelve years since his last match. A right-back, he let left-winger Einar Wilhelms escape him for the first goal after twelve minutes as France lost 2–0 at home.

Andy Ducat, who played Test cricket as well as international football, was brought back in 1920 after an absence of very nearly ten years – only to become part of the first England team to lose to Wales since 1882!

But none of these can match the remarkable international career of the one and only Albert Beuchat. Picked at full-back for Switzerland in 1911, he ran slap into the Hungarian attack, one of the best in Europe, which ran up nine goals without reply, five of them scored by the brilliant, spindly Imre Schlosser, the greatest goalscorer of his day. Poor Beuchat was immediately dropped, the First World War came along, and that seemed to be that.

Then, in 1923, after the Swiss had failed to win any of their last three matches, he was recalled against the very average Danes in Copenhagen. Again Switzerland lost – and didn't win either of the next two games Beuchat played in, both in the same year. Back into international limbo.

Amazingly, that wasn't the end of it. Eight years later, at the age of 41, he was picked yet again, against Italy, one of the strongest teams on the continent. Yet another defeat, 3–0 – and this time the great Albert's international days were numbered after five matches without a win spread over twenty years!

> *Stan Mortensen even had a final named after him. The Matthews Final.*
>
> **LAWRIE McMENEMY**

After picking up 31 disciplinary points, and a suspension, Brighton centre-half and captain Steve Foster spent the next weeks trying to persuade people to let him play in the 1983 FA Cup final, even going as far as the High Court, who turned him down. He had to sit out the match, which Brighton drew 2–2 against heavy favourites Manchester United.

In a gesture of solidarity, acting captain Tony Grealish had worn Foster's well-known headband when he led the team out.

There was never much doubt that big Steve would be back for the replay – or that Brighton wouldn't be able to repeat the performance. In the original match, Gary Stevens and Steve Gatting had coped well with United's strikers Frank Stapleton and Norman Whiteside. This time, with Gatting moved over to right-back, Brighton lost 4–0. During the match, the United supporters began a chant that ran along the lines of 'Steve Foster, what a difference you've made.'

There's only one way to describe Brazil's 1966 World Cup effort, and that is to openly declare that from beginning to end it was a total and unmitigated disaster. Hard to disagree with that – especially as it's the opinion of Pelé.

For some time before the finals, it seems that the CBD, the Brazilian sports federation, had been telling the media that a third consecutive World Cup win was there for

Steve Foster, at the head of his band, about to make a big difference to the result

the taking; all that was needed was a return to the heroes of 1962 and even 1958. After all, Pelé was still only 25...

Yes, but some of the others had been past their sell-by date for years. Hideraldo Luíz Bellini, for example, captain in 1958, had been left out for being too old in 1962! He was now 36, as was goalkeeper Gylmar dos Santos. Bellini's central defensive partner Orlando de Peçanha, also dropped in 1962, was brought back at 31. The once fantastic Garrincha was 32 and injury prone. Above all, Djalma Santos, arguably the best right-back of all time but now 37, kept Carlos Alberto Torres (winning captain in 1970) out of the squad. A scandal, a national joke.

Pelé saw it all coming. 'So many errors had been made, I would not have minded being dropped myself, since I was ready to concede our not winning a single game.' Somehow he held the old men together long enough to win the first match, against the destructive Bulgarians – but he was too badly injured to play in the next, in which poor old Djalma was exposed to the brilliance of Ferenc Bene. Hungary won far more easily than the 3–1 scoreline suggests, inflicting Brazil's first World Cup defeat in twelve years. Garrincha, in his fiftieth and last international, appeared on the losing side for the first time!

Brazilian manager Vicente Feola reacted by making nine changes for the make-or-break match with Portugal, including (hard to believe, this) the return of Orlando to face the mighty Eusébio. 'The European Pelé' scored twice, Brazil lost 3–1 again and were eliminated, Orlando and Bellini were never capped again.

Pelé again: 'In World Cup competition, against some of the strongest teams in the tournament, it was suicidal. But I suppose our directors put faith in the old dictum that "God is a Brazilian", forgetting that God also helps those that help themselves.'

Like every other country, Wales have picked a number of players who were found wanting at international level. Big Fred Jones, for example, was described as 'weak' and 'a complete failure' in his only match, against Scotland in 1893. Roger Evans, another one-cap man, 'was much criticised for an inept display' against Ireland in 1902.

But neither of these compares with the selectors' own performance in selecting Harry Hibbott against England and Scotland in 1885. A reasonable dribbler at club level, he was 'decidedly a failure' for Wales. And no wonder. He'd been capped five years earlier as a goalkeeper!

> *Such a positive move by Uruguay, bringing two players off and putting two players on.*
>
> **JOHN HELM**

André Egli, a world-class defender who won 77 caps, played for Switzerland from 1979 to 1994 but opted out of international football for more than three years. In his first game back, a European Championship qualifier at Hampden Park in 1990, he gave away the first goal by conceding a penalty for deliberate handball, then got himself sent off for a foul on Gordon Durie! Scotland won 2–1 and reached the finals by finishing one point ahead of the Swiss.

Eating disorders

(so does drinking)

If it's true that the Wolves players drank a concoction made from monkey glands before the 1939 FA Cup final, it didn't do them much good (thank goodness, or everyone would have to drink it). They lost 4–1 to underdogs Portsmouth.

The evening before their FA Cup first round match against Southend in 1968, non-League King's Lynn indulged in a steak dinner with all the trimmings, washed down with a cocktail of rum and eggs. They ran out 9–0 losers.

Gyula Zsengellér, one of the world's leading goalscorers, provided the pass that gave Ferenc Puskás an easy goal on his debut for Hungary in 1945. The following year, he wasn't quite so helpful.

At the dinner after a match with Austria, the team were given bananas for dessert, a rare treat in those straitened times. The 20-year-old Puskás, who'd never seen one before, looked towards Zsengellér to see how to go about eating one of these exotic fruits, then consumed it without any great enjoyment.

No wonder; Zsengellér had bitten into the skin, then watched with the rest of the team while Puskás ate his banana, skin and all.

Sitting down to a meal in the team hotel when he was a youngster with Fulham, Alan Mullery was faced with a bowl of water with a slice of lemon in it. With no cue forthcoming from the other players, he picked it up and drank the water – which of course turned out to be for rinsing his fingers after eating prawns.

Jimmy Cowan was one of the best half-backs of his day, a fierce tackler and good passer, the hub of the Aston Villa side that won five League titles and two FA Cups, including the Double in 1897. He won only three caps, partly because Scotland didn't pick players with English clubs until 1896 – and partly as a result of his performance against the Auld Enemy in 1898.

By all accounts, it was a very odd display. When he wasn't missing tackles, he was indulging in uncharacteristic dribbles that kept losing the ball. His team mates roundly blamed him for their 3–1 defeat: Neil Gibson, for one, felt that 'Cowan's play disheartened us all'; others that 'he was the cause of Scotland's defeat'. Newspapers of the day reported the crowd's reaction ('What are you playing at, Jamie?'). A strange business.

It came to light that before the game, some of the Scottish selection committee had been so concerned about Cowan's condition that a reserve was asked to take his place. Quite why this didn't happen in the end isn't immediately clear, especially as no-one who was there had any doubt: James Cowan was drunk. After his disorderly display, he didn't play for Scotland again.

Preparing for trouble

Before the 1970 FA Cup semi-final replay at Villa Park, Manchester United were staying at a hotel near Wolverhampton, as was a comely member of the opposite sex. With George Best in the United party, sex was the appropriate word. Unfortunately for the team, it took place only an hour or so before the match, during which Best, in Alex Stepney's words, 'had a nightmare match', or in his own, 'played like a big w**ker'. Within five minutes he'd put a good chance over the bar – then, clean through on goal, he fell over on the job, and lay there with his face in the mud. The crowd, he remembered, gave him the bird.

United again drew 0–0 with Leeds before losing a second replay.

Even Georgie didn't always have great success with the ladies. Nine years earlier, when he was a young apprentice not long in from Belfast, Eamonn Dunphy tried to set him up with a girl in a Manchester night club. But, even though she was apparently usually willing, the young Best was 'too small and quiet' for her. Thanks but no thanks.

A few years later, when any girl in the country would have been happy to date George Best, she realised her mistake. Too late now, I suppose? Definitely.

Needing to beat lowly Iceland at home to stay in contention for a place in the 1982 World Cup finals, Wales twice took the lead – but lost their rhythm when the floodlights failed, holding the game up for 43 minutes. Iceland drew 2–2 thanks to two goals from world-class forward Asgeir Sigurvinsson. Wales haven't reached the finals since 1958.

The Rest of Europe team that came to play a Great Britain XI at Hampden Park in 1947 had one or two defenders who weren't necessarily the best that could have been chosen (Petersen of Denmark, Ludl of Czechoslovakia) but were nevertheless expected to do rather better than lose 6–1.

Explanations? The British team was stacked with exceptional players (Matthews, Lawton, Mannion, Swift, Steel) – and the Rest's erratic little French keeper Julien Darui may not have done himself any good with his pre-match diet, which included glasses of wine with as many as twenty lumps of sugar in each! Essential for his stamina, he said. Well, picking the ball out of the net six times is hard work.

On the way back from shooting practice in 1878, a class from Clifton College in Bristol were travelling by train when one of them accidentally fired his rifle. The bullet went through the wall of the compartment, into the next – and killed one of their teachers, Alexander Fletcher Jones, who'd won his only cap for Wales just the year before.

Remember when Chrysler used Scotland's 1978 World Cup squad to advertise its cars? Their most unfortunate TV slot was after the 1–1 draw with unfancied Iran. The slogan: 'Both run rings round the opposition.'

Although goal nets were first used in major matches in 1891, they weren't in operation during the Ireland–England fixture three years later – the biggest mistake in the match, leading to another, by referee Tom Park. He allowed an equalising goal scored three minutes from the end by the 17-year-old Willie K Gibson – even though many in the crowd, and all the England players, had seen the ball go wide of the post. Luck of the Irish? It was their 13th match against England, the first in which they scored more than one goal, and the first time they avoided defeat.

What happened to the four Kilmarnock players who didn't turn up for a game in 1908 is a mystery – though not as big a mystery as the scoreline: the remaining players lost only 4–1 to Port Glasgow Athletic. The magnificent seven are thought to be the smallest quorum to take part in a complete first-class match in Britain.

The 1923 FA Cup final went ahead more or less as scheduled only because PC George Scorey's white horse inched the crowd back off the Wembley pitch. It made for an ideal story: the officer riding in on his white charger to save the day. West Ham didn't quite see it like that.

Their forwards, who'd scored five goals in the semi-final, were looking forward to attacking Bolton's defence on Wembley's big smooth surface. Inside-forward Billy Moore felt that his international wingers Dick Richards and Jimmy Ruffell could win them the match. Then the horse came along and wrecked everything.

West Ham trainer Charlie Paynter was sure the pitch was ideal for their style of play until 'that white horse thumped its big feet into the pitch. When the game started, it was hopeless. Our wingers Ruffell and

Richards were tumbling all over the place, tripping up in great ruts and holes.' To be fair, Paynter also blamed the hundreds of thousands of human feet, but his team could have done without the equine input. On the other hand, Bolton, who won 2–0, would gladly have kept him in sugar lumps for life.

When Burnden Park was chosen as the venue for the 1901 FA Cup final replay, the businessmen of Bolton made ready for the financial harvest that was coming their way, buying in enormous stocks of meat pies and souvenirs. And fair enough, you'd think: the drawn final had attracted 114,815 spectators.

Unfortunately, the good burghers hadn't done all their homework, and therefore didn't know that the railway company was refusing to issue cheap-day tickets. As a result, the crowd was only 20,740, the lowest for any FA Cup final this century, and many supplies had to be thrown away. For years afterwards, the black day was known as Pie Saturday.

By the time Grimsby Town finished building their Findus Stand in 1982, they realised it was so tall that it interfered with the television reception of the nearby houses. The club had to pay to have cable TV installed.

In 1991 the Red Star Belgrade v Panathinaikos European Cup match was held in Sofia because it wasn't allowed to take place in Serbia. When fighting broke out between Bulgarians and Greeks, the Bulgarian police tried to end it with a baton charge – against the Yugoslavs at the wrong end of the stadium!

Same season, same competition, same venue: this time Red Star v Sampdoria, which was top of the bill but only a supporting act to the main entertainment of the evening, provided by the Bulgarian police dog handler who couldn't handle his dog. The beast in question, having tried to attack everything that moved and finding nothing within its range, went for the handler himself when the hapless gent kicked over a smoke bomb canister. His fellow plods had to wade in amid clouds of smoke to save his bacon. The canine miscreant's punishment has never been revealed.

Whoever was responsible for the small dog that invaded the pitch when Brentford were playing Colchester United in 1970 wasn't responsible at all. The beast charged into Brentford goalkeeper Chic Brodie, damaging his cruciate ligament so badly that he was out for three months and played only seven more matches in the League.

Tough for Chic, who was later on the receiving end of Ted MacDougall's record nine goals in the FA Cup (see SCOTTISH GOALKEEPERS). 'If I ever catch up with that bloody animal,' quoth he, 'I'll blow its backside off with a shotgun.' For the dog owner, in the words of an American golfer, the sphincter factor must have been pretty high.

Turkey's results in Euro 96 were as bad as they come: the only team never to score a goal in three finals matches, all of which were lost. But perhaps their performance was affected by what they saw when they arrived at their hotel near Grantham.

Strutting on the lawns was a large bird which, in English, shares the same name as their country. Someone had booked them in at the same time as the annual charity golf tournament run by the British Turkey Federation.

When Yugoslav clubs Kotor and Bokeljan turned up to play their Third Division match in 1990, they found the pitch had been double-booked and a circus was taking place. Both teams were allowed in free.

Is it true that Harold Wilson set the date of the 1970 General Election for 18 June because it was the day after the World Cup semi-final? If so, it was risky to say the least. After losing to Ted Heath, he claimed that England's loss in the quarter-finals had cost him his job!

Italy's defeat by Argentina in the 1990 World Cup semi-final was entirely due to bad planning. They held it at the wrong stadium (it was the 17th international staged in Naples), allowed the wrong player to take the decisive penalty in the shoot-out (Roberto Donadoni was wearing No.17) and Toto Schillaci was foolish enough to put them ahead after 17 minutes. Obvious, really.

Heading for trouble

One of the North London derbies in 1968–69 was also a League Cup semi-final. The first leg, at Highbury, was goalless till forty seconds from the end, when Arsenal keeper Bob Wilson, now ITV's anchorman, hit a big clearance which Spurs right-back Joe Kinnear, now the Wimbledon manager, headed sideways straight to opposition striker John Radford, who drove the easy chance into the roof of the net for the only goal of the game. Tottenham lost 2–1 on aggregate.

> ## *It's headed away by John Clark, using his head.*
>
> **DEREK RAE**

Although an injury kept their captain Kevin Keegan out of the start of the 1982 World Cup finals, England reached the second round stage without him – but when they hadn't scored deep into the second half against Spain, they brought him on, together with another injured regular, Trevor Brooking, to look for the two goals they needed to reach the semi-finals.

Two chances fell to them, one good, one very good. Both were missed, first by Brooking when his left-foot shot went straight to Arkonada, then by Keegan, picked out unmarked at the far post by a cross from Bryan Robson. He headed wide ('I should have scored'), England drew 0–0 and were eliminated without losing a match, Keegan and Brooking played only 27 minutes each in any World Cup finals. It was the last England match for both of them, and for manager Ron Greenwood.

The final stages of the 1931 final were among the most dramatic in Scottish Cup history. After taking a 2–0 lead within twenty minutes, underdogs Motherwell were still leading by that score with only eight left. Although the prolific Jimmy McGrory pulled one back, the 'Well were still ahead in the final minute. Then Celtic right-winger Bertie Thomson sent in a left-footed cross and – so it's said – someone in the Motherwell defence shouted, 'Yours, Alan.'

Unfortunately, there were two Alans in the back line, McClory the goalkeeper and Craig the centre-half. The centre-half Alan got there first and headed it past the goalkeeper Alan for the most famous traumatic equaliser in Scottish Cup history. Craig knelt and punched the ground, Motherwell lost the replay 4–2 and didn't win the Cup till 1952.

Two years later, in fact, they lost to Celtic in the final again, thanks to a series of dreadful clearances (plus some indecision by poor McClory) which let Jimmy McGrory in to score again, this time the only goal of the game. 'Seldom has the Scottish Cup been won by such a soft goal.'

The 1979 final was also decided by a headed own goal, by Arthur Duncan, once an international winger, now the Hibs full-back, ten minutes from the end of extra-time in the replay against Rangers. It was Hibs' last appearance in the final. They haven't won the Cup since 1902.

Before the waters began to muddy, the George Graham managerial era was a time of great success at Highbury. Mind you, they might say he owed them one – and one they haven't been repaid.

After losing only 2–1 away to the great Ajax side in the quarter-final of the 1972 European Cup, Arsenal needed just a 1–0 win in the second leg at home to go through. With only 14 minutes gone, Johan Cruyff's throw-in found Ruud Krol, whose chip, intended for Arie Haan, was headed back by Graham to goalkeeper Bob Wilson – and past him for the only goal of the game. Ajax went on to retain the Cup, which Arsenal have never won.

Although Pat Bonner's fumble against the Dutch will be remembered as the blunder which knocked the Republic of Ireland out of the 1994 World Cup, the first goal in that match had already been scored; even without Bonner's slight of hand, it might well have been decisive.

After only ten minutes, Ronald Koeman put in a chip over full-back Terry Phelan's head, making him turn. The ball bounced high, and Phelan decided on a header back towards his defence. It didn't get there. Marc Overmars latched onto it, sped up the wing, and gave Dennis Bergkamp a comfortable tap-in. Phelan won only one more cap in the next twelve months.

Future TV presenter Bob Wilson (left), preparing his comments on future manager George Graham (right) as Arie Haan follows in

Handing it to them

Phil Neal the coach, stressing the importance of playing the ball to feet

Bobby Robson was in awe of the Danes before the vital European Championship qualifier at Wembley in 1983. Worried by the likes of Morten & Jesper Olsen, Lerby, Laudrup and Simonsen, he packed the team with defenders, including one of the least creative midfields ever to play for England (Ray Wilkins, John Gregory, Sammy Lee) – admitting to having 'exaggerated the Danes' ability in my mind...it sowed seeds of doubt in my players' minds...I put our rivals on a pedestal and knocked our own confidence so that we didn't challenge or work as a unit that night.'

Nevertheless England might still have escaped with at least a point but for a single mistake. Six minutes from half-time, Michael Laudrup knocked in a cross – and Phil Neal, with the goal in no immediate danger, handled it. Simonsen sent Peter Shilton the wrong way from the penalty spot.

The only goal of the game, it effectively sent Denmark through to the European finals at England's expense. It was Neal's 50th international match, and his last. In the one before, he'd scored an own goal. That and the one from the penalty were the only two Shilton conceded in a run of nine matches. Nine consecutive clean sheets would still be the England record.

There was no score in the 1966 Scottish League Cup final when Celtic full-back John Clark hit a free-kick into the holders' penalty area and – 'for some strange reason,' said Celtic's Bobby Murdoch – Rangers' centre half Ron McKinnon handled the ball. John Hughes converted the penalty, then another Celtic won 2–1 to take the Cup for the firs of five times in a row, and Rangers had to wait all that time before winning it again.

Celtic took the lead in the 1970 European Cup final, were outplayed for the rest of the match, survived thanks to the goalkeeping of Evan Williams, and were level with only three minutes of extra-time left. Then a harmless ball dropped over Bobby Murdoch's head near the halfway line and he handled it unnecessarily as it fell. Rinus Israel's free-kick led to the winning goal (see DEFENDANT DEFENDERS).

Hayes were struggling but holding out well enough in the 1931 FA Amateur Cup final when Wycombe Wanderers floated a ball into the box and one of the two Caesars in the Hayes defence panicked and handled it when there was no need. Holding saved Broderick's penalty but Britnell followed up to score the only goal of the game. It was the only time Wycombe won the Cup. Hayes never did.

Goalkeepers who used their hands...

Spain's home match with Argentina in 1952 was decided by a single goal, knocked in by Ricardo Infante after the Spanish goalkeeper Antonio Ramallets (see THE FINAL STRAW) had saved a free-kick which he should have left alone even though it was going into the net: it was indirect.

The 1970 League Cup semi-final, a Manchester derby, was decided in the same way. Two-one down from the first leg, United were 1–0 up and level on aggregate at Old Trafford when Francis Lee hit an indirect free-kick through the wall ('Idiot,' said his manager Malcolm Allison) and Alex

Stepney pushed it out to the feet of Mike Summerbee. City drew 2–2 and went on to win the Cup for the first time. United didn't win it till 1992.

The following year (1971), City showed that this kind of thing can happen to anyone. Holders of two major trophies, they reached the Cup-Winners Cup semi-final, lost the first leg at Chelsea 1–0, and went into the second with Allison suspended from the touchline – and above all a late choice in goal, young Ron Healey.

Three minutes from half-time, Keith Weller took an indirect free-kick for Chelsea, Healey fumbled it when he didn't need to touch it, and the ball crept in for the only goal of the game. Chelsea went on to win the final, City haven't won another European trophy.

> *I am a firm believer that if you score one goal the other team have to score two to win.*
>
> **HOWARD WILKINSON**

Tom Breen was one of the leading goalkeepers of his day, winning 14 caps for Ireland and the Republic of Ireland (1935 to 1947) and spending several seasons at Manchester United. But he staked his chief claim to fame in a single match, an FA Cup fourth round tie in January 1938.

When Barnsley won a throw-in near the corner flag, Frank Bokas sent it into the United penalty area, where Breen touched it as it drifted over his head and into the net. If he'd let it go straight in, United would have been awarded a goal-kick. Bokas was the first player known to have scored from a throw-in in English first-class football. Luckily for Tom, the match ended in a 2–2 draw and he kept a clean sheet in the replay.

Unsafe keeping

A separate section for a breed apart

David Seaman models the gloves he could have done with
against Mohamed Ali (see ENGLISH GOALKEEPERS)

Scottish goalkeepers

'Nuff said

Their antics began at the very beginning. After only ten minutes of the second international match, at the Kennington Oval in 1873, with England already leading 1–0, Alexander George Bonsor's unthreatening shot was saved by the Scotland captain Bob Gardner, who then slipped and fell over the line with the ball: the first goalkeeping blunder in international football. England won 4–2.

Jimmy McAuley was quite an all-rounder. First capped as a centre-forward, he scored for Scotland against Wales on his debut – then went on to be generally accepted as the best keeper of his generation (the original 'Prince of Goalkeepers'), conceding only seven goals in eight internationals (in a very attacking era) and never appearing on the losing side. Still, if Banks and Yashin could nod…

Dumbarton were leading 1–0 in the 1887 Scottish Cup final when Hibs forward Clark hit a weak shot which the great James dropped at the feet of Montgomery, who equalised. Dumbarton lost 2–1 and McAuley didn't play in another final.

Before the 1923 Scottish Cup final, Hibs' international goalkeeper Bill Harper hadn't conceded a goal in the competition. Naturally he was merely waiting for the appropriate stage to get into a book like this.

Ten minutes after half-time, he came out for a lob by Celtic half-back Jean [*sic*] McFarlane, misjudged it so badly that it bounced over his head towards goal, and had to watch while Joe Cassidy headed into the empty net for the only goal of the game. The following year, an unchanged Hibs team lost 2–0 in the final to Airdrie after Harper was baulked by one of his own full-backs.

On the list of players who won fifty caps, Allan Rough's name must be just about the most surprising. A large blond-haired keeper short of international class, he was picked so often (by Jock Stein, too – not just Ally McLeod) there must have been a shortage of credible alternatives. It sometimes cost Scotland dear.

Seven minutes from the end of the match against England at Hampden in 1978, he dropped Peter Barnes' average long cross for Steve Coppell to score the only goal of the game.

In the World Cup finals later that season, he let Iraj Danaiifar's shot in at the near post to give Iran a shock draw. In the finals four years later, Scotland were holding a surprise lead against the favourites Brazil when Rough positioned himself on the wrong side of the wall at a free-kick, allowing Zico to curl the equaliser into the other corner. Again Scotland didn't reach the second round.

But although he made enough of these errors for those south of the border to enjoy, what's remembered most about big Allan's presence is a *general* sense of insecurity. No keeper ever had a more appropriate name.

The daddy of them all still has to be the one and only Frank Haffey, who wasn't helped by Scotland's attacking style at Wembley in 1961 but nevertheless was at fault with at least four and possibly six of England's

England's No.8 scores England's No.8. Jimmy Greaves completes his hat-trick in 1961 against fallen Frank

goals. Strange, because in his only other international, the same fixture a year earlier, he'd conceded only one goal, and that a penalty, then saved another to preserve a 1–1 draw. Now he was on the receiving end of a 9–3 defeat, the most goals conceded by Scotland in a single match, and wasn't capped again.

The joke was quickly doing the rounds: What's the time at Wembley? Nearly ten past Haffey. And at King's Cross station after the match, cameramen asked poor Frank to pose for pictures – on Platform 9!

The Wembley hoodoo for Scotland keepers struck again in 1975, when Stewart Kennedy missed Gerry Francis' long shot and Kevin Beattie's high header to give England a 2–0 lead within seven minutes. They won 5–1 and Kennedy wasn't picked again.

Four years later, Scotland were 1–0 up with only a minute to go to half-time when Peter Barnes' weak mishit left-footer trundled past

George Wood into the corner. On the hour, Wood fumbled a shot to let Steve Coppell score from his customary three or four yards. Scotland lost 3–1.

One of the more uplifting developments of the mid '90s has been the rehabilitation of Jim Leighton, back in the Scotland team at 36. Light at the end of a very long tunnel.

After being an important part of the talented Aberdeen side that won two Scottish League titles, four Scottish Cups, a Scottish League Cup and the 1983 Cup-Winners Cup, he followed his club manager Alex Ferguson to Manchester United, where he did well enough for a year or so. Then the new decade came along and spoiled everything.

His confidence, which had been draining away throughout the 1989–90 season, seemed to have evaporated so much by the

FA Cup final, a 3–3 draw with Crystal Palace, that he was replaced by Les Sealey in the replay, which United won 1–0. Worse was to follow at the World Cup finals.

He'd already given a preview of what was to follow. In the last minute of the last qualifying match, at home to Norway, he'd let a very long shot slip past him for the equaliser. Luckily Scotland had only needed to draw.

They also only needed a single point from their last group match in the finals – which made a change after the wins required in 1982 and 1986 (see DEFENDANT DEFENDERS and CHANCES ARE A FINE THING). And they almost got it. Against group leaders Brazil, too.

There was no score with only nine minutes to go when Brazil's driving midfielder Alemão shot firmly but not overwhelmingly from the edge of the penalty area. It should have been a comfortable low save for Leighton, but nothing was simple for him at that time and he didn't hold the shot.

He blocked Careca's follow-up, but the damage had already been done. The ball bounced behind him to the left – and was almost on the line, on the verge of going out of play, before Muller squeezed it in from a very tight angle. On another day, in better times, Leighton's error would have gone unpunished. As it was, the 1–0 defeat knocked Scotland out of their last World Cup finals to date. He wasn't capped for another four seasons and didn't play for United again.

When they heard they'd be facing Bournemouth in the first round of the 1971–72 FA Cup, non-League Margate's defenders were naturally apprehensive. The Third Division club's main striker was the very prolific Ted MacDougall, later capped by Scotland.

Still, upsets happen – and one might have taken place here if Margate keeper Chic Brodie hadn't dropped the ball after just two minutes. MacDougall knocked it in and went on to score nine in the 11–0 win, the most by one player in a single match in the competition proper. Poor Brodie's League career had earlier been ended by a dog on the pitch (see PREPARING FOR TROUBLE).

> *It's a shame half-time came as early as it did.*
>
> **GORDON DURIE**

When Rangers keeper Ally Maxwell kicked the ball against Dundee United's Christian Dailly in the 1994 Scottish Cup final, he set up an easy tap-in for Craig Brewster – and ended all manner of sequences. The only goal of the game, it stopped Rangers from winning a) the Cup for the third year in a row, and b) their second successive Treble of League, Cup & League Cup – and gave United the trophy for the first time in their history after six defeats in the final.

And one honorary Scot

Maxwell's blunder was matched two years later, though this time it only affected a Double. At Wembley in 1992, Gilles Rousset won his last cap for France, conceding the goals (including one by Alan Shearer on his England debut) that ended an unbeaten streak of 19 internationals. At Hampden Park in 1996, he was in the Hearts team that took on all-conquering Rangers in the Scottish Cup final. Early in the second half, Brian Laudrup hooked a poor low cross straight at Rousset, who let it slip under his body.

It was Laudrup's second goal of the game and the killer for Hearts. Rangers manager Walter Smith's understatement ('It knocked the stuffing out of them a little bit') was put into perspective by Laudrup ('It was very important...a great blow for Hearts'). Whereas Rangers won 5–1 to achieve the Double for the third time in five seasons, Hearts haven't won any of the three trophies since 1963.

English goalkeepers

(For those who think the Scots have a monopoly on this kind of thing)

Ray Wood was once beaten by a shot from the touchline by Alfredo Di Stéfano as Manchester United lost to Real Madrid in the European Cup – but of course the daddy of them all from that kind of range has a more recent vintage.

The 1995 Cup-Winners Cup final was in its very last throes, about to go to penalties after holders Arsenal had equalised against Real Zaragoza. Throughout the 120 minutes, Spurs fans had been hoping that the one player on the pitch with any connection with their club might score the winner. So it proved, but he needed a little help.

Mohamed Ali Amar, known as Nayim, had played in the 1991 FA Cup final. Now with Zaragoza, he picked up the ball near the right-hand touchline about fifty yards from the Arsenal goal – and hit one of the most famous lobs in history.

Now, there have been worse goalkeeping blunders than David Seaman's here – after all, he can't have expected Nayim to shoot from that range – but his positioning wasn't what it might have been and he seemed to mistime his jump at the end. 'As soon as he hit it,' he admitted, 'I knew I was in trouble.'

As the great up-and-under came over, he backpedalled, went up, could only help it in, and lay on his side for several seconds inside the goal with the ball coming to rest on the goal-line in front of him and a look on his face that said it all. He'd had bad moments before (see CORNERED) but this was something else.

Mohamed Ali's sucker punch, delivered right on the final bell, gave Zaragoza their first European trophy for 31 years and prevented the Gunners from becoming the first club to retain the Cup-Winners Cup. All together now: unlucky, Arsenal.

Big Joe Corrigan developed from the butt of Manchester City supporters' jokes into one of the best goalkeepers in the world, denied more England caps by the presence of Shilton and Clemence. But those early days haven't been entirely forgotten, especially one televised moment that's been shown time and again.

City were already 4–1 down at home in 1970 to West Ham when Corrigan hit a punt towards the halfway line – then committed a cardinal goalkeeping sin by turning his back on the ball. A roar from the crowd had him looking across at team-mate Tommy Booth, who pointed to the ball, which was now in the City net. Big Joe's expression is still worth the licence fee.

His kick had gone straight to Ronnie Boyce, who'd volleyed it in as Corrigan walked back towards goal. City lost 5–1.

After losing the 1888 FA Cup final, probably through over-confidence [BLUNDERS VOL.1], Preston were back the following year as League champions. Against Wolves, playing in the final for the first time, in a match postponed till four o'clock because of the Oxford v Cambridge Boat Race, Preston scored after fifteen minutes and broke through again ten minutes later, John Goodall finding Jimmy Ross, whose mishit shot went between goalkeeper Jack Baynton's legs (*The Sportsman* said he 'badly muffed' it). Preston won the match to complete the first Double in the very first League season.

The 1893 FA Cup final, 'a very hard match but not a particularly scientific one', was decided by a single mistake, Everton goalkeeper Dick Williams letting an unspectacular shot from Wolves half-back Harry Allen slip past him for the only goal of the game. There was some standard British understatement in the *Sporting Chronicle*'s opinion that he 'ought to have stopped the ball which scored,' especially as he'd 'otherwise kept goal well.' Everton had to wait till 1906 to win the Cup for the first time.

Albert Iremonger had a high profile – at 6ft 5in, one of the highest in League history. In the course of a club record 564 appearances for Notts County (1904–26) he became so popular that a street in the city was named after him.

The story goes that during a League match against Sheffield Wednesday, he came up to take a penalty, hit the bar so hard that the ball rebounded almost to the halfway line, chased back, but was beaten to it by a Wednesday player who punted it downfield. He refused to give up, and got to the ball before it crossed the goal-line – then he kicked it into his own net. Go on, believe it. You know you want to.

When Joe Neenan gave away a penalty in a 1979–80 FA Cup replay, he not only condemned Scunthorpe United to defeat by a non-League club (the penalty gave Altrincham the only goal of the game) and cost his club a money-spinner at Anfield in the next round. He did himself no favours, either, especially when the game was over. Involved in that great post-match tradition, a nightclub scuffle, he chased one of his tormentors into an alley, where he meted out some corporal retribution, which landed him (and his team-mate, a cricketer called IT

Botham) in court. Neenan pleaded guilty and was fined £100, a fair-sized sum at the time. Botham didn't, and was acquitted.

Two clubs who reached the FA Amateur Cup final only once each were both undone by their goalkeepers when they got there.

In 1898 Uxbridge held their own against Middlesbrough until a cross came into the penalty area and Gumbrell punched it straight into the face of the Boro centre-forward Kempley, from which it bounced into the net.

In 1900 underdogs Lowestoft Town might have done better against Bishop Auckland if Ayres hadn't fumbled in the first two goals of the match. Lowestoft lost 5–1.

> *And now the familiar sight of Liverpool lifting the League Cup for the first time.*
>
> **BRIAN MOORE**

Goalkeeping slip-ups have decided a number of Amateur Cup finals since then. Even Bishop Auckland weren't immune. In 1906 they were 1–0 down against Oxford City but dominating the second half when the City centre-forward's shot was stopped by the Bishops' amateur international keeper Ernest Proud – who felt anything-but when he let the ball slip from his grasp, then, in his attempt to knock it behind for a corner, slapped it into his own net to present City with the Cup for the first time.

The following year, after a goalless first half, a weak shot from Purnell was pushed out by Stockton keeper Gary (his surname) to the feet of Russell, who put Clapton ahead in a match they won 2–1.

A bit harsh including Peter Bonetti in all this – his display in that 1970 World Cup quarter-

final looked worse than it was – but it can't be helped. All three of the West Germany goals looked preventable, especially the first, which Bobby Moore was very unhappy about in print: Franz Beckenbauer's shot was firmly hit but predictable, and it did go under poor Peter's body. Then, although Uwe Seeler's looping header looked lucky, Bonetti did seem to be in no-man's land – and he might have attacked Hannes Löhr's dropping header before Gerd Müller leapt up to score the winner. It's the first one which really clinches his place here – and cost him any more caps.

Shame, because before that match he'd conceded only one goal in six internationals, all of which were won – and 'the best three goalkeepers in the world are Lev Yashin, Gordon Banks and Peter Bonetti.' In Pelé's opinion, anyway.

Mind you, one of his England team-mates called the first West German effort 'a Weetabix goal', whatever that means. Maybe that's why he had three of them.

After drawing all three group matches in the 1958 World Cup finals, England had to play off against the USSR for a place in the quarter-finals, hoping that their team spirit would keep getting them through: they'd been 2–0 down against the USSR, twice a goal behind against Austria.

To try and offset the lack of quality up front, first caps were given to two Peters, Broadbent and Brabrook, who took the game to the Soviets. Even when Brabrook missed chances (shooting straight at Lev Yashin, hitting the post twice, handling the ball before putting it in the net) it looked only a matter of time before the first goal arrived.

Unfortunately, it came at the other end. With twenty minutes left, England took a goal kick. Colin McDonald, first capped in

Peter Bonetti has to hold up his hands for England's surrender of the World Cup – Gerd Müller's winner for West Germany in the 1970 quarter-final

Moscow just before the tournament began, had been one of the team's successes: safe hands, good temperament, no mistakes to speak of. Now, however, he tried to find Brabrook with the goal kick, sliced it straight to Yuri Falin, saw it pushed across to Yuri Voinov, on to the captain Nikita Simonian, then beyond Billy Wright to Anatoly Ilyin, who shot past McDonald's right hand.

When Brabrook had hit the post, the ball rebounded into Yashin's arms each time. When Ilyin hit it, the ball went in and England out. It was the only time McDonald was on the losing side in an international match.

> *If in winning the game we only finish with a draw, we would be fine.*
>
> **JACK CHARLTON**

England would probably have beaten Scotland in 1912 if goalkeeper Reg 'Tim' Williamson had stopped the shot which put them 1–0 down. Andy Wilson's effort went straight to him, but instead of going for it with his hands, he let it slip between his knee and the post. The 1–1 draw meant that the two countries shared the Championship.

At his peak, it was said of Gil Merrick that he had all the qualities a goalkeeper needs. Unfortunately this was no longer the general view after his last season of international football (1953–54), when he was unlucky enough to be England's last line against the great Hungarians, who won 6–3 and 7–1 – and he clearly hadn't recovered by the time he went to the World Cup finals at the end of the season.

There, despite conceding four goals in their first match, England reached the quarter-finals, where they faced the holders

Uruguay, the best side in the world after Hungary. England did well, too – at least in the outfield.

Five minutes before half-time, they were level at 1–1 and causing the Uruguayan defence problems, Stanley Matthews having perhaps his best ever international. Then Merrick pulled the rug from under them.

Jimmy Dickinson headed away a free-kick, the Uruguayan captain Obdulio Varela got to it 25 yards out and hit a high, curling shot which the England players expected Merrick to save. Instead he not only didn't do that, he didn't move at all as the ball dropped inside the post.

Worse followed early in the second half, Juan Schiaffino beating Merrick from a very narrow angle (confirmed by film of the match) to score the third, which killed England off. They pulled a goal back, but then Merrick didn't get down to cover Jávier Ambrois' optimistic cross-shot, and that was that. England didn't reach the semi-finals till 1966 – and Merrick, whose last international season cost 30 goals in ten matches, wasn't capped again.

The 1979 FA Cup final was a pedestrian game lit up by an incredible finish, Arsenal leading 2–0 at half-time, Manchester United scoring twice with only four minutes left, then the fifth goal of the game arriving in the very last minute.

Almost from the kick-off after United's equaliser, Liam Brady's pass sent Graham Rix towards the left-hand goal line, from where he pulled back a high cross, which United's 20-year-old goalkeeper Gary Bailey decided to come for. Bob Wilson, watching from only a few yards away, called it 'a naive and bad decision'.

The ball, curling away from goal, always had too much height on it. Bailey didn't get a touch, and had to watch as it fell behind him for Alan Sunderland to get to it before Arthur Albiston and push it into the empty net for the winner.

Bailey came back to pick up a winner's medal in both 1983 (saving Gordon Smith's famous last-minute shot – see CHANCES ARE A FINE THING) and 1985, the year in which he spoiled his first international, against the Republic of Ireland at Wembley, by letting Liam Brady's late shot from a tight angle squeeze in at the near post. It put an end to England's run of five consecutive clean sheets.

With only a minute to go in their FA Cup fifth round tie against Birmingham City in 1968, Arsenal were leading 1–0 when a very simple lob slipped through the fingers of Jim Furnell for the equaliser. It was a costly mistake for Arsenal (they lost the replay 2–1) and for Furnell, who'd been No.1 choice since 1963.

His reserve for all that time had recently been tempted to take a job as a physical education lecturer at Loughborough College, at last taking the hint that four First Division appearances in as many years meant someone up there didn't rate him. Now a single blunder had given him his chance – and neither of them looked back.

While Furnell drifted down to Rotherham and Plymouth, Bob Wilson became an important part of the side which won the 1970 Fairs Cup and the domestic Double in 1971. He won two Scotland caps before retiring at the top to go straight in at the same level with the BBC.

A well-known one, this. A tale of being snatched from obscurity for a chance of glory, which Gary Plumley didn't exactly grasp with both hands.

When Watford reached the 1987 FA Cup semi-final, they found themselves suddenly short of fit goalkeepers, and Graham Taylor had to send out an SOS for Plumley, who was by then running a wine bar.

Sadly, it seemed to show. His first test arrived within five minutes, a well-struck but simple enough ground shot from Clive Allen – which Plumley didn't hold and

Gary Plumley, by the post, wishing he was back behind the bar

Steve Hodge kicked in. After that, the deluge. Within half an hour, Tottenham were 3–0 up and on their way to Wembley after Plumley had let in Paul Allen's shot at the near post. Generally looking caught in the headlights throughout the match, which Spurs won 4–1, he went back behind the bar after it. Watford haven't reached the final since 1984.

Playing for non-League Marine in the first round of the 1995–96 FA Cup, Keith Procter ended a goalmouth scramble by pushing the ball in off his left-hand post to put Second Division Shrewsbury 1–0 up. They went on to win 11–2!

Phil Thompson, a mainstay of Liverpool's very successful back four in the 1970s and early '80s, winner of 42 England caps, was never a goalkeeper and just as well. Liverpool's reserve team coach when they won the 1992 FA Cup, he was leaving the team's London hotel after the final when he dropped the great trophy's lid, denting it so badly it didn't fit back on the rim.

All the world's keepers

Contrary to the popular myth, Brazil have usually fielded world-class goalkeepers, especially in the World Cup. Gylmar didn't concede a goal before the semi-finals in 1958, and only let in five in six games four years later. In 1974 Emerson Leão also kept a clean sheet in each of the first four matches, then let in only three goals in seven games in 1978. Carlos Gallo set a record by conceding only one goal in five matches in 1986.

Cláudio Taffarel lost little in comparison. In Italia 90 he was beaten only twice in four matches, in 1994 only three times in seven – and saved a vital penalty in the shoot-out that won Brazil the Cup. But the time in between included some hairy moments, and he was lucky to play in the '94 final.

Throughout the tournament he'd looked generally unsafe, especially on crosses, and gave away an important goal in the quarter-final. Before that, he'd been dropped by Parma for their victorious Cup-Winners Cup final in 1993.

Still, he seemed to have recovered by the start of the World Cup qualifying competition, keeping a clean sheet in the first match in Ecuador and saving Erwin Sánchez's late penalty in Bolivia. Then the roof, or rather the floor, fell in.

With just two minutes to go, Bolivian midfielder Marco Etcheverry worked some space on the left-hand goal line and knocked in a low cross which was no more than a gesture: there were no Bolivians in the six-yard area, and Taffarel bent down to pick the ball up unchallenged.

In Brazil they call what happened next a *frango*. When a man tries to pick up a hen, they say, it scuttles across his legs. Taffarel, covering his near post, reached down for the ball, which hit his left heel and went in. Cluck cluck, one of the worst-looking blunders ever seen at this level. A minute later, substitute Alvaro Peña went down the same left channel and shot home between Taffarel's legs. It was the only World Cup qualifying match Brazil have ever lost. Hard to believe, at that moment, that we were looking at the goalkeeper of the next World Cup winners.

What helped him was the way his Bolivian opposite number repaid his generosity. In the return match, Carlos Trucco bent down to an easy ball and let it slip behind him to present Raí with the first goal of a game which Bolivia lost 6–0. Both countries qualified for the finals.

By 1986, although they had several of the same players, France had come down from the heights of their European Championship win two years earlier, but were still good enough to reach the World Cup semi-finals in Mexico as they'd done in 1982, and against the same country.

West Germany had an even more uninspired team than in 1982 and reached the semi-final after losing to Denmark, beating Morocco with a last-minute free-kick, and winning their quarter-final on penalties. France have never had a better chance of reaching the final.

After only nine minutes, however, Patrick Battiston fouled Karl-Heinz Rummenigge on the edge of the box, and Felix Magath rolled the ball to Andreas Brehme, whose shot came through towards the near post.

Joël Bats had been the hero of the quarter-final, saving a penalty from Zico and making a string of excellent saves. Here he got down to the ball but let it slip under him in much the same way as Arkonada two years earlier (see THE FINAL STRAW). France have reached three World Cup semis but never the final.

Even before his amazing scorpion kick at Wembley in 1995, René Higuita had earned a reputation as one of the most eccentric of all goalkeepers, one who scored from more than 20 penalties in league matches and internationals and above all carried the role of goalkeeper-sweeper to extremes, i.e. sometimes as far as the halfway line. It often worked (Colombia have been a successful team in his time) but when it didn't, it didn't spectacularly.

The most glaring example of this took place during the 1990 World Cup finals. The very late goal which gave Colombia a draw with eventual champions West Germany took them into the knockout phase, where they faced Cameroon, the surprise package of the tournament. Billed as a colourful clash of styles, the match wended its tedious way into extra time, then turned on Higuita's singular approach to the job.

First he left too big a gap at his near post when Roger Milla broke through for the first goal of the match – then, with only eleven minutes left, he collected a back-pass and tried to dribble it round the same player.

It's a manoeuvre fraught with trouble for even the very best – and if the great Bobby Moore could lose a World Cup match by trying it [BLUNDERS VOL.1], so could an average international goalkeeper imitating a below average defender. Milla got a foot in, nicked the ball away, and ran on to put it into the empty net. He was the oldest scorer in any World Cup finals (a record he added to in 1994).

Colombia pulled a goal back but went out 2–1. This of course did nothing to change Higuita's ways (nor did the spell of imprisonment that made him miss the 1994 finals): that save against England was a talking point of the season.

If we're ever allowed to use the football cliché 'agonising', it has to be about Pat Bonner's dreadful fumble of Wim Jonk's

Higuita dribbles, Milla drools

shot in the 1994 World Cup second round match. The ball was hit straight at him from long range, he seemed to have his body behind it, but it slipped through his hands and in, giving Holland their winning 2–0 lead. We've all seen it several times and sympathise completely, of course we do.

However, it wasn't the worst-looking goalkeeping mistake in a World Cup. If you get the chance to see a video of the 1938 quarter-final between the hosts France and the champions Italy, grasp it with both hands, something Laurent Di Lorto should have done. It has to be seen to be believed, and words fail, but here goes.

Remember the old one about the keeper who put his head in his hands and dropped it? Pat Bonner after Holland's second goal

After only nine minutes, Italy's sharp left-winger Gino Colaussi ran onto a pass at the corner of the French penalty area (his left, the goalkeeper's right). Surrounded by three defenders, he tried a right-footed volley but didn't connect properly, looping the ball straight at Di Lorto, who hopped up for an easy catch – then pushed it away.

It wouldn't have been so bad if he'd knocked it straight out. Instead, he somehow palmed it sideways and slightly backwards, tried to follow it as it fell into the net, crashed into the post, and kicked the ball away in disgust. A genuine masterpiece, and all his own work. He didn't play for France again. Italy, presented with this first goal, won 3–1 and went on to retain the Cup.

Almost as hilarious was Stanislav Seman's boob in the 1982 World Cup finals. Czechoslovakia had held group leaders England to 0–0 for the first hour when Ray Wilkins hit a left-wing corner too close to the keeper, who went up for the easy catch – and dropped it in front of Trevor Francis, who volleyed the goal that ultimately stopped Czechoslovakia from reaching the second round. Seman, substituted twelve minutes later, wasn't capped again.

Three seasons earlier, another keeper's international career had been ended by a mistake that cost Czechoslovakia a match against England. Pavol Michalik was celebrating his 27th birthday, but Steve Coppell must have thought it was his when Michalik fumbled a low cross to let him in for the only goal of the game at Wembley.

Irish winger Peter McParland and Welsh keeper Jack Kelsey, their countries' stars in the 1958 World Cup finals, had made their debuts in the same match, at Wrexham in 1954. They'd been playing international football for only forty seconds when McParland lobbed the ball into the box and Kelsey misjudged it so badly that it drifted past him into the top corner. McParland remembered it as 'the first time I'd touched the ball, and Jack's first touch came when he fished the ball out of the back of the net.'

McParland scored twice in the 2–1 win, his only international goals till those World Cup finals (where his total of five was a British record before Lineker).

Kazadi Nwamba was one of the better players in the Zaire team that took part in the 1974 World Cup finals – which doesn't sound like much (they lost all three games without scoring a goal) but has to be taken in context: one of the best goalkeepers in Africa playing behind an undisciplined defence.

Zaire did well to restrict Scotland to 2–0 in their first match, but Kazadi fumbled in Joe Jordan's header. When three goals then went past him within 20 minutes against Yugoslavia, he was taken off – and was still wandering along the touchline when his substitute Tubilandu Dimbi let in the fourth. The 9–0 defeat, which equalled the World Cup finals record, made some of the team want to go home before the final match against Brazil. They stayed, and did better – but don't say that to the Scots.

With just over ten minutes to go, Zaire were only 2–0 down against that strange, physical travesty of a Brazilian side (Jairzinho lumbering around at centre-forward, etc) when Valdomiro Vaz Franco, a very ordinary winger, shot from the right. None too hard and just right for Kazadi to make a comfortable save on the ground.

He let it in, of course. At the near post. Under his body. The goal that sent Brazil into the second round and eliminated the Scots, who hadn't lost a match.

Manuel Bento had a mixed career at the highest level, sometimes brilliant, sometimes a liability. In his last international, at the 1986 World Cup finals, he made some good saves on the way to captaining Portugal to a 1–0 win over England. Liverpool, though, had fonder memories of him.

When Benfica came to Anfield in 1978, they were already 2–1 down from the home leg of the European Cup quarter-final, Bento having let Jimmy Case's shot go under his body for the equaliser then watched Emlyn Hughes' cross from virtually the touchline go over his head for the winner. Now he completed the three-card trick with the best of the lot, shaping to clear Ian Callaghan's shot with his left foot, missing, catching it with his right, and deflecting it in. A classic, shown on any number of repeats. Liverpool won 4–1 and went on to retain the Cup.

After losing 2–1 at home to a brilliant Red Star Belgrade team in the first leg of the 1991 European Cup semi-final, Bayern Munich played bravely and very well in the return, recovering from a goal down to take a 2–1 lead themselves. Extra time was only a minute away when an aimless cross by Sinisa Mihajlovic was deflected up in the air by Bayern sweeper Klaus Augenthaler.

Now, it could be argued that it was therefore his fault, but the ball was well within goalkeeper Raimond Aumann's reach – or would have been if he hadn't mistimed his jump. Instead of turning the ball over the bar, he flicked it into his own net and will have to live with the scorecard of Aumann own goal 89. Red Star went on to become the first Yugoslav club to win the Cup, Bayern haven't won it since 1976.

There would have been two English clubs in the 1984 UEFA Cup final but for a pair of errors by Hans van Breukelen, Nottingham Forest's Dutch goalkeeper, in the semi-final second leg which Anderlecht won 3–0 after losing the first 2–0. They lost the final to Tottenham, Forest haven't won a European trophy since 1980.

Two elementary errors by Bruce Grobbelaar knocked Liverpool out of the European Cup in successive seasons [BLUNDERS VOL.1] in the early eighties. More than ten years on, they were drawing 1–1 away to Spartak Moscow in the first leg of the 1992–93 Cup-Winners Cup when Grobbelaar was caught in possession and kicked the ball straight to midfielder Valery Karpin, who shot past him as he chased back. Then, after Liverpool had drawn level for the second time, a wild challenge gave away a penalty and earned Grobbelaar the red card. Liverpool lost 4–2 and were halfway to elimination.

Before that, another costly cock-up from the jungle man. In March 1988, Liverpool went to Goodison Park needing only a draw to break Leeds' all-time record of 29 unbeaten League matches from the start of a season. When a left-wing corner floated in, Grobbelaar went up for it above five other players, couldn't hold it, and was beaten by Wayne Clarke's low shot. It was the only goal of the game and only the third he'd conceded in 17 matches.

> *It'll be a shame if either side loses, and that applies to both sides.*
>
> **JOCK BROWN**

Milan have been a power in the European game for almost forty years, but they've had their downs as well as ups. In the 1979–80 European Cup, for example, a goalless draw away to Porto seemed to have set them up for a place in the second round. Then the Portuguese were awarded a free kick, which the Brazilian Duda curled over the wall but straight at Enrico 'Ricky' Albertosi, Milan's

39-year-old goalkeeper – who let it hit his chest, from which it bounced onto the post and in. It was the only goal of the tie, and typified the way things were soon to go for Milan and Albertosi: a famous bribery scandal saw the club relegated to Serie B and the player banned for life.

Spain came to Highbury in 1931 as one of the strongest teams in Europe, the first from outside Britain ever to beat a full England team. Their goalkeeper and captain Ricardo Zamora, first capped at 19, now 30 and at his peak, was widely regarded as the best in the world.

As the teams lined up, he asked the band to play something with a Spanish flavour – then marched along the touchline in time with the music from *Carmen* bowing to the crowds, which must have been as, um, different then as it sounds now. Certainly it prompted the England centre-forward Dixie Dean to bet his centre-half, Everton club-mate Charlie Gee, their £6 match fee that England would put five goals past the great celebrity.

It didn't take Dean long to start winning the money. The game had been going only three minutes when Jack Smith's moderate ground shot gave Zamora his first chance to show what all the fuss was about. He got both hands to it – then let it slip through them into the net. Seven minutes later he fumbled Tom Johnson's shot. Spain lost 7–1 and Zamora was dropped for the next match, a 5–0 win in Dublin.

Although he was forever remembered over here as something of a clown, this was definitely just a blip. Zamora went on being capped for Spain until 1936, playing marvellously and bravely in the 1934 World Cup finals. In 46 internationals played during an attacking era, he conceded only 42 goals, 10 of them in two matches against England. A great keeper, don't doubt it. Mind you, the performance at Highbury really was embarrassing. *Carmen*, for heaven's sake.

Ronnie Hellström was the best Swedish goalkeeper of all time, safe as well as spectacular, a star of the 1978 and especially 1974 World Cup finals – though he might not have appeared in either if he hadn't been forgiven for a dreadful blunder in the first few minutes of his very first World Cup finals match, against Italy in 1970.

There was no danger when Angelo Domenghini drifted in from the left wing after eleven minutes and hit a very moderate shot almost straight at Hellström, who went down and pulled the ball in to his chest (photographs show his hands cupped under his neck) – then let it spill out under his body and into the net.

Not only was it the only goal of the game, it was the only one Italy scored in their three group matches! If Hellström hadn't let it in, Sweden would have qualified instead. As it was, Italy went all the way to the final. Hellström was dropped from Sweden's two remaining matches in the finals.

Vladimir Beara was one of the all-time greats, star of Yugoslavia's excellent sides throughout the 1950s. He saved a penalty against England in 1956, another (from Puskás of all people) in the Olympic final four years earlier, and left an impression of almost balletic agility with everyone who saw him.

He also made relatively few mistakes – but one of these, in that same Olympic final, decided the match. Yugoslavia's forwards had had no effect on the Hungarian defence throughout the match, so they were always going to struggle if they fell behind, which they did halfway through the second half.

When Zoltán Czibor hit a long ball into the area, the balletic one dropped on it, then let it slip out. Puskás took full revenge from close range, Czibor scored a second two minutes from time, Hungary won the title for the first time.

It was the second successive Olympic final Yugoslavia had lost. They lost in the next as well, before finally winning their fourth in a row in 1960, the year after Beara won his last cap.

The rest of your football team are tall, they dwarf above you.

FRED DINENAGE

When Abel Resino let the ball slip through his hands against Barcelona in March 1991, it cost Atlético Madrid a point – but affected Abel even more, putting an end to his run of 13 consecutive clean sheets in the league, a world record run of 1,230 minutes without conceding a goal.

The final straw

Goalkeepers in international finals

Frantisek Planicka was probably the best keeper in the world throughout the 1930s, winning a world record 73 caps and captaining Czechoslovakia in the 1934 World Cup.

In the final in Rome, he caught everything as the Czechs led the aggressive hosts 1–0 with only eight minutes left, then braced himself for Raimundo Orsi's shot from the edge of the penalty area.

One of three Argentinians in the side, Orsi provided Italy's blue-collar teams with their one threat of the unexpected. Sleek-haired and thin, he had great ball control and a famous bodyswerve. But he was 32 now, off form in this match, always liable to try one thing too many with the ball. He tried one now, beating Josef Kostalek then Ladislav Zenisek to make an opening, and shaping to hit the obvious left-footed shot.

Then some trick of the blood made him change feet and shoot with the right, his weaker foot. A mistake, a nothing shot. The ball looped up and wandered weakly towards goal.

In the semi-final, Planicka had let an innocuous lob by Rüdolf Noack drift over his head for Germany's equaliser – but surely it couldn't happen again. This time the ball apparently wobbled in the air, but there's little doubt that it should have been saved without much trouble. Instead, to everyone's astonishment and the delight of the crowd, it wafted over his fingertips (he wasn't a tall keeper) and dropped in.

It was the end of the best opportunity Czechoslovakia ever had to win the World Cup (Italy scored again in extra time). Four years later, in a brutal World Cup match with Brazil, a broken arm put an end to Planicka's international career.

In 1962 the Czechoslovakian goalkeeping jinx worked its mischief again. They reached the World Cup final on the backs of a famous half-back line (Masopust–Popluhár–Pluskal) and especially some remarkable acrobatics by their balding 30-year-old keeper Viliam Schrojf, who'd been particularly brilliant in the 1–0 win over Flórián Albert's Hungarians in the quarter-finals.

In the final, Czechoslovakia scored first. If they'd held out for any length of time, against a slow, old (average age over 30), declining Brazil without Pelé, who knows? As it was, the decisive moment arrived only two minutes later.

Mario Zagallo gave the ball to Pelé's replacement Amarildo Tavares on the left-hand corner of the penalty area. Amarildo beat Jirí Tichy on the outside and homed in on Schrojf along the goal line. The keeper moved out to cover the cross, Amarildo shot between him and the near post: 1–1.

Czechoslovakia held out until twenty minutes from the end, then Schrojf missed Amarildo's cross from the left and Zito bundled it in from virtually under the bar. Eight minutes later, Djalma Santos hoofed a hopeful ball into the area, Schrojf dropped it and Vavá pushed it past him. As with Planicka in 1934, the best keeper in the tournament had cost Czechoslovakia the final. They've never reached even the semi-finals again.

Belgium surprised everyone by reaching the 1980 European Championship final, where they were holding West Germany to a 1–1 draw in the last minute. Then, when Karl-

Heinz Rummenigge's left-wing corner came over, Belgium's flamboyant goalkeeper Jean-Marie Pfaff came out when he should have stayed in, didn't get to the ball, and could only watch as Horst Hrubesch headed the ball into the net past the spot where Pfaff had originally been standing. The Germans took the title for a record second time, Belgium have never won it.

Spain reached the 1984 European Championship final after two very narrow squeaks: a last-minute goal against the holders West Germany, and a penalty shoot-out against Denmark in the semi-final.

Now, against France, the hot favourites (15–8 on) and talented hosts, they held out until ten minutes after half-time, when Salva was judged to have pushed Bernard Lacombe on the edge of the penalty area, and Michel Platini took the free-kick.

The French captain had already scored a record eight goals in the tournament (two hat-tricks, the winner in two other matches) and his free-kicks were famous: he'd put one past Peter Shilton earlier in the year and scored from another in the group match with Yugoslavia. Here he swept it low round the Spanish wall.

Not one of his best. Luis Arkonada had been saving better shots all fortnight, redeeming himself after a nervous World Cup at home in 1982. He dropped down to collect the free-kick, pulled it in to his body, then let it creep through and over the line before trying to scoop it back. France won 2–0.

Arkonada went on captaining Spain until a World Cup qualifier in Wrexham the following year. There he called for the ball then suddenly let it run through to Ian Rush, who tapped in the first goal of Wales' 3–0 win. Arkonada wasn't capped again.

Argentina weren't satisfied with their goalkeeping in the group matches of the 1930 World Cup. Although they won all three, they conceded three goals against the mediocre Mexicans and needed Luisito Monti to do his worst at centre-half to keep out the so-so French and Chileans. Before the semi-final they dropped Angel Bossio and brought in Juan Botasso for his first cap.

There wasn't much for him to do in the match, which Argentina won 6–1 against the muscular but naive Americans. In the final, against the hosts Uruguay, he conceded a goal after twelve minutes, but Argentina led 2–1 at half-time and their pure technique held Uruguay's physical approach: 2–2 with twenty minutes left.

When Uruguayan defender Ernesto Mascheroni robbed Francisco Varallo and pushed a pass upfield to Santos Iriarte, nothing much looked on. More of a striking winger than a provider, Iriarte hadn't done much of either despite the almost complete absence of any Argentinian marking. They left him alone again now, which seemed fair enough this time.

The distance of long-range shots grows in the telling (thirty yards seems to be the going rate) but Iriarte really was a speck in the distance. He seemed to shoot because there was nothing else to do. Botasso made no attempt to stop the shot till it was too late, then the newsreel shows him almost walking across before throwing up his arms (in horror?). Uruguay regained the lead, scored again in the last minute, and Argentina had to wait 48 years to win the Cup for the first time. Botasso (and seven others in the team) didn't play international football again.

After that, Uruguay stayed out of the World Cup for twenty years, then came back to gratefully receive some more goalkeeping help in the final match, which they had to win while the brilliant hosts Brazil needed only a draw. At 1–1 with eleven minutes left, Alcides Ghiggia scored the winner when Brazilian goalkeeper Moacyr Barbosa left a big gap at his near post – even though Ghiggia was only four yards out! It was the last time Uruguay lifted the Cup. Barbosa won only one more cap, three years later.

In the first half of the 1980s, Harald 'Toni' Schumacher was arguably the best keeper in the world. Confident and ruthless – the foul that hospitalised Patrick Battiston in 1982 still reverberates – he played for West Germany when they reached the World Cup final in 1982 and 1986.

Easily beaten by Italy in the 1982 decider, the West Germans were underdogs against Maradona & Co four years later. Nevertheless, Schumacher had kept a clean sheet in each of the last three matches, making several important saves (including two in the penalty shoot-out) in the quarter-final.

However, after twenty minutes of the final, he came off his line but didn't get anywhere near Jorge Burruchaga's high free-kick, leaving José Luis Brown free to head into an open net. Ten minutes into the second half, that first mistake in mind, he stayed back as Jorge Valdano approached from his right: 2–0. Six minutes from time, he stayed put again when Burruchaga ran in from the left: 3–2, the final score.

By the time the Germans won the next World Cup final, their third in a row, Schumacher was long gone in a gust of tale-telling (he called his autobiography *Blowing the Whistle*), winning just two more caps after the '86 final.

Brown heads in as Schumacher *(second left)* leaves German hopes high and dry

> *So that's 1–0, sounds like the score at Boundary Park, where of course it's 2–2.*
>
> **JACK WAINWRIGHT**

By 1960–61 Antonio Ramallets was coming to the end of a distinguished career, including ten years as Spain's first-choice goalkeeper. That season, the first signs of decay were beginning to show, especially in the 4–2 defeat by England at Wembley – but he was still No.1 at Barcelona, who were hot favourites to win the European Cup final after ending Real Madrid's five-year reign in the first round, their forward line containing four of the very greatest players of all time in Luis Suárez and the three Hungarians Kubala, Czibor and Kocsis. When one of the latter's famous headers put them in front against Benfica, the European Cup seemed to be all ready for Ramallets (Barça's captain) to pick up.

Within the space of two minutes around the half-hour mark, he'd effectively dropped it. First he rushed impetuously out of goal, allowing Cavém to push the ball square for José Aguas to tap in. Then – one of the worst blunders of his career – he went up for a ball headed back by his own defender Enrique Gensana, lost it (some say in the evening sun, though he was wearing a cap), knocked it against the post, flicked it away

that followed, he was now 35 and had just won his last cap, but seemed as calm and consistent as ever.

Benfica had to play the 1965 European Cup final at the San Siro, home ground of their opponents, who were also the defending champions: the brilliant but ruthless Inter. While Eusébio & Co struggled up front, the great Germano protected Costa Pereira from Mazzola, Suárez and Corso – at least until three minutes from half-time, when the ball reached Inter's electric Brazilian winger Jair da Costa on the right. He slipped as he fell, so there was no power in the shot, and Costa Pereira bent down to gather the ball.

It's true that the pitch was waterlogged in places – but a) not in the goalmouth, and b) all the more reason for him to get his body behind the ball. Instead it slipped between his legs and barely made it over the line as he scrambled after it under Germano's baleful eye.

It was Costa Pereira's last act on the world stage. Going off with a mystery injury (to the undisguised scepticism of his team-mates), he left the ten men to try and find their way through the Inter barricades, an impossible task. Germano was as composed in goal as he was dominating at centre-half, and Jair's goal was the only one of the game. It was the last time either side won the Cup.

Although by 1972 Inter were no longer the force of old, they were just as defensive – and a lot luckier. They reached the European Cup final by beating Borussia Moenchengladbach in a replayed match after losing 7–1, then Standard Liège on away goals and Celtic on penalties in the semi-final after two goalless draws, and were clear underdogs in the final against the great Ajax team.

They held out till half-time, then Ajax pushed right-back Wim Suurbier further forward, and the move paid off within three minutes of the restart. His high cross seemed about to be headed away by an Inter defender until Ivano Bordon intervened.

A keeper of real promise, later Dino Zoff's deputy in the national team, the young

after it had crossed the line, then held his head when the goal was given.

Barcelona didn't recover, and Ramallets' errors helped Zoltán Czibor to a unique and unwanted record: two major finals in seven years (the 1954 World Cup with Hungary), each time as one of the overwhelming favourites, each time a scorer, each time on the receiving end of a 3–2 defeat – and both in the same stadium! Barcelona had to wait another 31 years before finally winning the Cup for the first time.

In 1965 Alberto da Costa Pereira was in much the same position as Ramallets in '61. One of the best keepers in the world for a decade, a late starter who first played for Portugal in 1955, star of the great Benfica team which won that 1961 final and the one

Bordon had saved an important penalty earlier in the competition – but this, for Inter supporters, is a scene painful to recall (and write about). He knocked his own defender flat and they were both on the deck when Johan Cruyff rolled the ball into an empty net at the far post.

Without an attack worthy of the name, Inter didn't look like equalising. Cruyff headed a second, Ajax retained the Cup, and Inter haven't reached the final since.

Vicente Traín played in only one European Cup final for Real Madrid, in 1964 against Inter, who were leading 1–0 when Aurelio Milani mishit a half-volley from outside the penalty area. The ball landed slowly in front of Vicente, who fumbled it into the net. Inter won 3–1 and took the Cup at their first attempt and without losing a match.

> **ELTON WELSBY** *Magnifique, Eric.*
>
> **ERIC CANTONA** *Oh, do you speak French?*
>
> **ELTON WELSBY** *Non.*

Looking at the record books now, you'd think Eintracht Frankfurt were very much the underdogs before the 1960 European Cup final against the might of Real Madrid, who'd won the previous four – but it wasn't necessarily so. In their semi-final, the Germans had beaten Rangers 6–1 & 6–3! Some knowledgeable judges gave them a real chance.

They almost took it, too. Ahead after ten minutes, level after thirty, they were holding Di Stéfano, Puskás and Gento and troubling Real's less accomplished defence. Then the ball reached Real's Brazilian right-winger Darcy Silveira dos Santos, known as Canário (canary), who not only telegraphed his shot but hit it slackly, sort of slapped it towards

the near post. Eintracht keeper Egon Loy went down for it with all the time in the world, only to push it straight at the feet of Di Stéfano – a grenade against a trampoline if ever there was one – who smacked it in to give Real a lead they never lost.

Egg on Loy's face. He conceded seven goals (his team-mates bravely scored three), a record for any European final. It was Eintracht's – and his – only appearance in the final of the major competition.

With just eleven minutes gone in the 1970 Cup-Winners Cup final, Manchester City's Francis Lee kept possession out on the left long enough to get in a shot, which he hit well but from outside the penalty area. Górnik Zabrze's international keeper Hubert Kostka saw it all the way, got down to it, but let it come straight back out, more or less straight to the feet of Neil Young, who shot the first goal of the game. City won 2–1, the only European trophy they've ever lifted, against the only Polish club to reach a European final.

The following year, another English club owed part of their success in a European final to a goalkeeping mistake. Late in the first leg of the UEFA Cup decider, Leeds United were 2–1 down in Turin when full-back Terry Cooper finished one of his famous raids up the left with a cross that went too close to Juventus keeper Massimo Piloni – who flapped at it and could only watch as Mick Bates pushed it in from close range. The 2–2 draw allowed Leeds to draw 1–1 at home in the second leg (from which Piloni was dropped) and win the trophy on the away-goals rule. Juventus were the first side to finish runners-up in a European competition despite not having lost a game.

A generation later, Juventus had some help of their own, in the Cup-Winners Cup final of 1984 when the thirteenth minute proved unfortunate for Porto keeper José Alberto Teixeira, known as Zé Beto. Juve's

Beniamino Vignola received the ball unmarked just ahead of the centre circle, turned, and set off on a run which took him to the opposition penalty area, where he was forced wide by two defenders. Surrounded by five of the enemy, with no-one to pass to, he shot because there was nothing else to do.

Shot quite well, too, in the circumstances – but from the edge of the box and in clear view of Zé Beto. What followed looked worse than it was. The left-foot cross shot dipped and was well placed, but the keeper should nevertheless have saved it, or at the very least made the effort. Instead he seemed to check his dive, and ended in a useless crouch with his left hand on the ground as the ball went in at the far post.

The rest of the defence stood and looked hard at Zé Beto, then turned and trudged towards the centre circle. Juventus won the Cup-Winners Cup for the first and only time. Their win in the following year's Champions Cup made them the first club to take all three European trophies. By the time Porto won the Champions Cup themselves three years later, Zé Beto was no longer in the team.

Few keepers have contributed so much to their club's defeat in a European final as Stevan Stojanovic. (In the very first European Cup final back in 1956, Juan Alonso's fumbles had left Real Madrid 2–0 down – but as they recovered to win 4–3 he escapes a place in the Hall of Blame.)

Stojanovic wasn't so lucky. And yet he'd been one of Red Star's heroes in the 1991 European Cup final, keeping a clean sheet then producing a match-winning save in the penalty shoot-out.

Two years later he helped unfancied Antwerp reach the Cup-Winners Cup final at Wembley – only to present favourites Parma with their first European trophy. First, after nine minutes, he came out for a corner and fumbled it straight to the feet of Parma captain Lorenzo Minotti, who volleyed in. Antwerp equalised within two minutes, but on the half-hour Stojanovic again came off his line and missed a cross, leaving Alessandro Melli to head home. There was no way back from that – and Stojanovic completed his hat-trick with six minutes left, hesitating to come out for a square pass and leaving himself stranded as Stefano Cuoghi scored the third. It was the only European final Antwerp have ever reached.

After being at fault with both of Germany's goals in the Czech Republic's first match of Euro 96, Petr Kouba had generally kept goal well in the tournament, making the save in the penalty shoot-out that sent his unfancied team into the final. Their opponents there: the Germans again.

Again he did well enough, making important saves from Stefan Kuntz. Then, with 17 minutes left and the Czechs leading 1–0, he failed to come out for the long free-kick which Oliver Bierhoff headed in from close range. Four minutes into extra time, Kouba allowed Bierhoff's unexceptional deflected shot to slip through his hands and drop gently in off the post for the sudden-death winner. Penalty shoot-outs apart, the Czechs haven't beaten Germany since 1964.

Cornered

Goalkeepers who let them straight in

The 1929 Home Championship wasn't decided until the very last minute. With the home match against England petering into a goalless draw and the title apparently about to be shared by the big two, Scotland won a corner in the final seconds. Taken by Alex Cheyne, the young inside-right winning his first cap, it floated over goalkeeper Jack Hacking's head and went straight in, apparently the first goal scored direct from a corner in international football. Scotland took the title with maximum points and Hacking didn't play for England again.

In terms of the Richter Scale this defeat was a force eight gale

JOHN LYALL

If Hacking was the first, David Seaman was the last so far. Three years before his horror in Paris under Nayim's lob (see ENGLISH GOALKEEPERS), he'd let Jozef Chovanec's low cross in at his near post against Czechoslovakia, becoming the latest keeper to concede a goal direct from a corner in an England match.

Even the very best aren't immune. Lev Yashin [see GOLD KEEPERS] let one in straight from a corner against Colombia in the 1962 World Cup.

After an exciting 3–3 draw, the 1964 Cup-Winners Cup final went to a replay, which was decided by a single goal, MTK's keeper

Ferenc Kovalik letting a corner by Sporting Lisbon winger João Morais go straight in over his head. It was the only European final either club's ever reached.

Bob Wilson's misjudgment in the 1971 FA Cup final cost Arsenal a goal [BLUNDERS VOL.1] but not the match and the Double. Just as well, because to lose your club one trophy in a season is unfortunate, to lose two...

Arsenal, defending the Fairs Cup, were a goal up in the first leg of their quarter-final against Cologne at Highbury when Wilson allowed a corner by Karl-Heinz Thielen to drift over his head and go straight in for the away goal that eventually cost Arsenal the tie.

With only thirty seconds of the first half left, Chelsea were well on top against Arsenal in the 1950 FA Cup semi-final: leading 2–0, and about to clear the corner kick which Freddie Cox hit too close to their goal.

Chelsea's Welsh international left-back Billy Hughes was in the right place, about four feet in front of the near post. Unchallenged by any Arsenal player, he went up for the header, but the ball was too high, whereupon Chelsea's other full-back John Harris called for goalkeeper Harry Medhurst to catch it.

Too late. Medhurst, having expected Hughes to head clear, didn't touch the ball till it had crossed the line, punching it into the roof of the net. A goal so close to half-time revitalised Arsenal: they came back to draw 2–2, won the replay, and went on to lift the Cup. Chelsea had to wait exactly twenty years to reach the final again.

In a Third Division match at Valley Parade in January 1984, both goalkeepers – Eric McManus of Bradford City and Peter Litchfield of Preston North End – conceded a goal direct from a corner.

For nearly two hours, BCC Lions of Nigeria looked likely to retain the African Cup-Winners Cup in 1991. Taking a 3–2 lead from the home leg of the final against Power Dynamoes of Zambia, they went further ahead in the second leg thanks to an own goal after 27 minutes, and were level at 1–1 (4–3 ahead on aggregate) until Richard Sikanyika's corner went over the head of goalkeeper Addingi (who hadn't played in the first leg) and straight in. Power Dynamoes, now ahead on away goals, became the first Zambian club to win a major African club title.

And one who didn't let the ball straight in, but definitely had a hand in it

Liverpool's tradition of using brilliant but spectacularly fallible goalkeepers (Lawrence, Clemence, Grobbelaar) has been maintained by David James, who might well have been capped by England by now but for the odd aberration.

Actually, he was on the fringe of selection for the Euro 96 squad, and seems to have become safer in recent times, never more so than in the 1996 FA Cup final. Or at least most of it.

Until five minutes from the end, he was probably its man of the match, catching everything and making two excellent saves. Then, with extra time on the way, he came for a corner from his left, punched it out weakly, and Eric Cantona drove in the only goal of the game to give Manchester United the Double for the second time in two seasons.

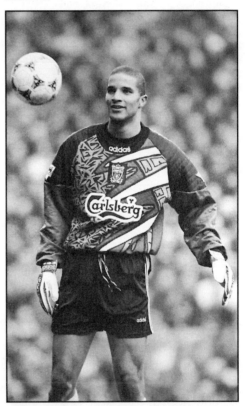

Man United are the Cup favourites, but David James gives them only a puncher's chance

Gold keepers

The best doing their worst

In Leipzig in 1963, Gordon Banks let Peter Ducke's unremarkable long shot slide under him to give East Germany the lead. It was the 500th goal conceded by England.

The match at Hampden Park in 1964 was heading for a goalless draw when Banks came out for a corner, shouted 'mine' – and was left in no man's land as Alan Gilzean headed the goal that gave Scotland a share of the Championship.

Against Scotland three years later, he admitted making the 'cardinal sin of not guarding my near post properly' to allow Jim McCalliog, on his debut, to score the winning goal.

Great keeper though he was (he apparently saved more than a hundred penalties in first-class football) it was said that if Lev Yashin were 'told to go from A to C and change trains at B, he would forget where he was supposed to change.' These lapses of concentration were occasional but occasionally critical; in fact it could be said that they knocked the USSR out of two World Cups...

In 1962, they led the mediocre Colombians 4–1 but were held to a 4–4 draw after Yashin had let in a goal direct from a corner. Then, in the quarter-final against the hosts Chile, he was beaten first by Leonel Sánchez's free kick then Eládio Rojas' ground shot – both from over thirty yards, the second such a bad miss that Rojas hugged him for it!

Four years later, in England, redemption; journalists voting big Lev the best keeper in the tournament. But even here it ended badly. The USSR were a goal down in the semi-final against West Germany when Franz Beckenbauer dragged the ball to his left and shot from outside the penalty area. Yashin made no attempt to save, thinking the ball was going past his right-hand post. Instead, it went in – and the look on his face, when he turned back, said it all. It was the furthest the USSR have ever gone in the World Cup

If any world-class keeper could match Yashin when it came to conceding goals from long range, it had to be Dino Zoff, who fully earned his World Cup winner's medal at the age of 40 with a single save, holding Oscar's header on the line two minutes from time to preserve the marvellous win over Brazil in 1982. That came from inside the penalty area. From further out, it was sometimes another story. In important matches too.

In the 1978 World Cup finals alone, he let in two famous long-range strikes: Arie Haan's 35-yarder that confirmed Holland's place in the final at Italy's expense, and Nelinho's drive from a very tight angle that helped Brazil win the third-place final.

Most traumatically of all, Felix Magath beat Zoff with a high shot from outside the area after only nine minutes of the 1983 European Cup final, the goal that allowed underdogs Hamburg to beat a Juventus team that was arguably the strongest (and most expensively assembled) club side of all time: six of the Italian World Cup team plus Bettega, Platini and Boniek. The European Cup was just about the only major trophy Zoff never won.

In the late '70s, Nottingham Forest had the Indian sign on Liverpool, knocking them out of the European Cup, beating them in a League Cup final and semi-final. But the FA Cup was never going to be Brian Clough's happy hunting ground, as Peter Shilton proved at home against Liverpool in the fourth round in 1979–80 when he dropped a simple high ball for Kenny Dalglish to score the first goal in a 2–0 win. The season before, he'd let substitute Yasuhiko Okudera's weak ground shot slip through for Cologne's equaliser in the European Cup (cue headline: Forest Sunk By Jap Sub).

Shilts had his fingers burned in internationals too: e.g. when he admitted to trying to make too good-looking a save against Poland at Wembley, costing England a place in the World Cup finals; when he failed to hold a simple low cross, letting Mirandinha score an equaliser for Brazil at Wembley (and encouraging Newcastle to buy the scorer, so it was a double error); when his failure to stop a 30-yard free-kick against Uruguay ended England's 17-match unbeaten record; and in his 125th and last match, the third-place final of Italia '90,

when he lost concentration on his goal line, allowing Roberto Baggio to rob him and set up the first goal in England's 2–1 defeat.

Pat Jennings stands comparison with any of the great keepers from any country. A world record 119 caps, hands like hams, almost total reliability.

'Almost' is right. Four seasons after moving from Tottenham to Arsenal, he came back to White Hart Lane for an FA Cup match in January 1982 – and gave his old club a belated leaving present, allowing Garth Crooks' weak left-footer to trundle under his arm for the only goal of the match. 'It's the worst goal I've let in during the whole of my career.' Spurs went on to retain the Cup.

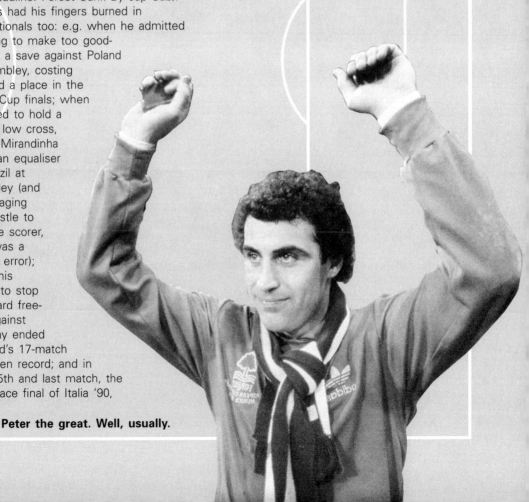

Peter the great. Well, usually.

Defendant defenders

Gary Stevens wins this one, but there's a Ruud awakening to come

Stuart Pearce's under-hit back pass against San Marino in 1993 made no difference to the result (England won 7–1) but it did set up a little moment of football history, allowing Davide Gualtieri to score after less than nine seconds, certainly the fastest goal in an England match and possibly in any international. It was Gualtieri's first for San Marino, making him their joint all-time record scorer!

Although his crosses led to several goals at international level, and Jimmy Hill once described him as 'the athletic right-back that England need', Gary Stevens rarely looked the constructive wing-back England could have done with – a point illustrated in several decisive matches.

Playing for Everton in the 1986 FA Cup final, he gave the ball away for Jan Mølby to set up Liverpool's equaliser on their way to a 3–1 win that gave them the Double. In the World Cup finals later that season, Stevens went AWOL at the far post when Carlos Manuel scored the goal that cost England their opening game against Portugal.

In the 1988 European Championship finals, England needed at least a point from the match against Holland, and had already hit the woodwork twice when the ball drifted over Stevens' head on the touchline, leaving him facing his own goal. His hesitation (according to his manager Bobby Robson, 'He didn't know what to do') allowed Ruud Gullit to rob him and find Marco van Basten in the penalty area.

Worse, as Van Basten turned to set up a shooting chance, Stevens made a desperate attempt to redeem himself by lunging in, and drilled the ball past Peter Shilton. Van Basten went on to be credited with the only hat-trick scored against England since 1959 as a 3–1 defeat virtually eliminated England, but that first goal was definitely a Stevens OG, as seen on TV.

Finally (phew), in the 1989 Scottish Cup final, Stevens' attempted back-pass to goalkeeper Chris Woods let in Joe Miller to score the only goal of the game for Celtic and deny Rangers the Treble.

Cardiff City, the only Welsh club to reach the FA Cup final, did it twice, first in 1925, when they kept a clean sheet for the first half-hour before the Sheffield United right-half Harry Pantling hit a hopeful crossfield ball towards his left-winger Fred Tunstall. Newspapers of the day were unanimous that the other right-half, Cardiff's Harry Wake, should have had no trouble cutting the pass out. Instead he missed the ball completely and Tunstall's low shot provided the only goal of the game. The *South Wales Football Express* can't have been the only publication to run the obligatory headline 'Wake Not Awake'. By the time Cardiff won the Cup for the first time, two years later, he was no longer in the team.

In the course of his long career with Celtic, his only professional club, Billy McNeill played 831 matches and won just about everything: nine League titles, seven Scottish Cups, six Scottish League Cups, 29 international caps. A classic centre-half, good in the air, he captained Celtic to their win in the 1967 European Cup final. Amazingly, in each of the next three seasons, his mistakes knocked the club out of the same competition.

In their very first defence, the first leg of the first round in 1967–68, Celtic were 1–0 down at home to Dynamo Kiev when McNeill misjudged a long clearance from goalkeeper Evgeny Rudakov and hit it against Anatoly Byshovets, who ran on to score his second goal of the game. Celtic lost only 3–2 on aggregate.

The following season, a 0–0 draw in the San Siro was wasted in the unlucky 13th minute of the return. Again McNeill failed to cut out a long pass, again the opposition's top striker (Pierino Prati) ran on to score, again Celtic lost at home, this time by just this single goal on aggregate.

In 1970 Celtic went all the way to the final (in the San Siro), took the lead against Feyenoord, and were still level three minutes from the end of extra time. Then, yet again, a long ball, this time a quickly taken free-kick from Rinus Israel, caught McNeill out. As it drifted over his head, he took several steps backwards, then handled the ball in the penalty area as he fell over. The referee played advantage and McNeill was squatting on his heels as another opposition leading marksman, Ove Kindvall, lifted in the winner. It was Celtic's last appearance in the final.

> *I don't really believe in targets because my next target is to beat Stoke City.*
>
> **RON WYLIE**

Scotland went into the final match of the 1904 Home Championship needing to beat England to win the title, but lost everything after only eighteen minutes when a dreadful miskick in the penalty area by full-back Jimmy Watson presented the ball to the last person he wanted to see with it, record goalscorer Steve Bloomer, who knocked in the only goal of the game. Watson's play deteriorated to the point where he was described as an 'out and out failure'. It was the first time Scotland had failed to win a match during a Championship.

The 1922 Home Championship was also decided by a single goal in an England–Scotland match, again the fault of a defender. Just past the hour, as England keeper Jerry Dawson was preparing to make a clearance after catching the ball, his left-back Sam Wadsworth, a highly-rated player making his international debut, wandered in front of him.

Dawson's clearance kick hit Wadsworth and rebounded towards goal, where Andy N Wilson rolled it into the unguarded net. The full-back accepted the blame, but it was Dawson who didn't play for England again.

Having lost to Blackpool in the FA Cup semi-final of 1948, Tottenham faced the same club in the same round five years later. Again the match was heading for extra-time when Blackpool pumped a long ball upfield in the last minute, where it was intercepted by Alf Ramsey, Spurs' slow but intelligent England right-back, who'd been outstanding throughout.

Instead of thumping the ball upfield, Ramsey remained true to character by passing back to goalkeeper Ted Ditchburn. The ball, badly under-hit, didn't get there. Jackie Mudie beat Ditchburn to it and scored the only goal of the game. While Blackpool went on to win the Cup in the Matthews Final, Tottenham didn't reach the final again till 1961.

In October 1975 England went into the crucial European Championship match in Bratislava needing a draw to stand a good chance of qualifying for the quarter-finals, took a 26th-minute lead through Mick Channon and seemed in command of things with only a minute to go to half-time.

Then Marian Masny took a corner and Zdenek Nehoda was unmarked when he headed the equaliser, unmarked because Ian Gillard, a rawboned left-back short of international class, was standing inside the near post.

This doesn't sound much of an error and needs some explaining – but it enraged England manager Don Revie for the rest of his career. Gillard became a byword in discussions with full-backs. Always stand holding the post at corners, Revie told them. 'Don't do what Ian Gillard did in Czechoslovakia. His positioning stopped him from challenging Nehoda for the cross.'

A small point? Perhaps, but big matches are sometimes decided on these things. Two minutes after half-time, Masny beat Gillard and crossed for Dusan Gallis to head the winner. Big Ian wasn't capped again and Czechoslovakia went on to win the Championship despite having lost their first group match 3–0 at Wembley in Revie's first game in charge.

Jack Charlton was regarded as something of a wounded hero after the England–Scotland match at Wembley in 1967 – but there was more to it than that.

Scotland were leading 1–0 when pacy little Bobby Lennox attacked down the left wing and Charlton, the Footballer of the Year, came across to intercept. Mistiming his run so badly that it left him no chance of making the tackle, he went through with the challenge regardless.

He hit wee Bobby's knee so hard it forced a stud back through big Jack's boot and into his toe, which was broken. He soldiered on up front, and even scored England's first goal – but there were only five minutes left by then and Scotland were 2–0 up against a defence disorganised by the loss of its big centre-half (the injured Lennox had scored the second). England lost 3–2, their first defeat as world champions.

After their lucky draw in the 1901 FA Cup final (see BRITISH REFEREES), Sheffield United led Tottenham 1–0 at half-time in the replay and were level at 1–1 when their captain Ernest Needham tried to clear his penalty area.

The Nudger was one of the leading players of his day, a short, hard, tireless half-back who won 16 England caps spread over

eight years. It was generally agreed that he hadn't put a foot wrong throughout either match of the final. Until now.

The attempted clearance barely left his boot, went straight to Tottenham winger Tommy Smith, and finished low in the net. Spurs' 3–1 win made them the first non-League club to win the Cup.

After losing 3–2 to a late penalty in the first leg of the 1971–72 League Cup semi-final, Tottenham were leading 2–1 at home in the last minute of normal time when Chelsea took a free-kick on the Spurs left. None of their dead-ball kicks had amounted to much throughout the match, and this one by Alan Hudson kept up the shoddy work, mishit low into the goalmouth.

Tottenham's England full-back Cyril Knowles had so much time (and not a blue shirt in sight) that he changed feet to clear it with his stronger left, missed it completely, stumbled, and watched as the ball trickled over the line. Not nice, Cyril, not nice at all. The final whistle went immediately and Knowles was dropped from the team almost as quickly.

> *Hodge scored for Forest after only 22 seconds, totally against the run of play.*
>
> **PETER LORENZO**

There were only eight minutes left and the 1981 European Cup final between Liverpool and Real Madrid was heading, goalless, for extra-time when left-back Alan Kennedy chased a throw-in into the left-hand side of the Real penalty area.

The ball was too far ahead, sitting up for defender Rafael García Córtes to clear it on the volley. Probably distracted by the charging Kennedy, he took his eye off the ball and missed it completely, a famous TV air shot. Kennedy ran on to score the only goal of the match and Real haven't won the Cup since 1966.

In the 1921 FA Cup final, the Wolves defence coped very well with Tottenham's dangerous forward line throughout the first half, right-back Maurice Woodward doing particularly well against the tricky little England winger Jimmy Dimmock.

Eight minutes after the break, Dimmock set off on a run, beat Val Gregory, then lost control. The ball ran on to Woodward, who controlled it for a moment, then lost it, knocking it straight back to the winger, who ran on to beat goalkeeper Noel George with a ground shot.

Dimmock was a well-known individualist who scored match-winning goals – but this was one of the luckiest of his career. Wolves didn't win the Cup again till 1949.

For a year, Mike Duxbury was a fixture in the England side that beat a dreadful Brazil in Rio but also had some very poor results – which he had something to do with, allowing crosses to go over his head for Michel Platini and Mark McGhee to head in for France and Scotland, then crowning it all by treading on the ball at Wembley for Sergei Gotsmanov to run on and score for the USSR, all in 1984. Duxbury was on the winning side in only four of his ten internationals before Bobby Robson recalled Viv Anderson.

For virtually a decade, Norman Hunter had been Bobby Moore's reserve in the England team, winning only 23 caps from 1965 to the beginning of the 1973–74 season. Then, when Mooro's mistakes lost the World Cup qualifier in Poland [BLUNDERS VOL.1], stormin' Norman was brought in as No.1

choice for more or less the first time. A 7–0 home win over Austria didn't prove much either way, but the same team was retained for the return with the Poles, who needed a draw at Wembley to reach the finals. England had to win.

There was no score, and goalkeeper Jan Tomaszewski was already writing himself, rather frantically, into the record books when

The Hunter hunted

Hunter chased a loose ball out to the right-hand touchline.

Grzegorz Lato went with him – but even the Polish winger's famous speed couldn't get him there in time. The leg biter had all the time he needed.

Easy to say in hindsight – but perhaps true nonetheless – that this was the problem. Too much time. Who knows what went through Hunter's mind? That putting the ball out for a throw-in would have looked too crude so close to the touchline, confirming people's belief that he wasn't in Moore's class when it came to using the ball? Whatever, he hesitated long enough for Lato to go in and win the ball, run on, wait for the other winger Robert Gadocha to cross his path on a dummy run, and find Jan Domarski, whose ground shot beat Peter Shilton at the near post. Catastrophe. If Hunter had always wanted to play like Bobby Moore, he had now.

England equalised, but Tomaszewski and a series of close shaves combined to make sure Hunter's contribution to Polish footballing history wasn't wasted. They went on to finish third in the finals, playing some of the most exciting soccer ever seen in a World Cup.

For England, Alf Ramsey, and before long Norman Hunter, the end of a road. The way all three had approached the game in the early '70s, they weren't missed in the World Cup.

If it's any consolation to the great limb-nibbler (it isn't), his great predecessor was prone to this kind of thing more often than we sometimes remember. That aberration against Lubanski wasn't Bobby Moore's only disastrous attempt to dribble past an attacking player. Two years earlier, in an almost equally important game, the first leg of the 1972 European Championship quarter-final at Wembley, he committed the cardinal sin of trying to carry the ball out of his penalty area and gave it straight to Gerd Müller, of all people, who helped set up West Germany's first goal. Their second, which put them ahead 2–1, came from a penalty after a foul by Moore.

Scotland went to Naples and their final qualifying match for the 1966 World Cup with nothing but defence in mind. A draw would force a play-off against Italy on neutral ground – and there was nothing left to attack with, as manager Jock Stein admitted. Injuries and the refusal of club managers in England (including well-known Scots like Busby and Shankly) to release players had deprived Scotland of a plethora of world-class players: Jim Baxter, Denis Law, Billy McNeill, Willie Henderson, goalkeeper Bill Brown. Forced into playing Ron Yeats as an extra centre-half, Stein sent out a defensive team and hoped for the best.

For a while, he got it. With Billy Bremner dominating Italy's playmaker Gianni Rivera and Ron McKinnon solid in central defence, Scotland held out for 38 minutes. Then Eddie McCreadie, who'd been doing so well at full-back, suddenly miskicked in front of goal, allowing the prolific goalscoring winger Ezio Pascutti to smash the ball in.

Scotland, with no cutting edge up front, rarely looked like scoring, lost 3–0, and didn't reach the finals until 1974. Jock Stein resigned immediately after the match.

By far the two best sides in the competition reached the 1993 European Cup final, where a lapse in concentration from one handed the trophy to the other. A poor, bad-tempered first half was coming to an end when Marseille won a corner on the Milan left. Abedi Ayew, immodestly nicknamed Pelé, took it, Rüdi Völler missed it, but it fell just right for Basile Boli to head it across towards the left-hand side of the goal – and in.

Not only should someone have got to the ball ahead of Boli, who was short for a central defender, but Milan had broken the first professional rule of defending a corner: there was no defender on the line.

The only goal of the game, it ended Milan's run of ten straight wins in the competition, made Marseille the first French team to win a European trophy, and deprived Italy of a clean sweep of the three European trophies that year.

Opinion seems to be divided as to whether there was a great defender trying to get out from under the fairly regular haplessness of Ian Ure. Although his career included spells with big clubs (Arsenal and Man United), it was punctuated by entire periods of poor form, laced with out-and-out errors. One of the most unforgettable (for Bob Wilson, among others) gave Third Division Swindon Town a boost of confidence – and their first goal – in the famous 1969 League Cup final.

The match was played on a typical Wembley mudheap of the time. On that kind of surface, Ure should have known better than to simply shepherd the ball back to Wilson, who shouted at him three times for a solid back pass. When this finally got through to big Ian, he was too close, over-hit the ball, and saw it cannon off Wilson's legs to Peter Noble, who squared it into the goalmouth for Roger Smart to open the scoring.

Arsenal's equaliser, only four minutes from time, was too late to dent Swindon's confidence, and two fine goals by Don Rogers won the Cup in extra time. Arsenal didn't win it until 1987, and John Francome Ure never won a major trophy in England.

> *He'd no alternative but to make a needless tackle.*
>
> **PAUL ELLIOTT**

After being 1–0 down for almost the entire match, then equalising in injury time, West Germany had just taken an extra-time lead against Italy in the famous World Cup semi-final of 1970 when they conceded a free kick on the edge of their area. Gianni Rivera took it, floating it towards the right-hand post.

One reporter described the kick as being 'hit as softly as if he was kicking crystal', which may have been true if rather painful, before going on to say that it dropped at Tarcisio Burgnich's feet at the far post. Well yes it did, but there was more to it than that.

Rivera kicked the crystal too firmly, too far ahead of his nearest team-mate and straight to Sigi Held, standing all on his own as a kind of sweeper behind the wall. Quite what he was doing there is unclear: he was a winger, a star of the 1966 final, and by no means a natural defender.

He demonstrated that here, letting the ball bounce off his chest straight to Burgnich, a rugged world-class right-back who was equally unaccustomed to appearing in the other penalty box. This, gratefully received from Held's mistake, was his second and last goal in an eventual 66 internationals.

Italy, let back into a match that was slipping away from them, went on to win 4–3. By the time West Germany reached and won the final four years later, Held had played his last international.

When the great Neil Franklin went looking for a living wage in Colombia in 1950, he left a hole in England's central defence that no one could adequately fill. Just before the 1950 World Cup finals, too.

Bill Jones of Liverpool was given a go, two goes in fact, before the centre-half spot was handed to his tall Liverpool club-mate Laurie Hughes, who did well in the tournament, making very few mistakes. Unfortunately one of those was decisive.

After losing to the USA, England needed to beat Spain to force a group play-off, and were level at half-time after having a goal disallowed. Five minutes into the second half, the Spanish outside-left and captain Agustin 'Pirru' Gainza put over a high cross, Hughes missed his clearance kick, and the stocky centre-forward Zarra beat goalkeeper Bert Williams to the ball before you could say his full name: Telmo Zarraonandia Montoya.

It was the only goal of the game and England, supposedly one of the favourites, were eliminated. Partly because of injury, Hughes wasn't capped again.

Few defenders have had such a traumatic time while playing for England as poor Russell Osman. And yet the potential seemed to have been there.

He played alongside Terry Butcher in the centre of Ipswich Town's defence, they made their international debuts in the same match, and were clearly being groomed (by their former club manager Bobby Robson, now in charge of England) for a long international partnership. Then, very soon, while Butcher was starting out on the road to his 77 caps, it all went horribly wrong for Osman.

Not only did England win only two of the eleven matches he played in, but these included some of the worst defensive performances of their time. It wasn't so much a case of blatant errors by Osman (though he did give away the late penalty in Copenhagen that gave Denmark a draw and helped them qualify for the European finals) as a general feeling of dread (in him too?) whenever the ball approached the England defence, especially on the ground.

The rollcall of horror: Spain, Switzerland and Norway 1981: all 2–1 scorelines camouflaging three famous disasters; finally Denmark 1983: the 1–0 defeat that cost England a place in the European Championship finals

> *Oh, he had an eternity to play the ball, but he took too long over it.*
>
> **MARTIN TYLER**

The 1958 FA Cup final is remembered mainly for the Nat Lofthouse shoulder-charge, which may have been legal, that deposited Harry Gregg in the net for Bolton's second goal. Big bad Nat against the team everyone sympathised with after the Munich air crash.

But the first goal turned out to be the winner, and it was a Manchester United defender's fault, Stan Crowther staying back when the others moved up to catch Bolton offside. A shot by Bryan Edwards was deflected to Lofthouse, who scored from close range. Crowther, who'd played for Aston Villa when they beat United in the 1957 final, missed the chance of becoming the first player to win the Cup in consecutive years with different clubs.

Two into one don't go

(but sometimes should)

England would almost certainly have beaten Scotland in 1887 but for two gross defensive errors. First, goalkeeper Bob Roberts spoiled his international debut by catching a free-kick which he should have left alone, and was charged over the line for the goal that put Scotland 2–1 ahead.

Then, after England had equalised, John Marshall crossed from the right, Roberts and his left-back Percy Walters left it to each other, and another new cap, Jimmy Allan, rolled the winner into an empty goal.

Blackpool, in their first FA Cup final (1948), were 1–0 up against Manchester United after half an hour. When the United captain Johnny Carey set up his winger Jimmy Delaney for a cross from the right, there seemed no danger: Delaney's high lob was too far ahead of any United forward.

Then Blackpool keeper Joe Robinson left it to his centre-half Eric Hayward, who left it to him: one of the best-known (and best-looking) televised Cup Final blunders. Jack Rowley nipped in, rolled the ball away from them, and touched it into an empty net for the equaliser. United went on to win the Cup for the first time since 1909, Blackpool had to wait till 1953 for their only win, by which time neither Robinson nor Hayward was in the team.

The 1977 League Cup final was easily the longest English cup final ever played, Everton and Aston Villa drawing 0–0 and 1–1 and going into the last two minutes of extra time in the second replay still level at 2–2. Then the Villa substitute Gordon Smith put

in a low right-wing cross which was deflected into the path of Everton defender Terry Darracott, who was at the near post with no Villa player near him. Instead of hoofing it to safety, he let it run behind him (did he get a call from keeper David Lawson?) straight into the path of Villa striker Brian Little, who tapped in his second goal of the game, one of the softest ever to decide a cup final. Everton have never won the League Cup.

Cardiff City's win in the 1927 FA Cup final is best remembered for goalkeeper Dan Lewis' fumble [BLUNDERS VOL.1] – which might not have been decisive if Arsenal had taken their chances, especially the one brought about by Sid Hoar's long cross into the area. Cardiff keeper Tom Farquharson came out, the ball bounced on the penalty spot and went over his head, Jimmy Brain and Charlie Buchan ran in to head it into the empty net.

At the last moment, they left it to each other, it went harmlessly wide, and 'between us we missed the golden opportunity of the game'. By the time Arsenal won the Cup for the first time, three years later, neither Buchan nor his inappropriately named team-mate was in the team.

Tottenham, back in European competition after seven years, were holding out comfortably in the first leg of the 1991–92 Cup-Winners Cup quarter-final, away to Feyenoord, when Paul Allen and keeper Erik Thorstvedt got their wires crossed and allowed the ball to run to the unmarked József Kiprich, who knocked in the only goal of the tie. It was Spurs' last appearance in Europe to date.

The 1968–69 FA Cup quarter-final between Manchester United and Everton was decided by a single gift goal. A long cross into the United box landed between goalkeeper Alex Stepney and centre-half Steve James. Goalkeeper left it to centre-half, centre-half left it to goalkeeper, resulting in what Stepney later (much later) called 'a hilarious after-you-Claude cameo'. Everton centre-forward Joe Royle scored the easy goal.

In 1980 it was more a case of after-me-Claude-or-we'll-both-suffer. Nottingham Forest, favourites to win the 1980 League Cup final, handed Wolves the only goal of the game in similar circumstances, except that this centre-half (Dave Needham) didn't hear a call from this goalkeeper (Peter Shilton). They collided under a long ball, leaving Andy Gray with an empty net. Had Forest won, they'd have been the first club to take the trophy three years in a row.

Seven minutes from the end of England's game in Finland in 1956, Colin Grainger took a corner, substitute Nat Lofthouse headed it on, and Dennis Wilshaw moved in to try and force it home – but the Finnish defence had it covered.

Then substitute goalkeeper Aarre Klinga and full-back Vaino Pajunen left it to each other. By the time Klinga dived, the ball had already gone in off a post.

The goal made no difference to the result (England won 5–1) but did big Nat a bit of good. It was his second of the game and his 29th for England, equalling the national record set by Vivian Woodward in 1911.

Alan Hansen's skills set him apart from other defenders (which is where he should have stayed)

Alan Hansen won only 26 caps for Scotland, one of the criminal records. Is this why?

Needing to beat the USSR in their final group match to qualify for the second round of the 1982 World Cup finals, Scotland led at half-time but were being held to 1–1 with only seven minutes to go. Then the Soviets lofted a long ball towards their dangerous winger Ramaz Shengelia out on the left touchline. Either Hansen or Willie Miller should have completed the simple clearing header; instead, both went for it at the same time, we have to admit the collision was fun to watch, and Shengelia ran on to swerve past a stationary Allan Rough. Scotland equalised with two minutes left, but the draw put the USSR through.

Rough justice

Justice for the rough

Eric Cantona's attempt to kick racism out of football

What better to kick-start this chapter than Eric Cantona's little aberration at Selhurst Park? Sent off against Crystal Palace in January 1995, he was making his way along the touchline when a spectator was so keen to express his opinions that he came down several steps to do it. Cantona, taking umbrage at the language used to express them, reacted with one of the most famous drop-kicks in football history.

Those are the bare bones. Palace banned the spectator for the rest of the season, but his wounds were apparently salved by some tabloid financial balm. Cantona, and Manchester United, paid rather more dearly.

Although the club immediately fined him two weeks' wages and suspended him for the rest of the season, it wasn't enough for the FA, who increased the ban to the end of September (United manager Alex Ferguson said he didn't think 'anyone in the history of football will get the sentence he got unless they had killed Bert Millichip's dog'). A civil court imposed a prison sentence, commuted to 120 hours of community service. Among everything else, the ban cost him the captaincy of the French team (he hasn't played for the national team since and was left out of Euro 96).

Cantona's rehabilitation the following season was almost preposterously fairytale: Footballer of the Year, scorer of the only goal in five critical League matches plus the FA Cup final, in which he captained United as they became the first team to win the Double twice. As he climbed the Wembley steps to pick up the Cup, he reacted to being spat at by Liverpool fans with just a shake of the head and a pitying smile. Meanwhile, his abuser at Selhurst Park, charged with using threatening behaviour, was in contempt of court for attacking one of the lawyers! Revenge complete.

Which makes that drop-kick all the more significant. Cantona's ban surely cost United the Championship in 1995 and perhaps the Double (they lost 1–0 in the FA Cup final); they would have been the only club to win four successive League titles. Cantona, who'd already won the title with Leeds, would have been League champion an incredible five times in a row. The headline player of his time, alright.

Ahmed Gora Ebrahim, a player with South African club Rabali Blackpool, was escorted from the ground in a police van after drop-kicking his own coach, the Austrian-born Walter Rautmann, who'd substituted him!

Chelsea must have suspected that the 1994 FA Cup final wasn't going to be their day when Gavin Peacock hit the bar. Their opponents, Manchester United, had already won the Championship that season, but Chelsea had twice beaten them 1–0 in the League, Peacock scoring both goals. Now, in the first half at Wembley, his fine long-range lob beat Peter Schmeichel but came back off the woodwork.

There was still no score after an hour, then Ryan Giggs won a challenge with Steve Clarke out on the left and toed the ball to full-back Dennis Irwin, who knew he was just inside the Chelsea penalty area and can be seen on TV bracing himself for the inevitable foul as Eddie Newton comes across to challenge.

The midfielder, so effective in the first half, brought Irwin down for an unarguable penalty, Eric Cantona sent Dmitry Kharin the wrong way from the spot, did exactly the same five minutes later, and United won 4–0 for their eighth FA Cup success (equalling the record) to complete the Double for the first time. Chelsea haven't won a major trophy since 1971.

If ever there was a year which proved that crime doesn't pay it was Alessandro Costacurta's 1994. First-choice central defender for Milan and Italy, he missed the two biggest finals of the year (European Cup and World Cup) after being suspended for a mixture of red (for fouling Jürgen Klinsmann) and yellow cards. To crown it all, when he did manage to play in a major decider, the World Club Cup in December, he gave away both goals, including a penalty, and was sent off five minutes from time.

Towards the end of the 1962–63 season, it was clear that one or other of the Manchester clubs would be relegated from the First Division. In the crucial match at Maine Road, City took an early lead through Alex Harley and looked as if they were going to take both points until keeper Harry Dowd rugby-tackled Denis Law in the area.

There had been no need. Law was chasing a diagonal ball 'which I had little hope of catching'. Albert Quixall's penalty drew the match, United stayed up and went on to win the FA Cup. City were relegated by just two points.

> *A late consolation goal for Middlesbrough, and they won't take any consolation from that.*
>
> **RAY STUBBS**

Cameroon excited everyone by reaching the quarter-finals of the 1990 World Cup – but how much further might they have gone but for their disciplinary record?

In their first group match, the famous 1–0 win over reigning champions Argentina, they had two players sent off: André Kana Biyick and Benjamin Massing, both for fouling Claudio Caniggia, the second with a spectacular assault that seemed to start halfway across the pitch.

There were so many subsequent bookings that they had to play England in the quarters without four regulars, then lost the match by conceding two penalties for fouls on Gary Lineker after leading 2–1. No second chance

in 1994: a spent force by then, they didn't win a match and lost the last 6–1.

Ian Wright has scored well over 100 goals for Arsenal, including some of the most spectacular in the Premier League. But the other side of his game, as they say, has never been very far below the surface. When he was booked for an unnecessary foul in the first half of the 1994 Cup-Winners Cup semi-final second leg, no-one was unduly surprised. He was banned from the final, which Arsenal won, played in it the following year (Arsenal lost) and has never won a European winners' medal.

Even more talented players have had that 'other side'. Johan Cruyff, for example, was never slow in expressing his opinions to referees, which earned him a booking in the 1974 World Cup final he'd been expected to dominate. Back in 1966, it wasn't the opinions that made refs nervous.

Both his first two internationals were European Championship qualifiers. In the first, his goal helped Holland draw with Hungary. In the second, against Czecho-slovakia, he was sent off for hitting East German referee Rüdi Glöckner. Holland lost the game 2–1, and Cruyff's subsequent suspension also cost them the next two away matches in the championship, by only a goal apiece. They failed to qualify for the quarter-finals.

Giacomo Bulgarelli was a talented ball-playing midfielder who won 29 caps for Italy, scoring twice on his debut during the 1962 World Cup. In the finals in England four years later, he was made captain in the third group match, against North Korea.

On the half-hour mark, going into a late tackle on the opposition's midfield link man, Pak Seung Jin, he succeeded only in tearing his own knee ligaments so badly that he had to be stretchered off. Within ten minutes, Italy went a goal down, which they were unable to pull back with ten men. But for Bulgarelli's foul, they might have qualified for the quarter-finals, thereby escaping the volleys of rotten fruit that greeted them back home after that famous defeat.

In 1984 Aberdeen won the Scottish Cup for the third year in a row – but didn't take the lead in the final until Celtic captain Roy Aitken had been sent off for fouling Mark McGhee, who scored the winner in extra time.

Zbigniew Boniek's reputation as one of the best strikers in the world was established by the 1982 World Cup finals, especially his marvellous, varied hat-trick against Belgium. However, in the match immediately after that, with Poland needing only a draw against the USSR to qualify for the semi-finals, he picked up an unnecessary booking.

It was his second of the tournament and he had to miss the semi, one of the most crucial suspensions in any World Cup. Without him, Poland rarely looked like scoring against Tardelli, Collovati, Scirea & Co, lost 2–0, and haven't reached the semi-finals since.

João Saldanha had been such a vehement critic of the Brazilian team for so long that in the end the patience of the powers-that-be snapped and they made him national coach!

What sounds like something done for a bet, a recipe for disaster, was an immediate success. Saldanha built the team round the Santos club (Pelé, Carlos Alberto, Clodoaldo, etc), keeping the same squad throughout the World Cup qualifiers. Brazil won all six,

beat world champions England, and established themselves as favourites for the 1970 finals.

Then, with the tournament in sight, Saldanha's famous short fuse kept getting in the way. Dishing out criticism from the press box was one thing, taking it another. It reached the point where Pelé knew that 'whenever we saw a group in one corner of the pitch we automatically knew João had invited someone there to settle things with fists.'

But it wasn't the fists that provided the last straw. Eventually Saldanha was discovered at the home of a particularly vociferous critic – brandishing a revolver. Luckily for everyone, it misfired and the crowd (he had audiences for this kind of thing by now) took it away from him.

The Brazilian FA sacked him and he had to go back to reporting the World Cup triumph he'd helped prepare.

After winning only 2–1 at home in the 1975 European Cup semi-final, Leeds United did marvellously well to draw the return 1–1 in Barcelona – but there was a big minus in the late sending-off of their big, warm-tempered stopper Gordon McQueen for 'an unnecessary piece of retaliation' which cost him a place in the final, where both of Bayern Munich's goals in a 2–0 win highlighted weaknesses in the centre of Leeds' defence. They've never reached another European final.

Needing to beat Holland to qualify for the 1974 World Cup final, the holders Brazil were undone by Luis Pereira, of all people, a world-class stopper who'd been one of their stars of the tournament.

It was a harsh, very physical match – and the Dutch weren't angels, partly because they knew they'd better not be. Before the game, their great left-back Ruud Krol had thought that Brazil were a dirty team. True, said his team-mate Arie Haan, 'but we can be dirty too.'

Every Brazilian player suffered an injury of some kind, Marinho Péres' (a gash from knee to ankle) being merely the worst. But that one was in revenge for Johan Neeskens having been knocked cold – and anyway the Brazilian fouling was generally clumsier, less sophisticated, more blundering if you like. And some of their challenges were unquestionably grotesque. Zé Maria was one of the best full-backs in the tournament, but try telling that to Johan Cruyff, whom he rugby-tackled in the first half.

The culmination – of an approach that helped cost Brazil the match – was Pereira's sending-off for an amazingly blatant foul on Neeskens. Brazil lost 2–0 and didn't reach the final for another twenty years.

You'll be hoping this run of injuries will stop earlier than it started.

ANDREW GIDLEY

Argentina, managed by the notorious Juan Carlos Lorenzo, abandoned their traditional attacking game, massed in defence, and qualified for the 1966 World Cup quarter-finals by conceding only one goal in three games.

Their opponents England hadn't conceded any at all, but had drawn 0–0 with the very defensive Uruguayans and taken their time scoring against little Mexico. And now Jimmy Greaves was out injured. Much nibbling of nails at Wembley, especially as the three Argentinians up front (Onega, Artime, Más) were of the highest class.

Behind them, most influential of all, strolled their 6ft 3in captain and one-man half-back line Antonio Rattin, the focal point of every match. Including this one.

Argentina, who had a real chance of winning the tournament, let alone this

match, threw it away in a welter of fouls and argument. Three were booked, but the referee couldn't keep up with the number of niggling obstructions and late tackles. Más brought down Alan Ball, Rattin fouled Bobby Charlton and Roger Hunt within a minute, Peters was hit from behind.

Ten minutes from half-time, the referee, Rüdolf Kreitlein, a balding West German dwarfed by Rattin, reached the end of his tether and sent the Argentinian captain off. For a while, he wouldn't go. Then the whole team threatened to go with him. Eventually he was given a police escort to the changing room, taking his team's chances with him. England struggled to win 1–0.

The unabashed Lorenzo went on to manage the Lazio team who brawled with Arsenal in the street after a Fairs Cup match, the Atlético Madrid who had three players sent off against Celtic in the European Cup, and Boca Juniors when they kicked their way to winning the 1977 Libertadores Cup!

Argentina eventually won the World Cup in 1978 and 1986, but the old ways returned with a vengeance in the 1990 tournament, in which they reached the final but gave themselves little chance of winning it.

To begin with, they had to play it without four regulars, all banned after receiving two yellow cards – and in the match itself they incurred the first two sendings-off in any World Cup final – Pedro Monzon and Gustavo Dezotti – and were down to ten men by the time they conceded the only goal of the game, from a penalty given for a foul. Remembering the Hand of God (BLUNDERS VOL.1), few shed tears for Maradona except Maradona himself.

Enough's been written about the great serial early bathers – Willie Johnston, Mark Dennis, Vinnie Jones – but here's a peculiar example of the breed, one who struck only in a particular part of the country: Nigel Pepper of York City was sent off three times in 1990–91, all against Darlington.

Talking of Vincent Peter Jones (we were bound to in a chapter like this), the only surprise about his international career for Wales was that it took him four matches to get sent off – and he was once booked within four seconds of the start of a match.

But even he hasn't been sent off in the first minute of a match (as far as we know), so Bobby Houston of Kilmarnock holds one over him. Four minutes into the second half of the match with Partick Thistle in November 1979, he came on as sub, put his foot in, and was sent off at once.

However, the fastest sending-off from the start of a match seems to have been that of Ambrose Brown of Wrexham, who left the field after only twenty seconds at Hull City in 1936 – possibly because he had some festivities to get back to: it was Christmas Day! Wrexham lost 1–0.

Stoke City centre-forward John Ritchie was sent off within thirty seconds of coming on as sub in the UEFA Cup match against Kaiserslautern in 1972. Stoke lost 4–0.

Marco Etcheverry was Bolivia's big hope for the 1994 World Cup, a skilful midfielder who was particularly impressive against Brazil in the qualifiers. Bolivia had lost every match they'd ever played in the finals, without scoring a goal, but they had genuine hope this time, if not against Spain and the holders Germany, at least against South Korea. Then injury got in the way. Etcheverry was out for most of the season and wasn't fit enough to start the opening match of the finals, against the Germans.

He stayed on the bench till eleven minutes from time, coming on to try and pull something out of the hat with Bolivia trailing 1–0. It was his first competitive match for six months, but in the end fitness didn't come into it.

Before long, he allowed himself to get involved in a needless touchline fracas with two of the German players – and was sent off by Mexican referee Arturo Brizio Carter. Bolivia lost the match and achieved nothing in the finals beyond their first ever point and first ever goal (a deflected one at that), though it might all have been different if their most talismanic player had had a World Cup finals career of more than four minutes!

Three Plymouth Argyle players were sent off at Port Vale in 1974: Steve Davey, Davie Provan, Bobby Saxton. Argyle lost 2–1.

Two years later, three Oxford United players were sent off at Blackpool: John Shuker, Mick Tait, Peter Houseman. Oxford lost 2–0.

Oldham Athletic were challenging for the First Division title when they played Middlesbrough in April 1915. In the second half, a penalty was awarded for a foul by their full-back Billy Cook – who reacted more strongly than most, to put it mildly.

His argument with the referee, who ordered him off, went on so long that the match was abandoned with more than half an hour left. The result stood – a 4–1 defeat for Oldham – and they finished second in the League, only a point behind Everton, easily the closest they've ever come to winning the Championship.

Cook was suspended for a year and ordered to pay the cost of an inquiry.

After holding holders Tottenham to a draw in the 1982 FA Cup final, Second Division QPR were hit by a goal after only six minutes of the replay, Graham Roberts running into the penalty area to be tackled by Tony Currie, a creative midfielder who didn't normally expect to have to do this kind of thing. No surprise then that he didn't do it too well, bringing Roberts down with a misjudged tackle. Glenn Hoddle's penalty was the only goal of the game. It was QPR's sole appearance in the final.

When their goalkeeper Andoni Zubizarreta was sent off after only nine minutes against Denmark in November 1993, Spain's chances of reaching the World Cup finals were in real jeopardy, especially as the ten men had to win to qualify. This they somehow did – so the repercussions of Zubizarreta's foul were purely personal.

His automatic ban from the first game of the finals meant that his replacement Santiago Cañizares had to play an entire friendly match to bed him into the team, so Zubizarreta missed the last game before the tournament – which put an end to his world record of 86 consecutive internationals.

George Best was one of the very few players to have been sent off twice in internationals: against Scotland in 1970 (for throwing mud at English referee Eric Jennings) and Bulgaria in 1973. Each time his dismissal disrupted Northern Ireland's chances: they lost both matches without scoring a goal.

Manchester United lost what chance they had of getting a result from the first leg of the 1969 European Cup semi-final when John Fitzpatrick was sent off in Milan – but it had probably always been on the cards: the player he kicked was Kurt Hamrin.

The little Swedish winger had been an international star for fifteen years, scoring four goals in Cup-Winners Cup finals for Fiorentina and Milan. In the 1958 World Cup semi-final, his skilful, impudent dribble clinched victory over defending champions West Germany – but only after defender Erich Juskowiak had been sent off for

retaliating against him, whereupon Sweden took the lead for the first time.

Things repeated themselves here in 1969. Not only did Hamrin provoke a sending-off, he scored an important goal: the 2–0 defeat proved just enough to knock the holders out and send Milan to the final, which they won easily. Even if United had come prepared for Hamrin's wiles, there wasn't much they could do once he picked Fitzpatrick as his victim; the length of his fuse was well-known.

Peter Sillett was the big young right-back and captain of the Chelsea side which won the club's only League title (1955). His penalty, the only goal of the game against Wolves, clinched the title. A month later, in his first match for England, his clumsy foul on Jean Vincent conceded a penalty from which Raymond Kopa scored the only goal of the game. A neat about-turn. Sillett wasn't capped again after England lost two matches and drew the other on the close-season tour.

Legia and LKS went into the last match of the 1992–93 Polish season with the same number of points, so both needed a good win to have a chance of taking the title. At the end of the afternoon, it was clear that some nefarious dealings had been going on: LKS had won 7–1, Legia 6–0 away. An investigation showed that both clubs had made illegal arrangements with the opposition; the blunder was in making it so obvious: they'd simply scored too many goals. Both were docked two points, handing the title to Lech Poznan.

In the second round of the 1994 World Cup finals in the USA, Brazil were being held 0–0 by the hosts when their left-back Leonardo

Nascimento de Araújo was involved in a tussle on the touchline with Tab Ramos.

Probably the best left-back of the tournament so far, more of an attacker than a defender, Leonardo proved that now by lashing out and catching Ramos with his elbow. He collapsed, Leonardo was invaded by Americans, there was never a more inevitable red card.

Ramos, hit in the temple, was apparently not too far from death. Leonardo's sending-off didn't cost Brazil too dearly (they hung on with ten men throughout the second half to win 1–0 and went on to lift the Cup) but it cost him a place in the final. The chance may never come again.

At Hampden in 1983, Uruguay lost to Scotland for the first time, thanks partly to Jorge Barrios, who was sent off for tripping. Nothing too unusual in that, except that in this case the victim was the referee!

Les Cocker, the old Leeds and England trainer, had a scar on his lip, wherein lies a tale.

Playing for Stockport County against Mansfield in 1949–50, he found himself up against George Antonio, an inside-forward of Italian extraction. Cocker kept up a stream of ice-cream jokes throughout the game, during which he was knocked cold, waking up in the changing room with a bruised face and a lip that needed stitches.

He never knew what hit him, though George Antonio probably had some idea. As Cocker sat waiting for the team bus to drive off, he saw Antonio walking by, not looking up but licking an imaginary ice cream. Violence of the tongue, as it were.

Talking of which, Semilde, who was playing with Urubuetama in a Brazilian regional league match, must have regretted mouthing off at referee Luíz Vila Nova, who flattened him with a right cross!

Stoichkov gets ready for take-off

In the and-about-time-too slot, that brilliant and bristling Bulgarian Christo Stoichkov was banned for one match and fined £2,400 after playing for Parma against Roma in 1995 – for taking a dive in the penalty box.

Rüdi Völler's still the only player to score twice in a match in two separate European Championship final tournaments, which might have been three if he hadn't been injured in the first match of the 1992 competition, when he was Germany's captain.

They reached the final without him, but missed his firepower and bristling forward play throughout the event, drawing 1–1 with the CIS, losing 3–1 to Holland and 2–0 to Denmark in the decider.

That decisive injury? Mostly his own work. While fouling the CIS defender Oleg Kuznetsov in the first half, he broke his own arm.

For more than a decade, the World Club Cup acted as a sparkplug for some satisfyingly extreme violence (Celtic v Racing, Man Utd v Estudiantes, etc). The first bad blood was spilled in 1963. Milan, 4–2 up from the home leg, led Santos (minus Pelé) 2–0 at half-time, only to concede four quick goals which forced a bad-tempered play-off on the same ground. After 34 minutes, Milan's captain Cesare Maldini, Paolo's dad, usually a very collected sweeper, suddenly entered into the spirit of things with a thumping foul in the area. Dalmo's penalty produced the only goal of the game. Maldini and Ismael of Santos were sent off, goalkeeper Luigi Balzarini carried off, a vivid tradition established.

In late 1995, a head butt followed by a punch led to Dumbarton goalkeeper Ian McFarlane being automatically suspended after reaching 24 penalty points – for being sent off twice in the same match!

Domingos da Guia was the most famous defender of his time, at least in Brazil. A very slow full-back (it's said that he only walked if he couldn't stand still) who survived on excellent positional play, he won 25 caps from 1931 to 1946, impressing Italy's famous manager Vittorio Pozzo in the 1938 World Cup finals. Mind you, Pozzo could afford to be magnanimous: Da Guia had helped Italy reach the final.

The Brazilian attack, without the brilliant Leônidas [see PICK OF THE WEAK], were held to a goalless first half, in which their defence had suffered the tortures of the damned against Italy's robust forward line, none more so than Domingos, whose style of play wasn't best suited to coping with a centre-forward as thrusting as the great Piola. Five minutes after half-time, Italy went ahead. Five minutes after that came the incident that decided the match.

Piola had brushed Domingos aside time after time, which eventually became once too many for the artistic full-back, who tripped the artisan centre-forward in the penalty area. Peppino Meazza sent the goalkeeper the wrong way with the penalty, which turned out to be the winning goal. Italy went on to retain the Cup, which Brazil had to wait another twenty years to win for the first time.

And no justice for one who wasn't rough (but should have been?)

The 1912 FA Cup final seemed about to go on for ever. What made it so interminable was the latest instalment of the Barnsley clean-sheet saga. The Second Division side had already kept nine of them in the tournament – and their team was patient as well as rugged: six of those matches had been goalless draws, including the final against West Brom. Now, in the replay, more of the same: deep into injury time and still no score.

Then, with only two minutes left, the Barnsley inside-right Harry Tufnell broke clear on the halfway line and began his run in on goal, pursued by international left-back Jesse Pennington – and it soon became apparent that only a professional foul would save it for West Brom.

But, unlike his England partner Bob Crompton, Pennington didn't go in for that sort of thing. Fair-haired and fair, he chased Tufnell all the way looking for the chance of a legal tackle. It didn't come, the shot did instead, and Pennington, one of the leading players of his day, never won a Cup winner's medal.

Barnsley, who lifted the Cup for the only time in their history, began their defence of it the following season with – what else? – a goalless draw.

Don't invade the pitch, it always fights back

In the 1984–85 Cup-Winners Cup, Celtic had to replay their second round home leg after the Rapid Vienna left-back had been hit by a mystery object (controversy here; Celtic claimed that Rapid changed their version of events three times). When the replayed match took place, at Old Trafford, Celtic found themselves one down after 18 minutes, 4–1 on aggregate – which was too much for some of their supporters. Just past the hour, one ran onto the pitch and attacked goalkeeper Herbert Feurer. Towards the end, another went for Peter Pacult, who'd scored the Rapid goal. Celtic lost 1–0, were fined £17,000, and had to play their next European home match behind locked doors.

More repercussive still was the missile that landed during the first leg of a European Cup tie in 1971–72. By then Inter were no longer the formidable world champions with an impregnable defence – as Borussia Moenchengladbach now proved in the second round.

The Germans, about to become one of the strongest teams in Europe throughout the decade, already fielded some of its best players – Netzer, Heynckes, Vogts, Wimmer – who proceeded to pull Inter apart. By half-time, the Italians were 4–1 down. After injuries and the sending-off of Jair had reduced them to nine men, they lost 7–1, by far their biggest defeat in European competition.

Not for long. With the score 2–1, their centre-forward Roberto Boninsegna had been hit by a can of soft drink thrown from the crowd. Not so soft: it allegedly knocked him out. UEFA overturned the result and made Moenchengladbach replay the match in West Berlin. They drew it 0–0 and went out 4–2 on aggregate, whereupon Inter went all the way to the final. Moenchengladbach didn't reach it till 1977.

> *We've been saying this both pre-season and before the season started.*
>
> **LEN ASHURST**

Sometimes you try to do a bit of good instead of a bit of naughty – and look where it gets you

In 1934–35 Brighton & Hove Albion allowed Arsenal to use the Goldstone Ground for special training before FA Cup ties, which allowed the Gunners to get used to the pitch – on which they beat Brighton in the Cup that year!

When Skonto Riga arrived in Aberdeen for the second leg of the UEFA Cup preliminary round in 1994–95, they discovered that midfielder Alexey Semenov had left his boots back in Latvia. Aberdeen gave him a pair, which he used to score the goal that knocked them out of the competition.

Daft azza brush

Because of the booking, I'll miss the Holland game. If selected. PAUL GASCOIGNE.

Few have ever doubted the man's talent, but even fewer disagree with the title above, coined by Bobby Robson, who gave Gazza his first England cap. All that potential, as seen in Italia 90, has never been quite fulfilled. It's true that injuries have had something to do with it, but the worst of these was all his own work.

Not that it was by any means the first or the last. Booked the first time he started a game for England, he began the New Year in 1991 with a sending-off, his third so far – and of course the tears that made him a household nickname flowed from his booking in the World Cup semi-final, which meant he'd have missed the final if England had reached it.

Earlier in the tournament, against Belgium, Gascoigne was booked before setting up

Even the referees retaliate nowadays: Gazza books himself into a booking

David Platt's last-minute winner. In the quarter-final, his unnecessary foul on Roger Milla gave away the equalising penalty. Four years later, more of the same. In England's last home match in the World Cup qualifiers, he volleyed the second goal in a vital 3–0 win over Poland – then earned a completely pointless booking by elbowing an opponent in the face (he was lucky not to be sent off), which kept him out of the next game, the decider in Rotterdam. The last vestiges of midfield creativity went with him, England lost 2–0 and didn't qualify for the finals.

But the great party piece, which caused all the injury problems, had taken place back in 1991, when his multi-million pound transfer to Lazio was seen as the move that would save Tottenham's financial bacon. His last match for the club was to be the FA Cup final.

He started it as only Gazza could, in every sense. Kissing Princess Di's hand instead of shaking it, then launching a chest-high kick at Garry Parker. Many referees would have sent him off for that alone. Roger Milford later admitted that the decision to let him stay was a mistake: 'Yes, I was guilty. I didn't stick to the laws, but I just couldn't bring myself to do it.' At the very least he should have issued an urgent talking-to, anything to reduce the adrenalin which had been pumped up in the Wembley tunnel and was now swamping all common sense. Only a few minutes later, Gascoigne threw himself at Gary Charles on the edge of the Tottenham penalty area.

You could feel the impact from here. Charles was hurt alright – but he landed on top, with the daft one's knee twisted underneath him. A typically fierce Stuart Pearce free-kick exacted the appropriate punishment, and the guilty party was stretchered off. The knee injury (the dreaded ruptured anterior cruciate ligament, which has ended a number of professional careers, Brian Clough's among them) delayed the move to Rome for nearly a year and ensured that it was never a success: too few appearances as a result of too many injuries arising from the original. The subsequent, endless lack of fitness affected his contribution to the England team right up to Euro 96.

Meanwhile, even when he was winning the Double and the Player of the Year award in Scotland, it wasn't all plain sailing. Already booked five times, he received a one-match ban for a head butt on Aberdeen's John Inglis that was investigated by the police. On the day they announced they wouldn't be taking further action, he was sent off against Borussia Dortmund. Then, farcically, he was booked against Hibs for 'booking' the ref!

A player of his skills has been sinned against as well as sinning, of course, never more crucially so than in the World Cup qualifier against Holland at Wembley in 1993.

England took a 2–0 lead after 23 minutes and would surely have won the match if Gazza hadn't been on the receiving end of a Dutch elbow in the face. Until then, he had been the driving

The most traumatic moment of the 1991 FA Cup final – Gary Charles winces at what it's about to do to Gazza's career

force, running at the defence to make the second goal. When he had to stay in the changing room at half-time, England's impetus was lost with him. They were held to a 2–2 draw, as crucial a result as any in Holland's qualification for the finals ahead of them.

A crushed cheekbone forced Gascoigne to wear a grotesque protective mask in subsequent matches. Neither the Danish referee Peter Mikkelsen nor his linesman spotted the foul. After incidents like this, small wonder if Gazza feels he has to be Gazza, warts and all.

British referees are the best in the world

(at this kind of thing)

It's fair to say that the South Americans were not enamoured of some of the decisions given against them by European referees at the 1966 World Cup finals (Rattin sent off against England, two Uruguayans against West Germany, Pelé fouled out of the tournament). Pelé himself, for instance, was convinced ('I have heard it said since, and I firmly believe it') that FIFA president Stanley Rous had 'instructed these referees to go easy on the "virile" game played by the European teams against the South Americans.' Certainly some of the decisions by English and German referees are still hard to fathom.

Against Bulgaria, Pelé was kicked so often by Dobromir Zhechev that he had to miss the next game. When he came back, for the vital group match with Portugal, the grotesque, crippling double foul by João Morais that forced him to limp off wasn't punished by so much as a booking.

The Uruguayans certainly lost their heads against West Germany – but they'd had some pretty severe provocation. The score was still 0–0 when Pedro Rocha's header from a corner was clearly handled under the bar by Karl-Heinz Schnellinger. The dejected Uruguayans lost 4–0 after being reduced to nine men.

Take a bow, Kurt Tschenscher, George McCabe – and Jim Finney, once described by Jimmy Greaves as 'one of the few good referees we have in this country'.

As Jim Finney sends off the Uruguayan captain Horacio Troche, Wolfgang Overath gets ready to play keep-ball against nine men

Tongues wagged when Ferenc Puskás was brought back as captain for the 1954 World Cup final. Kicked on the knee in the group match with West Germany, he'd missed the quarter-final and semi, matches Hungary won 4–2 without him. He's only half fit, they said (he often was), he looks rather thick round the waist (ditto) and the team doesn't need him (hm).

He was also the most extravagantly talented and influential player of his generation, one-footed in the extreme but with a left foot that could juggle the soap in the showers. Hungary, now unbeaten in 32 internationals, were always better with him than without.

Even in the final, whose top and tail he influenced heavily. After only six minutes, József Bózsik to Sándor Kocsis, a tackle by Werner Liebrich (who'd crocked Puskás in the group match), a loose ball. The great man gleefully kicked it in.

Hungary led 2–0, hit a post, forced Werner Kohlmeyer to kick off the line, but were overhauled 3–2 with only five minutes left. Even then there was time for Toni Turek to make yet another save and – crucially – for Puskás to run onto Mihaly Tóth's pass and squeeze it under Turek in the last minute.

Apparently the film of the match shows him onside when he reached the ball, and it's hard to find any commentator who didn't believe it was a perfectly good goal (Puskás had, after all, run past a defender to reach the pass) – but the linesman, Mervyn Griffiths, an authoritarian, high profile Welshman, left his mark on the final as he was perhaps always likely to do by flagging for offside. English referee Bill Ling took his word for it, and Hungary, arguably the greatest team of all time, became the best not to win the World Cup.

While Tottenham, the reigning League champions, were making a good attempt at retaining their title, Huddersfield Town's place in the First Division was in the balance when they went to White Hart Lane in early April 1952 (they won only a single away match in the League all season). Nevertheless their rugged team held out well enough and would surely have gone back with a precious point but for a referee with eyes in the back of his head.

There were only two minutes left when Spurs won a corner, taken by their skilful international inside-forward Eddie Baily, who drove the ball in – and into the back of referee W Barnes, who'd positioned himself along the goal-line between the corner flag and the near post. The referee was knocked over, the ball came back into Baily's path, he centred, big Len Duquemin headed the only goal of the game, Huddersfield were relegated.

They didn't go down without a fight, or at least some frank and meaningful discussions, not least by their chairman who went looking for the referee after the match. The goal, of course, was quite illegal, Baily having touched the ball twice – but the League management committee and an FA inquiry backed the decision and the result stood.

The referee's explanation? That another player had touched the ball before Baily's second cross – confirmed by linesman A Cook. Since no-one else in the ground appears to have seen this, it's gone down as one of the biggest mistakes of its kind in League history. Huddersfield spent only one season in the Second Division before being promoted, but – like Eddie Baily's touches – it was one too many.

Tottenham's last realistic chance of retaining the title that year disappeared in the North London derby at White Hart Lane. Needing to win to keep pace at the top, they were level at 1–1 when referee GW Tedds stepped in front of centre-half Harry Clarke's clearance kick and teed the ball up for Arsenal's Alex Forbes to score the winner. Spurs had to wait nine years to win the Championship again.

> *Good challenge by Wright, but an unfair one.*
>
> **BRIAN MOORE**

Three clubs in a row – Tottenham in 1982, Manchester United 1983, Everton 1984 – won the FA Cup after losing that season's League Cup final to Liverpool – but Everton should probably have won both, held to a 0–0 draw by Alan Hansen & Co after the stylish defender had clearly handled in the area.

The incident stemmed from yet another error by Bruce Grobbelaar (see ALL THE WORLD'S KEEPERS), who allowed himself to be robbed by Adrian Heath on the edge of the penalty area. Heath hooked the ball towards goal and Hansen blocked it with his thigh then his hand. Referee Alan Robinson didn't give a penalty, Liverpool won the replay 1–0, and Everton have never won the League Cup.

Two years later, Robinson turned down Everton claims for a penalty in the FA Cup final – against Liverpool.

Scottish referee Alastair Mackenzie didn't endear himself to the Northern Ireland players or fans during the home match with England in 1971, first by disallowing George Best's cheeky kick over Gordon Banks' head when he was about to kick clear, then – more importantly – by allowing England's goal after Francis Lee had clearly handled the ball before passing for Allan Clarke, who may have been offside, to go round Pat Jennings for the only goal of the game, which cost Northern Ireland the Championship.

> ## *Referee Norlinger is outstanding in the sense that he stands out.*
>
> **GEORGE HAMILTON**

After holding European champions Liverpool to a goalless draw in the 1978 League Cup final (18-year-old Chris Woods played a blinder), Nottingham Forest held out again in the replay – and won the match when John O'Hare was brought down just outside the box.

There's little doubt about that. TV replays confirm it – and Liverpool defender Phil Thompson had been careful where he committed the foul. FIFA referee Pat Partridge wrongly awarded the penalty, John Robertson scored the only goal of the game from it to give the Clough regime its first trophy with Forest, Thompson was fined for saying he'd deliberately tripped O'Hare outside the area, and Partridge further endeared himself to Liverpool by booking Ian

Callaghan for an innocuous offence, his first caution after more than 800 matches!

In the third round of the 1900–01 FA Cup, Tottenham were struggling to hold out 1–1 at Reading when goalkeeper George Clawley made a half save and left-back Sandy Tait prevented a certain goal by punching the ball out from under the bar. Despite fierce protests from the home side, the referee gave a goal kick. Tottenham won the replay 3–0 and went on to become the last non-League club to win the Cup...

...despite the worst refereeing error in any FA Cup final, even worse than Percy Harper's bloomer which cost Arsenal the trophy in 1932 [BLUNDERS VOL.1].

Spurs had just taken a 2–1 lead in the final when Sheffield United's left-winger Bert Lipsham sent in a shot which Clawley knocked down in front of him. As soon as he'd picked it up, burly Walter Bennett barged him over the goal line – but not between the posts.

As both sides prepared for the obvious corner (which the linesman had signalled), referee Arthur Kingscott suddenly awarded a goal. His subsequent explanation – that the ball had crossed the line when Clawley fumbled the original shot – rebounded on him when the cameras (it was the first final to be filmed) proved that it certainly hadn't. The match was drawn 2–2.

Luckily for Kingscott (who was allowed to referee the replay), Tottenham won it 3–1.

One of the most momentous penalty decisions of all time was somehow the most predictable. After he'd awarded the first spot kick in any World Cup final (to Holland in the first minute, 1974), you felt it in your bones that Jack Taylor was going to give one back to West Germany. Sure enough, when Bernd Hölzenbein cut in from the left and went over Wim Jansen's leg...

Hölzenbein keels over and Jack Taylor cuts Holland adrift in the World Cup final

Hugh Johns, commentating for ITV, wondered aloud if any contact had been made. Even if Taylor couldn't have been expected to know that Hölzenbein was a notorious diver in the Bundesliga, he should surely have given the defender the benefit of the doubt. Instead he judged that Jansen 'was certainly not going for the ball'.

For the Dutch, the Wolverhampton butcher's cut was the deepest. They've never won the World Cup. And no Englishman's refereed another World Cup final.

Arthur Holland was one of the leading referees of his day, taking charge of both the FA Cup final and the European Nations Cup final in 1964 – yet two years earlier, in the Coventry–Southend match, it had taken him several minutes to realise that both teams were playing in blue and white..

...which wasn't the worst mistake of its type. In the match against Glasgow in 1930, the Sheffield captain Jimmy Seed noticed that he kept passing to the referee, whereupon he asked him to change his shirt: J Thomson was wearing the same colour (white) as the Sheffield team.

One of the strangest pieces of refereeing in international football took place during the Scotland–England match at Hampden in 1929. There was no score when England were awarded an indirect free-kick inside the Scottish penalty area – and the entire Scottish team retired behind the goal line, which was only five or six yards away from the ball. The entire team, that is, except goalkeeper Jack Harkness, who stood to one side against a post, apparently worried that the shot might hit him and go in. Weird.

Even more odd was the reaction of English referee Arnold Josephs to what happened next. When Russell Wainscoat tapped the ball sideways for another England player to shoot home, one of the Scottish defenders charged it down. Since he couldn't have been ten yards away when the kick was taken, a retake should have been ordered. Instead Josephs allowed Scotland to clear the ball. They went on to win 1–0, Wainscoat won only this one cap, and Josephs didn't referee another England match.

> ## *I think you and the referee were in a minority of one, Billy.*
> **JIMMY ARMFIELD**

Manchester City needed to win their last League match of the 1937–38 season, at Huddersfield, to stay in the First Division – and seemed to have done just that when a typically ferocious drive from Alec Herd rebounded from the stanchion inside the goal. Peter Doherty, City's great inside-forward, remembers seeing it hit the 'iron stay' and come back out. The referee, however, thought it had hit the bar, and didn't give the goal. City lost 1–0, were relegated, and didn't come back up until after the war.

The chapter dealing with the incident in Doherty's book was called Dear Blunderers. Like the title.

Towards the end of the 1969–70 season, Aston Villa scored at Leicester City but the referee didn't award the goal. Instead, although even the Leicester keeper admitted that the ball had gone in and come back out off the stanchion, he waved play on. Villa, clearly deflated, lost 1–0 and were relegated to the Third Division by two points.

The 1912 FA Amateur Cup final went to a replay, then to extra time in the replay, then to the last minute of extra time – and still little Eston United had no luck. One of their players was about to knock in the equaliser when he was pushed over by Stockton's right-back Loney. Everyone in the ground saw it, except the referee, who'd turned his back as the ball came over! Stockton won the Cup for the third time, Eston never did.

After holding Manchester United to a 2–2 draw in the 1958 FA Cup semi-final, Second Division Fulham fell 4–3 behind in the replay but seemed to have forced extra time when Johnny Haynes chested down a cross from the left into the path of Roy Dwight, who knocked it in – only for the referee to disallow the goal for handball by Haynes, a decision which disappointed Haynes' team-mate Jimmy Hill – and Haynes himself, who was adamant afterwards that he didn't use his arm. From the free-kick, United moved upfield to score the winner.

The following year Dwight scored in the final for Nottingham Forest – but neither Haynes nor Hill (nor Fulham, for that matter) ever won a winner's medal.

Steve Bloomer was, arguably at least, the greatest English goalscorer of all time: 352 in League matches as well as 28 in only 23 internationals (a world record at the time and, but for a dubious goal credited to Vivian Woodward, an England record till 1956), including at least one in each of his first 10 matches (a world record that still stands) and a record 8 at the highest level of his day, i.e. against Scotland. But it should have been 9, and 29 in all.

He scored in seven different matches against the Scots, including his last, in 1907, by which time he was 33 but still very much a threat, as he proved by scoring England's equaliser after 40 minutes. He also had two goals disallowed, one correctly, the other preposterously. Taking Woodward's pass, he actually beat two defenders before scoring: impossible for him to have been offside.

The papers agreed. 'Only a referee's error prevented England taking victory... The error was so clear that Bloomer may be forgiven his breach of etiquette... I should not be surprised to learn that Mr Robertson has decided never to accept such an appointment again.'

In fact Tom Robertson took charge of the game with Ireland the following year, one of a record 20 (some say 21) England matches he refereed. His mistake in the 1907 match cost England a win (they drew 1–1), gave the Championship to Wales for the first time, and marred Bloomer's last international.

The only goal of the England-Scotland match in 1913 was scored in the imagination of Scottish referee Alex A Jackson, for which his countrymen didn't thank him. He awarded it after the England centre-forward Harry Hampton, who liked nothing better than shoulder-charging goalkeepers, had

tried one of his specialities on the famous Jimmy Brownlie, who liked nothing better than repelling this kind of boarder. This time there's little doubt that a) the charge was illegal, and b) the ball didn't cross the line, as several players, English as well as Scottish, confirmed. The goal handed England the Home Championship outright for the last time before 1930.

Whether that was a penalty or not, the referee thought otherwise.

BRIAN MOORE

Fifteen minutes from the end of the Irish Cup final in 1899, the holders Linfield were leading Glentoran 1–0 when one of their defenders punched the ball away from an open goal. According to contemporary reports, it was as clear as day – but the referee didn't give the penalty, whereupon the Glentoran team walked off the field, forfeiting the Cup, which they didn't win again until 1905.

Foreign referees

...are equally as good

The brunette falls on the pitch. Ronald Koeman begins his assault on England's World Cup chances

England, needing at least a draw and probably a win in Rotterdam to qualify for the 1994 World Cup finals, were more than holding out against the likes of Koeman, Bergkamp, Rijkaard and Bryan Roy when the game turned on a single incident just after the hour, one captain (Ronald Koeman) tackling the other (David Platt) as he raced clear on the edge of the Dutch penalty area.

We're using the word 'tackle' loosely here. It's something the mighty Koeman was never particularly good at. One of the game's great long passers, he also scored dozens of goals for PSV, Barcelona and Holland, mainly from dead-ball kicks. Whenever he put foot to ball, 'dead' was the operative word; witness the only goal of the 1992 European Cup final. His covering in defence, however, was never so decisive – and Platt proved it yet again by beating him to this long ball. Koeman pulled him back by the shirt in plain view of everyone in the stadium, including the German referee Karl-Josef Assenmacher.

He didn't give a penalty, which was the right decision – but he allowed Koeman to stay on the pitch, which definitely wasn't. FIFA's directive left no room for a referee's discretion: a foul which denied the attacker a clear scoring opportunity had to be punished by a red card. Assenmacher showed the yellow.

Two minutes later, after England had done nothing with the free kick, Koeman blasted one of his own against the England wall, tried again when Paul Ince was penalised, and chipped the retake into the top corner. England manager Graham Taylor, vividly caught on camera telling the linesman that his compatriot had 'cost me my job', was right about that (he lasted just one more match) and about the fact that 'that blond man shouldn't have been on the pitch' to score the first goal.

The blond in question agreed: 'Yes. Sure. Of course. Very lucky for us.'

Holland's 2–0 win effectively took them to the finals, where Koeman's defensive shortcomings were exposed once and for all. England stayed at home – as did Assenmacher, dropped from the FIFA list.

In the finals themselves, Kurt Röthlisberger was sent back to Switzerland after admitting that he should have given Belgium a penalty against the holders Germany for Thomas Helmer's foul on Josip Weber. The Germans won 3–2 to reach the quarter-finals.

BLUNDERS VOL.1 highlighted three of Diego Maradona's Hands of God, two of which helped Argentina on the way to consecutive World Cup finals. Lo and behold, another of his underhand manoeuvres has come to light, the one which won his club their only European trophy.

In the first leg of the 1988–89 UEFA Cup final, Napoli were 1–0 down to Stuttgart with just over twenty minutes to go when they took a corner from the left. A defender's header reached Fernando De Napoli, whose cross from the right, headed on by Andrea Carnevale, found Maradona near the left-hand angle of the six-yard box.

He chested it down on the volley but knocked it too far ahead of him. No matter, there was always that trusty left arm in reserve. This stopped the ball long enough for him to lift it back across goal with his equally adept left foot. When the ball hit the arm of defender Karl Allgöwer less than a yard away, Greek referee Gerasimos Germanakos gave a penalty.

Stuttgart's protests, that Allgöwer couldn't have had time to lift his arm deliberately, were waved away and Maradona added insult to injury by taking the kick himself and sending Eike Immel the wrong way. Napoli went on to win the leg 2–1 and take the Cup on a 5–4 aggregate. It was the only European final either club's ever reached.

Argentina, champions in 1991 & 1993, might well have become the first country to win the South American title three times in a row but for a Peruvian referee's white stick. In their 1995 quarter-final against world champions Brazil, they were leading 2–1 with ten minutes left when Jorginho's low cross into their penalty area was knocked in by Tulio Pereira – after what TV replays confirmed as the clearest case of heavenly hands since the divine Diego. Even the Brazilians recognised the fact; one of their columnists called it 'an illegal goal of top pedigree, of untouchable pedigree. I would let Tulio's goal marry my sister.' Referee Alberto Tejada gave the goal, Brazil went through on penalties.

Somebody up there had some kind of conscience. In the final, Tulio put Brazil ahead against the hosts Uruguay but was the only player to miss in the penalty shoot-out which decided the title. He later admitted that the goal he scored to give Botafogo the Brazilian title for the first time had also been illegal.

One of the most flagrant examples of perverse arbitration had no effect on the great scheme of things, perhaps not even on the match itself, but it was a classic of its kind, still baffling after all these years.

In the 1970 World Cup finals, little El Salvador had lost their opening match and were expected to be absolute cannon fodder for the hosts Mexico in their second. Instead, they held out surprisingly easily until injury time at the end of the first half – then, while one linesman, Jack Taylor of England, was trying to let the referee know that time was up, the other, Keith Dunstan of Bermuda, signalled a throw-in to El Salvador.

It's possible that the referee, Ali Kandil of Egypt, overruled him – but if he did (and it's by no means certain) he didn't make it obvious to anyone except the Mexicans. Certainly the El Salvadoreans were getting ready to take the throw-in – and were amazed when the Mexican captain Gustavo Peña kicked the ball to Aaron Padilla, whose cross was missed by Enrique Borja but put in by Jávier Valdivia. One-nil – and all hell about to break loose.

The El Salvadoreans surrounded Kandil, imploring him to go and talk to Dunstan. Nothing doing. When he brandished his yellow warning disc, several of them turned their backs, inviting him to take their numbers. When they refused to restart the game, Kandil fetched the ball himself and put it on the centre spot. When they kicked it into the crowd, he blew for half-time.

In the second half, dispirited beyond endurance, El Salvador did nothing except try to kick as many Mexicans as they could. They lost 4–0. It was the last match Ali Kandil ever refereed in any World Cup finals.

Mexico weren't short of good fortune in that home tournament. In the next match, needing a draw with Belgium to reach the quarter-finals, they were gifted a penalty after fifteen minutes, awarded by the Argentinian referee Angel Norberto Coerezza after Léon Jeck had cleared the ball then Valdivia had fallen over his leg. The Belgians protested for more than two minutes before Peña's kick produced the only goal of the game.

In the quarters, with no such help forthcoming, Mexico lost 4–1 to Italy.

Coerezza wasn't finished yet. Among all the usual talking points from England's famous defeat by West Germany (Bonetti, Ramsey's

substitutions, Seeler's apparently lucky header), the disallowed goal seems to have been quietly forgotten – which is odd, because it was the most contentious moment of the match; the incident, more than any other, which cost England the chance of saving the game.

West Germany were 3–2 ahead in extra time when Francis Lee, who should have made the score 3–1 (see VERY LITTLE GREY CELLS), made amends by beating Karl-Heinz Schnellinger on the goal line and pulling the ball back for Geoff Hurst to drive it past Sepp Maier. Coerezza disallowed the goal.

Hard to understand why. Lee hadn't fouled Schnellinger, and he'd pulled the ball back, so Hurst couldn't have been offside. It was the last match Coerezza refereed in any World Cup finals – too late for Belgium and England, who didn't appear in the tournament for another twelve years.

In those same quarter-finals, Uruguay and the USSR were locked in a drab 0–0 draw with only three minutes of extra time left – then Luis Cubilla reached the goal line in the inside-left position, found his way barred, and turned his back towards the posts with Valentin Afonin behind him. As he tried to shield the ball, he ran it out of play. Afonin turned away and the other defenders relaxed – whereupon Cubilla, given the room he'd been looking for, crossed for substitute Victor Espárrago to head in at the near post.

Dutch referee Laurens van Ravens looked to his linesman, Bobby Davidson of Scotland, who allowed the goal despite angry protests from the Soviet players. On television and from the press box, the ball could be seen clearly crossing the line. It was the USSR's last match in the finals till 1982.

No need to go into great detail about Geoff Hurst's over-the-line 'goal' in the 1966 World Cup final (enough's been written already) – but it still raises a point or two.

First, the ball definitely didn't cross the line. Photographs, showing the position of its shadow, prove that. Secondly, neither the linesman Tofik Bakhramov nor the referee Gottfried Dienst had any business awarding the goal.

Bakhramov, although he had an unobstructed view of the incident, was a long way back, nowhere near the goal line. Dienst, who obviously had his doubts, shouldn't have taken the word of an official whose viewing position was anything but ideal. Incidentally (perhaps more than that), Dienst had also allowed a similar goal in the European Cup final five years earlier.

Only two of the Germans (Beckenbauer and Overath) were in the team that won the Cup in 1974. The others all knew what they wished upon Herr Dienst. One publication spelled his name Goodfried.

France were leading 3–1 against Kuwait in the 1982 World Cup finals when Alain Giresse scored a perfectly legal goal – only for the Kuwaitis to protest because they'd heard a whistle, apparently blown in the crowd. Play was held up for seven minutes, a fracas that involved the appearance on the touchline of the Kuwaiti general manager Al-Sabah, a sheikh in all his robes calling the players off.

When play was eventually restarted, Soviet referee Miroslav Stupar annulled the goal and gave a dropped ball. France still won 4–1, but the Kuwaitis were censured and fined £7,000 (a drop in the ocean of oil) and Stupar didn't referee another game in any World Cup finals.

During the 1958 World Cup finals, Bobby Robson had two goals disallowed, one for a foul on the famous USSR keeper Lev Yashin, the other for handball against Austria. In each case, Robson swore he'd done nothing illegal. The two decisions cost England a place in the quarter-finals.

Now that more than ten years have passed since the Heysel disaster, perhaps it's no longer in doubtful taste to mention that the only goal of that final, the Michel Platini penalty which made Juventus the first club to win all three European trophies, was given for a foul (by Gary Gillespie on Zbigniew Boniek) that not only looked accidental but was clearly committed outside the penalty area – though it's understandable if Swiss referee André Daina had other things on his mind.

> *The referee didn't change his mind. He merely amended his view.*
>
> **FA SPOKESMAN**

Inter, winners of the European Cup in 1964 and 1965, went into the 1967 final as underdogs when Luis Suárez and Jair da Costa dropped out, scored within eight minutes, and set up their famous defensive stall to hold out against Celtic's all-out attack.

They nearly made it, too. With Giuliano Sarti making save after astonishing save, they were still ahead after an hour – then Jim Craig overlapped on the right and squared the ball for the other full-back Tommy Gemmell to smash it home from the edge of the penalty area. Celtic's victory, inevitable after that (without Suárez and Jair, Inter had no counter-attacking springboard), was acclaimed as a triumph for attacking football over Italian negativity – but there was more to it than that. West German referee Kurt Tschenscher might have disallowed their equaliser.

A photograph shows the ball in the net and Sarti pointing to two areas in front of him. Not just the usual half-hearted protests of a team conceding a goal, either. Still frames from the BBC's recording show two

Celtic players in offside positions on the six-yard line, close to Sarti and directly in his eyeline. A famous reign ended in that moment – and another one didn't start: the following season, Celtic went out in the first round.

> *There are eleven men sitting on yellow cards and that's a very uncomfortable position to be in.*
>
> **JOHN MOTSON**

After Leeds United's traumatic 1975 European Cup final, much was made of Peter Lorimer's disallowed goal, the violence in the stands, and the Parisian riot police's reaction to it – all of which took attention away from the performance of French referee Michel Kitabdjian (Leeds manager Jimmy Armfield said simply, 'He was awful') whose biggest mistake wasn't so much Lorimer's goal as his blind eye towards Franz Beckenbauer in the first half.

The Bayern captain had another great game that night, but he'd never been wholly comfortable in man-to-man situations (witness his rugby tackle on Malcolm Macdonald earlier in the year). Here he first appeared to handle the ball to stop Lorimer breaking through, then undoubtedly tripped Allan Clarke a few yards from goal with only Sepp Maier to beat. The great man admitted as much after the game: 'I did foul him. But the referee was in a bad position... Leeds were unlucky because they were the better team on the day.' Their 2–0 defeat marked the end of an era.

In the 1978 World Cup finals, Canadian linesman Werner Winsemann and Swiss referee Jean Dubach combined to give one of the worst penalties in the competition's history (an Argentinian journalist called it the

original Hand of God) when the classy French sweeper Marius Trésor fell on the ball while making a clean tackle. If they hadn't, Argentina wouldn't have reached the second round of a tournament they eventually won.

Leo Horn, one of the leading referees of his time, awarded Real Madrid a contentious penalty in the European Cup final of 1957 (Enrique Mateos had been flagged offside before being brought down), then tidied up the ledger by refusing Real an obvious penalty in the 1962 final before awarding a less obvious one against them. Eusébio's kick gave Benfica the lead for the first time on the way to retaining the trophy.

Northern Ireland, who'd beaten the hosts Spain earlier in the tournament, went into their match with France needing to win to reach the 1982 World Cup semi-finals. Although the French were favourites, they were a fragile team (England had beaten them 3–1 in their first group match) who might have struggled to break the Irish down if they'd fallen a goal behind. This they did, though the record books don't show it.

Halfway through the first half, captain Martin O'Neill broke through to score a well-worked goal – only to have it disallowed for offside by Polish referee Alojzy Jarguz. Wrongly. Replays show that O'Neill was behind the last defender when he received the ball.

Within seven minutes Alain Giresse had put France ahead and they went on to win 4–1. The only other time Northern Ireland reached the World Cup quarter-finals they lost 4–0 in 1958 – to France.

Having drawn with world champions Italy in Milan on their 1939 tour, England were fully expected to beat a weak Yugoslav team five days later – and would probably have done so if speedy Frank Broome, who scored England's equaliser, hadn't been rugby-tackled in the penalty area when clean through. French referee Georges Capdeville, who'd taken charge of the 1938 World Cup final, waved play on (Ivan Sharpe called it 'the worst decision I have seen in football'). Yugoslavia won 2–1, their only victory in thirteen internationals.

For Republic of Ireland supporters, Sofia 1977 is still a red rag memory, the day they'll always believe they were refereed out of qualifying for the World Cup finals. Others agreed, including Michel Hidalgo, the manager of France, who were in the same group: 'I have no doubt that they would have won without the referee.'

Just before half-time, Steve Heighway crossed to the far post, cutting out the goalkeeper, and Don Givens moved in to head the equaliser – only to be clearly pushed by Boris Dimitrov. No penalty.

The Irish got their equaliser early in the second half, then began to dominate. On the hour, Heighway beat Dimitrov and put over another far-post cross, Gerry Daly headed back, veteran player-manager Johnny Giles drove it home. The Greek referee Nikos Zlatanos disallowed it for no obvious cause. Daly had headed the ball back, so there was no offside, and no-one had been fouled.

Finally, 14 minutes from the end, Zlatanos punished Jimmy Holmes' clean tackle with a free kick which was deflected in off Giles. The Republic lost 2–1 and failed to qualify.

After winning the very first World Cup match, 4–1 against Mexico in 1930, France needed a draw against the second favourites Argentina to stay top of their group, but were 1–0 down when their quick left-winger Marcel Langiller ran through on goal – only for the Brazilian referee Gilberto de Almeida Rego to signal the end of the match.

Disappointing for the French – but they didn't realise how much so until they reached the changing room, to be informed that the referee had lost track of the time. He'd blown his whistle six minutes early!

The match was restarted and the missing minutes played out, but too late for France, who couldn't break through again. They were eliminated, Argentina went on to reach the final.

In all the euphoria surrounding Denmark's win in the 1992 European Championship, few noticed (and even fewer cared) that Kim Vilfort's clinching goal in the final was scored after he'd controlled the ball with his arm. Swiss referee Bruno Galler didn't see it.

Euro 96 was littered with refereeing blunders, some that didn't affect the overall picture (John Collins of Scotland getting away with handball in his own area against Holland; Pierluigi Pairetto awarding that penalty in the final after Matthias Sammer had brought down Karel Poborsky outside the box and the linesman, perfectly placed, kept his flag down) and some that cost teams their place in the tournament.

Antonio López Nieto, for example, crowned his performance in the France–Holland quarter-final by giving the Dutch a free-kick for handball even though the offence was clearly committed inside the French penalty area. Then, in the penalty shoot-out, his finicky insistence on replacing the ball did Clarence Seedorf no favours: he was the only player to miss a kick.

In the Bulgaria–Romania game, Peter Mikkelsen of Denmark booked Tsanko Tsvetanov when Daniel Borimirov committed a foul, and didn't award a goal when Dorinel Munteanu's shot crossed the line after hitting the bar. Romania lost 1–0.

Finally, England won their torrid quarter-final against Spain after Marc Batta of France had disallowed a goal by Julio Salinas, who was shown to have been definitely onside.

Doubting Thomas

It's hard to think of another referee who attracted controversy like Clive Thomas from Treorchy. He was successful here (FA Cup final 1976) and abroad (FIFA list) but his name was made by a series of specific incidents. Even before he sent off three players in a single European Championship semi-final in 1976, his profile was high. In the years that followed, he was sometimes as important an element as either of the teams.

In 1981 he outraged not a few in two of the biggest matches of the season. In the FA Cup semi-final, he awarded a late equalising penalty to Wolves after Kenny Hibbitt, in many people's opinion, had simply

Clive Thomas points out the exact second his World Cup career ended

fallen over Glenn Hoddle's leg. Thomas himself admitted 'that if I had a chance to relive those moments, I would not now give the penalty.' He didn't referee the replay, which thankfully Spurs won.

In the League Cup final, he allowed the goal that gave Liverpool a 1–0 lead over West Ham, even though Alan Kennedy's shot had passed right over Sammy Lee lying offside on the ground. Not interfering with play, said Thomas. Right in my line of vision, thought goalkeeper Phil Parkes. West Ham manager John Lyall was angry enough to make an unwise reference to cheating, for which Thomas reported him to the FA. West Ham lost the replay 2–1.

Back in the 1978 World Cup finals, Thomas had blown the final whistle a fraction of a second before Zico headed in a corner against Sweden, a remarkably accurate piece of time-keeping which deprived Brazil of a 2–1 win. Thomas later pointed the finger at the Brazilians themselves, for wasting time over taking the corner, but it looked a pettifogging decision (one journalist called him 'technically correct but naive') and FIFA seem to have agreed: he refereed just that one game in the tournament.

But Clive's crowning moment had arrived in another semi-final, a Merseyside derby in 1977, one of the most vivid FA Cup matches in years. Everton had just made the score 2–2 and were chasing the winner when their winger Ronnie Goodlass crossed, Duncan McKenzie helped the ball on, and Bryan Hamilton deflected it in for what would have been the winner if Thomas hadn't disallowed it.

He probably didn't help himself by not explaining *why* immediately after the match, instead saying, 'Watch TV tonight, you'll see it then.' In his autobiography, he revealed that he'd ruled Hamilton offside, adding that 'the cameras did prove me correct.'

Well, it doesn't look as conclusive as that on the screen, and even the Liverpool captain Emlyn Hughes thought it an iffy decision. Above all, linesman Colin Seel was already on his way back to the halfway line, 'satisfied with the goal'. To add insult to Evertonian injury (like West Ham, they were beaten in the replay), Thomas added in his book that he could also have disallowed the goal for handball!

Invited (mischievously?) to make a speech at an Everton dinner, he was listened to in complete silence for half an hour. No applause but no barracking. When he sat down, the first question from the floor brought the house down. 'Mr Thomas, what I'd like to know is this. Why didn't Hitler bomb Treorchy first?'

Officials who didn't measure up

Portsmouth started 1989–90 with goalposts that were several inches too low, but no-one noticed for the first three months of the season – and the hackneyed German reputation for efficiency took a bit of a blow before the start of the 1974 World Cup final in Munich when English referee Jack Taylor saw that the corner flags were missing.

In a 1930 World Cup match, the United States' trainer came onto the pitch, put his bag down so hastily that he broke a bottle of chloroform, and was so overcome by the fumes that he had to be helped off the pitch! Note: like everything else in this book, this is a true story.

Early in 1995 the Pro-Line company in Canada issued 1,940 pools coupons, of which no fewer than 1,690 turned out to be winners. The company paid out $783,000, all because the matches on the coupons were in the English league – and had ended forty minutes earlier! Spokesman Don Pister said, 'It was our mistake,' which shows how well British understatement travels.

Although no-one condoned the post-match riot which caused the 1909 Scottish Cup final to be rendered null and void, it might have helped if the Scottish FA had actually mentioned to the crowd that extra-time wasn't included in the rules. The paying customers, thinking that perhaps this was a ruse to inveigle them into forking out for a third replay, made their displeasure known setting fire to pay boxes among other things They were kept well informed from then on

Switzerland had something of a rude awakening on their African tour of 1983 After winning their first match, agains supposedly their strongest opponent Algeria, they lost to the Ivory Coast and Zimbabwe and drew in Kenya. Mind you, wasn't entirely their own fault. No team ever had so much bad luck with penalties

In Zimbabwe they twice took the lead only to be hauled back each time by a spc kick awarded by local referee Sanyka, befor losing to a goal four minutes from time. I Kenya they missed a string of chances an had three penalty appeals turned down fc glaring fouls, again by a local referee, Sa Ali. Above all, they were beaten by the Ivor Coast's late penalty after their own defence Heinz Lüdi had been fouled (!), which wa bad enough. Worse, Zahoui's kick wasn easy to miss: the groundsman had painte the penalty spots two yards too close to th goals!

When the first European Cup was bein arranged (1955–56), the English Leagu champions were naturally invited compete. The Football League, fearing fixture escalation (well, they weren't to wrong...), put pressure on Chelsea not take part. Their chairman Joe Mears agree It was a mistake. They never appeared the competition again. The following ye Manchester United refused to bend t knee, entered, and reached the semi-fina

Northern Ireland's first appearance in the World Cup finals (1958) ended in honourable defeat in the quarter-finals after a gutsy win in a group play-off, and they were rightly welcomed home as the little people who'd done more than could have been expected.

And yet, right at the end, they did themselves no favours. That's putting it mildly. George Raynor, English coach of the Sweden team that reached the final, put it differently: 'It was here that Northern Ireland made a complete hash of things.'

It's probable that they wouldn't have survived the quarter-final whatever happened (this was the France of Kopa, Fontaine, Piantoni et al) but the Irish had drawn with defending champions West Germany earlier in the tournament, so they would have had *some* chance – if their officials hadn't exhausted them beforehand.

Due to play the French in Norrköping only 48 hours after a play-off in Malmö that required extra-time, they got there the hard way. Raynor, who knew Sweden's transport system as well as anyone (he first coached the national team in 1946), was aware that they 'could have travelled in comfort by fast train from Gothenburg to Stockholm, and Norrköping is but an hour on a fast train from the capital, or they could have flown to Stockholm in under an hour from Gothenburg. But instead they spent hours in the discomfort of a motor-coach.'

The Irish held out till a minute from half-time before weariness set in. They lost 4–0 and didn't play in the finals again till 1982.

Although the top two teams from the 1949–50 Home Championship would qualify for the World Cup finals, the Scottish FA announced that they'd only go there as British champions. So when their team lost 1–0 at home to England, they were as bad as their word and made them stay behind, despite the protestations of captain George Young and the rest of the squad.

Scotland missed out on some important experience of a stressful tournament. When they deigned to take part four years later they were humiliated 7–0 by Uruguay.

Manchester City officials must have regretted being found guilty of making illegal payments to their players. An FA inquiry ordered them to transfer four of the recipients in 1906: Jimmy Bannister, Herbert Burgess, Jimmy Turnbull, and the great Billy Meredith. They moved only as far as Manchester United, helping them to win the League title in 1908 and 1911 and the 1909 FA Cup. City didn't win either competition again until 1934.

> *What I said to them at half-time would be unprintable on the radio.*
>
> **GERRY FRANCIS**

When Brazil's famous 38-year-old goalkeeper Gylmar dos Santos Neves was recalled for his last international, against England in 1969, it was a mainly sentimental gesture: the award of his 100th cap. A presentation was made by Brazilian officials, he helped Brazil win 2–1 and was given a rousing send-off by the Maracaná crowd.

Just one thing. It wasn't his 100th international. Later, too late for another recall, it was discovered that he'd won 'only' 95.

Ah, but Brazil regard matches against club sides and the like as full internationals, don't they? Um, no – that's an old British wives' tale. And even if they did, it wouldn't have saved the Brazilian FA's blushes: including such matches, the one against England was his 103rd!

In the days when rules were tighter, you had to be born in a country to play for it. But even then a few managed to slip the net, none more often than Fred Hughes, who won six caps before being banned from playing for Wales: it had taken English officials two years to discover that he'd been born in Cheshire.

It may add some balm to the wounds of Estudiantes' victims in the World Club Cup (Man Utd, Celtic & Feyenoord) to learn that the Argentinian club's three consecutive successes in the Libertadores Cup (1968–70) cost money as well as friends. It transpires that they made the mistake of promising their players enormous bonuses, which ate up the club's finances at such a rate that they faced bankruptcy for a while and the president shot himself.

The organisers of the first FA Cup final held at Wembley (1923) should have made the match all-ticket. Instead, an estimated 200,000 people swarmed into the stadium, covering the pitch, delaying the kick-off, and perhaps helping to score one of the goals (it's said that when Bolton winger Ted Vizard ran along the touchline, he took a rebound from a spectator before crossing!). The final's been all-ticket ever since.

The 1923 match programme had assured its readers that 'Spectators will have a fine view of the game from all points in the Stadium.'

The following clubs didn't take part in the FA Cup – Sheffield Wednesday in 1886–87, Birmingham City 1921–22, QPR 1926–27 – each time because someone in the office forgot to post the entry form!

The crowd getting a close view of the Wembley pitch, as advertised

The German FA not only bowed to the threat of a violent minority by cancelling the match with England in 1994, they presumably had something to do with arranging the fixture in Berlin on April 20th – Adolf Hitler's birthday!

Mind you, if every old Nazi's anniversary is going to be removed from the calendar, how many days will be left? This isn't as facetious as it sounds: Germany also cancelled their game against Wales in April 1995 because it coincided with the birthday of Hitler's deputy Rüdolf Hess!

Whoever drafted the new laws relating to corner kicks soon had to change them in 1925, after Everton's international winger Sam Chedgzoy had exposed a loophole by dribbling the ball from the corner flag straight into the net for the only goal of the home

game against Tottenham. The rule specifying that the player taking the kick can't touch the ball twice in succession came in at the end of the season.

It may not be a true story, but seems a plausible explanation for one of the biggest mismatches of all time. Read on, it's fun.

When Orion entered the Scottish Cup in 1885–86, they were surprised not to receive any notification as to whom they were playing in the first round. This, it seems, is because someone at the Scottish FA had sent the invitation not to Orion FC but to Orion Cricket Club!

Quite what the cricketers thought of this hasn't been recorded, but they seem to have been willing souls, because they upped sticks and travelled to play the big ball game, undeterred by the fact that they didn't have football jerseys, shirts or boots.

During the match itself, it's said that the opposition goalkeeper didn't touch the ball even once, and that Orion would have conceded even more goals than they did if goal nets had been in use; the time spent recovering the ball saved them from a bit of a thrashing.

Relatively speaking, that is. They lost 36–0 and their opponents' right-winger John Petrie scored 13, both still records for a British first-class match, though Aberdeen Rovers tried to get in on the act by losing 35–0 to Dundee Harp on the very same day.

The mistaken invite had produced one of the great matches in football history. Orion's opponents were First Division Arbroath. On the way to the match, the cricketers had changed their name (why, nobody knows – but what a famous moniker it now is) to Bon Accord.

Aston Villa's 3–1 win over Chelsea in the 1920 FA Cup semi-final spared the blushes of the event's organisers. The rules of the competition forbade holding the final on the ground of either finalist – but that season the FA had arranged for it to be held at Stamford Bridge, even though Chelsea were a First Division side and therefore had as good a chance as most of getting there. By the time Chelsea reached the semis, it was too late to move the final to another stadium – so Villa's win came in the nick of time.

UEFA weren't so lucky in 1957 and 1965. For some reason, they arranged for the European Cup finals in those years to be held on the grounds of clubs who were not only the Cup holders but the best teams in the world at the time, so they had every chance of reaching the final again and playing it at home! Sure enough, Real Madrid and Inter won without conceding a goal between them. Neither of their opponents, Fiorentina and Benfica, who protested in vain, have won the Cup since then.

Standard Liège haven't won *any* European competition, though they might have had more of a chance against Barcelona in 1982 if they hadn't had to play the Cup-Winners Cup final in the Nou Camp. They lost 2–1 after taking the lead.

> *We got the winner up there with three minutes to go, but then they equalised.*
>
> **IAN McNAIL**

After resigning their place in the League in 1908, Stoke City's directors decided, for some reason (financial inducement?), to sponsor Tottenham's application to take their place. Then they changed their minds – but too late. Tottenham were accepted, Stoke weren't allowed back in for another eleven years!

After having to make 120 arrests at matches in Bournemouth and Weymouth in May

1991, the police complained that the Football League had ignored their requests to move the fixtures. League president Bill Fox admitted it had been an error to hold the matches on a bank holiday weekend and insist that the kick-offs stayed at 3pm.

The Verona city authorities planned to name a new stadium after one of their old players, Aldo Olivieri, who'd kept goal for Italy in the 1938 World Cup final. Arrangements were in place for the inauguration in March 1996 when someone suddenly discovered that the honour would have to be postponed: Olivieri wasn't dead. 'Thanks for the thought,' quoth the sprightly 86-year-old, 'but I plan to be around for a little while longer.'

In 1992–93, Fiorentina were going along perfectly well in mid-table when they lost 1–0 at home to Atalanta – whereupon they suddenly sacked their experienced coach Gigi Radice.

An error. New man Aldo Agroppi couldn't get the best out of world-class players like Brian Laudrup, Stefan Effenberg and Gabriel Batistuta. Fiorentina won only three of their last twenty league matches and were relegated to Serie B for the first time in 55 years.

The government's identity card scheme. Laid to rest January 1991. RIP.

The last word on the subject (it really does leave you speechless) goes to Workington Town, who were relegated after finishing bottom of the Third Division in 1966–67. At the start of the season, they'd increased the size of their board to thirteen, which meant they had more directors than full-time players!

Grounds for complaint

(and getting caught by nets)

It's still widely believed that Sheffield United's unstoppable slide in the 1970s was caused by a new stand. Until then Bramall Lane had only three, plus an open space where the pitch backed against the cricket ground of the same name. This gave it a distinctive, famous appearance, but the club had long muttered about suffering 'such a freak as a three-sided ground'. So, when United were promoted back into the First Division in 1971, they gave the cricket club two years' notice. By August 1973, the ground which had hosted Test cricket had staged its last County Championship match.

The £750,000 price tag on the new cantilever stand weighed on United almost immediately. With little left over for transfers, they nosedived from the First to the Third, then (in 1981, for the first time in their history) the Fourth.

In 1966, World Cup star Jack Charlton opened a golf driving range which Halifax Town had introduced at one end of their Shay ground – but the money-making scheme didn't make much: the arrangement was abandoned as soon as it dawned on the club that the roofs of the stands were being peppered with wayward golf shots.

Some groundsmen must have done their job none too well at the end of the last century, when a rash of complaints about their pitches led to any number of replays.

For example, in a Scottish Cup match in 1889, Celtic suffered a shock 1–0 home defeat by Clyde but protested that the referee shouldn't have allowed the match to take place on a waterlogged pitch. They

succeeded in having it replayed, won it 9–2, and went on to reach the final...

...where, amazingly, they were up to the same tricks. Again the pitch was sub-standard, again they had the original result overturned (a 3–1 defeat by Third Lanark) – but enough was now enough. Third Lanark took the Cup 2–1.

In 1892–93 it was Celtic's turn to be on the wrong end of a protest, this after winning a Cup match 1–0 on a frosty pitch. Queen's Park won the replay 2–1.

After losing to a powerful Darwen team 3–1 in the 1891 FA Cup, little Kidderminster protested about the pitch, won the right to a replay – and surely wished they hadn't. Darwen, their danders up, won 13–0!

The 1890 FA Cup quarter-final between Sheffield Wednesday and Notts County was replayed twice, the first time because of an unsuitable pitch. Wednesday won 5–0, lost the replay 3–2, then took the third match (after protesting about an ineligible player) 2–1. They went on to become the first club to reach the FA Cup final after losing during the competition.

Although goal nets had been in general use since about 1892, the final design still hadn't been perfected by 1908–09. That season, West Bromwich Albion scored a goal against Blackpool – but the net had been pulled so tight that the ball shot straight back out and the referee assumed it had come back off the woodwork! Remarkably, this happened twice more in the same match, and although West Brom won it easily, those goal nets made all the difference to their promotion challenge: they missed going up into the First Division by 0.0196 of a goal!

Football bloomers

(and other items of clothing)

Not all here for the beer – Tottenham players after the 1987 FA Cup final

Towards the end of 1986–87, Tottenham unveiled a new playing strip which was to be worn from the start of the following season. However, as the club had reached the FA Cup final, they decided to parade the new kit at Wembley.

A consignment of shirts was duly delivered in time for the final. However, some of the players asked for short-sleeved ones, and no-one noticed that this batch didn't have the logo of the club sponsors, Holsten, on the front. As a result, some of the team played in sponsored shirts and others in Holsten-free tops. Tottenham (less of a team than usual?) lost an FA Cup final for the first time, then fired the club secretary.

After the match, a rival brewing company ran a press advertisement that showed a photo of Glenn Hoddle, minus logo, with the caption: 'I bet he drinks Carling Black Label.'

The 1894 FA Cup first round match between Preston North End and Reading was played on a Deepdale pitch that was dale deep in mud. The home side improvised by coating their boots in black lead and knocking metal studs or bars into the soles – and their Welsh international goalkeeper Jimmy Trainer wore a raincoat during a second-half downpour. Reading, who didn't do any of these things, lost 18–0, still their worst ever defeat.

The wrong footwear caused John Robinson some embarrassment in 1975. He usually went to Upton Park in shoes with platform soles, but this time had his working boots on, and got stuck so firmly in the turnstiles that it took four men to pull him out. John Robinson weighed 35 stone.

When Stan Richards arrived at Maine Road in 1946 to play his first game for Wales, he found he'd forgotten his boots. Replacements were found, but he didn't score against England – or win another cap.

The proliferation of new team strips in recent times (occasionally for commercial reasons?) has led to a number of eye-catching little numbers which haven't met with universal admiration – especially one or two goalkeeping jerseys, notably the riot of colour worn (and designed) by Mexico's Jorge Campos in the 1994 World Cup, and David Seaman's England top which was likened to a tube of Refreshers.

Most hilarious of all? Perhaps the grey strip worn by Manchester United away to Southampton in 1995–96: 3–0 down at half-time, the players changed their shirts because they said they couldn't see who they were passing to!

Whatever possessed Manchester City to play in the 1933 FA Cup final wearing red shirts and white shorts (United's colours!)? Naturally they lost, 3–0.

During the 1990–91 season, 15-year-old Kashim Abdul of the Bangladeshi Northern Eagles in Manchester offered to wash the team kit, but used curry powder instead of washing powder and turned the shirts yellow. Well, that's what it says here.

Two national folk heroes emerged from the Faroe Islands' shock win over Austria in 1990: Torkil Nielsen, who scored the only goal – and goalkeeper Jens Martin Knudsen, who made save after important save.

Knudsen's woollen hat achieved immediate fame around Europe, probably providing sartorial inspiration for a whole generation of goalkeepers – until former Danish international Allan Simonsen was hired as the Faroes' manager.

The bobble hat wasn't suitable, he announced. Never mind that it was a lucky charm; people didn't take the team seriously while he was wearing it. It had to go.

And go it did, whereupon the exposed Knudsen conceded five goals in each of the next three games.

The 1958 FA Cup semi-final replay between Manchester United and Fulham was played on a wet Highbury pitch – but Fulham's Gibraltarian goalkeeper, the spectacular but not always spectacularly reliable Tony Macedo, decided not to wear gloves. According to Bob Wilson, 'It proved a costly error.'

Macedo had played very well in the first match, but the gloves were off for him after this one: he gifted United their first goal by dropping a simple centre, was blamed for at least one of the others, and didn't need to be told that he'd had a shocker: 'I had begun to worry about having a bad match at the wrong moment. And so I did, in the game that mattered most.' Fulham lost 5–3 and had to wait till 1975 to reach the final for the first time.

In a Division 2 match in December 1892, Burslem Port Vale lost 10–0 to Sheffield United, still the worst home defeat in Football League history, much of which was self-inflicted. A contemporary paper recorded that 'The Port Vale goalkeeper lost his spectacles in the mud.'

Footballers and superstitions have always gone hand in hand, but Jeff Hall, the Birmingham City and England right-back, was something else.

On a tour of the West Indies in 1955, an FA team were playing at Kingston's Sabina Park. Hall had given his boots to a cobbler to change the studs, but when he arrived at the ground, the work hadn't been done. Still, it wasn't going to take long and there was enough time. The cobbler set to work.

Unfortunately, he started with the left boot – and Hall always insisted on putting his right boot on first. So, while the crowd and the two teams waited, Hall did the same, resisting every entreaty from those around him. Eventually, with the crowd growing restless, he was persuaded to put the left boot on first while the cobbler finished work on the right. Hall got both on his feet just in time to join the rest of the team as they walked out onto the pitch.

Big mistake, that. Putting the wrong boot on first. The footballing gods didn't create these superstitions for nothing. Within two minutes, Hall went up to head a ball – and was headed himself, in the jaw by an opponent, an accident that required him to have six stitches and take no further part in the match, which he left without having touched the ball!

Perhaps it was always on the cards that Arsenal might lose to Walsall in the 1932–33 FA Cup; their new players were nervous before the match, especially the untried centre-forward Charlie Walsh who had such a bad game [BLUNDERS VOL.1]. According to his team-mates, he started putting his boots on before his socks.

With friends like these...

There's never been a good time to score an own goal against yourself. JOHN GREIG

The quality of Tottenham's players (Hoddle, Ardiles, Villa, Crooks, Archibald) was expected to win them the 1981 FA Cup final against a Manchester City team that was undeniably combative (Paul Power, Gerry Gow) but short of the highest quality (Kevin Reeves, Gerry Gow). In the event, it took a while for the class to out. The ineffectual Villa was substituted, and with only eleven minutes left Tottenham were trailing 1–0 when they were awarded a free kick on the edge of the City area.

As so often, the ball was tapped by one player then stopped by another for Glenn Hoddle to shoot, something he did better than anyone else in the League from that range. Not this time, though. TV cameras, directly behind the shot, show that it was sailing over the right-hand end of the City wall towards the waiting hands of Joe Corrigan, who'd moved to his left with all

the time in the world to make a save that probably wasn't going to be necessary: the kick seemed to be going wide

Enter Thomas Hutchison from stage left. A leggy Scottish winger who'd played well in the 1974 World Cup, long Tommy was 33 by now but still a class act (he was playing League football ten years later). Indeed, it was his rare diving header that had been dividing the teams since the 29th minute. Now, at the free kick, he decided to sweep up behind the wall.

Unnecessary from the start, it became downright disastrous when Hoddle's chip hit doubting Tommy's shoulder, sent Corrigan the wrong way, and sailed into the other side of the net. Hutchison became only the second player to score for both sides in an FA Cup final, Spurs escaped with the draw and played infinitely better in the replay to win it 3–2 (the reprieved Villa scoring twice,

Tommy Hutchison (far right) shoulders the blame for Tottenham's equaliser in the Cup final

including one of the great Wembley winners), City didn't reach the final again and haven't won the Cup since 1969.

Ten years later, Tottenham's winner in the final was an own goal by Des Walker [BLUNDERS VOL.1].

In 1984–85, Tottenham were the UEFA Cup holders. Their quarter-final against Real Madrid was decided in the first leg when Emilio Butragueño got to the goal line and pulled the ball back low across the box, Ray Clemence got a touch, and Spurs captain Steve Perryman turned it into his own net for the only goal of the tie. It was Spurs' only home defeat in European competition.

In the second leg in Madrid, Perryman was the victim of a vicious tackle by Jorge Valdano (who said he'd mistaken him for Graham Roberts!) which ripped his sock and ankle pad, leaving stud marks around his Achilles tendon. Perryman's mind was set on revenge ('and to an extent that took over from my other responsibilities'), which duly arrived in the second half, a really spectacular kick doubling as a professional foul ('I knew it was him and this was my chance, so I took it'). He walked off without waiting for the red card, Real went on to win the Cup.

Spain were probably favourites to win the 1924 Olympic soccer title. The best team on the continent, fitter than the skilful Uruguayans, they'd lost only one of their last eleven matches, winning eight in a row. When their first round opponents Italy lost 7–1 in Budapest just before the Games (scoring from a penalty when they were 7–0 down), things looked promising.

Still, the Italians had forced a goalless draw with Spain two months earlier – and now looked likely to earn another. There were only four minutes left, and no goals in the match, when Italy's Adolfo Baloncieri shot from the edge of the area. A skilful

playmaker and striker, he eventually scored 25 goals in 47 internationals, but clearly wasn't about to do that here. His shot was going wide until the Spanish captain Pedro Vallana stuck out a foot and deflected the ball in for the only goal of the game.

Italy beat Luxembourg before losing to the Swiss team who reached the final. Spain, who won their next nine matches, had to wait till 1992 for the Olympic gold medal.

The Boss says that games in hand are no good unless you turn them into points. What he's saying is that games in hand aren't much good unless you turn them into points.

DAVID PLATT

Leslie Compton lived most of his sporting life in the shadow of his brilliant younger brother Denis. Both played cricket for Middlesex, but only Denis reached Test level (5,807 stylish runs at 50.06). Both picked up an FA Cup winners' medal with Arsenal in 1950, but Denis won twelve wartime caps to Leslie's five. One was a cavalier crowd-pleasing winger, the other a solid, unspectacular centre-half. 'Nuff said.

But big Leslie, a late developer, bided his time. In 1950, still looking for a replacement for the irreplaceable Neil Franklin, England gave Leslie a full, official, senior cap, something Denis never won.

The big man was 38 by then, and although England beat Wales and he was given another chance, the centre-forward he was marking, the rumbustious Trevor Ford, scored twice.

A week later against Yugoslavia, when Nat Lofthouse celebrated his first cap by scoring twice in four minutes, that seemed to be that. Although this was one of the most talented teams Yugoslavia ever fielded

(Beara, Mitic, Vukas, Zlatko Cajkovski), they were 2–0 down only four minutes from half-time.

Then Compton, on his own Highbury pitch, turned a cross into his own net. Yugoslavia scored another to become the first foreign country to avoid defeat in England, and Big Les wasn't capped again.

The following year, France became the second, at the same stadium, by the same score – but would have won (they've never done so in England) if Abdelkader Firoud hadn't scored an own goal four minutes from the start of his debut, the only goal he scored in international football.

And now for the goals from Carrow Road where the game ended nil-nil.

ELTON WELSBY

In their last match of the 1978 World Cup finals, Austria won 3–2, the first time they'd beaten West Germany since 1931, thanks to an own goal by the German captain Berti Vogts, once a world class man-marker (he'd kept Cruyff on a leash in the 1974 final) but now in decline. His deflection of Walter Schachner's header levelled the match at 1–1, the Germans lost to a European side for the last time before the 1982 World Cup final, and Vogts didn't play international football again, finishing with 96 caps.

Having drawn at home in the first leg of the 1961 Fairs Cup final, Birmingham City held an expensively assembled Roma team to a goalless draw for almost an hour – then right-back Brian Farmer put through his own goal. Roma's 2–0 win gave them the only European trophy they've ever won,

Birmingham (who've never won one) lost in the final for the second successive year.

Liverpool, struggling against Borussia Dortmund in the 1966 Cup-Winners Cup final, equalised through Roger Hunt from Peter Thompson's cross after the ball had gone out of play, and were finally beaten by a bizarre goal in extra-time.

Lothar Emmerich put Sigi Held clear, Tommy Lawrence saved, the ball went loose on the right, and Reinhard Libuda's long high cross, amid much falling about in the Liverpool goal area, was knocked past Lawrence by his own captain, the huge centre-half Ron Yeats.

Dortmund became the first German team to win a European trophy. Liverpool have never won the Cup-Winners Cup.

In 1971, needing a draw at Villa Park to stay in the Third Division, Reading recovered from the horror of conceding a second-minute goal to draw level in the second half, and were holding out well until striker Terry Bell came back to defend at a corner – and headed past his own keeper.

This could just as easily have been filed under BRITISH REFEREES, since Leo Callaghan, in his last League match in charge, missed a blatant push on Bell by Geoff Vowden – but let's see it as a culmination instead: it was Reading's sixth (some say ninth) own goal of the season. They went down on goal average and took four years to get back out of the Fourth Division. Bell had just been voted club player of the year.

When Reading right-back and player-coach Stewart Henderson put through his own goal against Brentford in the first League match of 1979–80, it mattered most of all to his own goalkeeper, the short and reliable

Steve Death, putting an end to his run of 1,103 minutes without conceding a goal in the League, including the last 11 games of the previous season.

It's still the all-time League record, but would have been even longer but for Henderson. When he sliced his attempted clearance, Death – seeing his record disappearing towards goal – rushed to get to the ball and was concussed in a collision, which meant he couldn't remember anything about the goal afterwards. Just as well for the hapless defender, who didn't have to face Death in the changing room.

Henderson didn't play in another League match for over six months, appearing in only three all season.

Three Sheffield Wednesday players got themselves into the record books by scoring own goals in the same League match in 1952 – Norman Curtis, Eddie Gannon and Vince Kenny – which made all the difference to the scoreline: West Brom won 5–4.

Two years later, three Rochdale players joined them: George Underwood, Harry Boyle, and Dan Murphy. Carlisle United, all contributions gratefully received, won 7–2.

No coincidence, surely, that both matches were played over the festive period: the first on Christmas Day, the other on Boxing Day.

Even more bizarrely, two Leicester City players had got in on the act against Chelsea seven days before Rochdale's feat. The same act. Stan Milburn and England international Jack Froggatt hit the ball at exactly the same time (as they confirmed later) to record the only joint own goal in League football.

Three ADO Den Haag players scored own goals in the second leg of a UEFA Cup match at Molineux in 1971–72 (one of them wasn't particularly appreciative of Derek Dougan's pat on the head!), helping Wolves on their way to the final.

After only six minutes of the home match against England in 1957, Wales' left-back, the normally reliable Mel Hopkins, passed back to his keeper – and passed him, an own goal that set England on the way to a 4–0 win. Wales didn't beat England at home again until 1980.

And Ritchie has now scored eleven goals, exactly double the number he scored last season.

ALAN PARRY

Scotland looked certain to beat Wales at home in the 1978 Home Championship, especially when Carl Harris hit the bar and Brian Flynn missed a penalty. Then, in the last minute, with Scotland leading 1–0, Willie Donachie hit a back-pass to goalkeeper Jim Blyth, who was at the far side of the goal when the ball went in by the post. Scotland didn't win any of their matches in the Championship that year (all played at Hampden), hardly the ideal send-off for those fateful World Cup finals.

The holders Milan reached the final of the 1974 Cup-Winners Cup, but didn't play like champions when they got there, retreating into typical defence and handing the initiative to the underdogs Magdeburg. Three minutes from half-time the attitude began to cost them dear, Enrico Lanzi turning the ball past his own keeper. With nothing happening for Milan up front, it was already the decisive goal. Magdeburg won 2–0 to become the only East German side to win a European trophy and Milan missed the chance to become the only club ever to retain the Cup-Winners Cup.

The 1978–79 UEFA Cup final was one of the most anonymous of all, at least in Britain, Borussia Moenchengladbach beating Red Star Belgrade 2–1 on aggregate after two dull games. And few of us here remember the name of Ivan Jurisic. Yet his was a unique feat in major finals.

Red Star were leading 1–0 at home after an hour of the first leg when he knocked the ball past his own keeper for the equaliser. Then, after 15 minutes of the return, he fouled Allan Simonsen in the penalty area, conceding the penalty that Simonsen converted for the only goal of the game. Red Star had to wait till 1991 to win a European trophy for the first time – and the immortal Jurisic is still the only player to score an own goal and give away a penalty in the same European final.

The fastest own goal in British first-class football appears to have been Pat Kruse's urgent effort in 1977: eight seconds. Torquay really gifted the opposition a point that day: Cambridge United's other goal in a 2–2 draw was also an own goal!

Alan Mullery wasn't just the first player to be sent off while playing for the senior England side (1968), he was also apparently the only one to score an own goal in the League before any of the opposition had touched the ball! This happened after only thirty seconds of Fulham's game with Sheffield Wednesday in 1961. The rest of the team seem to have taken their cue from Mullers in this one: they lost 6–1 at home!

Deep into extra time in the 1982 Scottish Cup final, Rangers centre-back Colin Jackson hit a weak back-pass to keeper Jim Stewart, who had to rush out to kick it clear, which

he did – but only as far as the stomach of Aberdeen's Neale Cooper, who pushed it into an empty net.

It wasn't by any means a decisive goal, but it epitomised the way things had gone for Rangers after they'd taken the lead and still been level 1–1 at full-time: this was Aberdeen's fourth in a 4–1 win. It gave them the Cup for the first time since 1970.

John Bailey, a Liverpool supporter as a boy, had the misfortune to score an own goal for them while playing for Everton in 1981: a spectacular televised header for the only goal of the game. 'I've never had so many free drinks off Liverpudlians.'

But even this wasn't the most famous in a Merseyside derby. That accolade still belongs to one which didn't affect the scoreline (Liverpool won 3–0) and certainly not the League title (Everton won by nine points). For some reason, Sandy Brown's header at Goodison in 1969 became a thing of folklore: in some Sunday league matches, an own goal is still referred to as a Sandy Brown!

When Liverpool centre-half Dick White lobbed the ball over his own keeper in an FA Cup match in 1959, he provided one of the famous shock results. Scored with only nine minutes left, it turned out to be the winning goal for non-League Worcester City.

Wimbledon were a non-League side when they went on their famous FA Cup run in 1974–75, beating Bath and Kettering to set up a match against First Division Burnley – then winning that too, 1–0, with the bearded Dickie Guy doing great things in goal.

But even that didn't compare with their most heroic tie, the two games that followed, against the might of Leeds United, which made Guy a household name. In the original match, which drew Elland Road's biggest crowd of the season, he saved everything that came his way, including a penalty which Peter Lorimer, the hardest shot of his day, chose to side-foot.

The goalless draw set up a replay at Selhurst Park, where Wimbledon and Guy simply carried on as before, holding out till ten minutes from the end, when a very average shot by Johnny Giles would have been comfortably saved if it hadn't been deflected by Dave Bassett, later Wimbledon's manager. Guy knelt and beat the ground with his gloves.

As errors go, it wasn't the worst ever made – but it gets in here because a) Bassett had conceded the penalty at Elland Road, so let's say he sort of deserves it, and b) it put an end to Wimbledon's sequence of 765 minutes without conceding a goal in the competition. They won it in 1988 of course, but even Dave Beasant's penalty save in the final [BLUNDERS VOL.1] doesn't eclipse Dickie Guy as *the* Wimbledon goalkeeper in the FA Cup.

In their last League match of 1990–91 Derby County lost 2–0 to Luton Town, which made no difference to them (they were already relegated) but kept Luton in the top flight and sent Sunderland down. Luton's first goal was an own goal scored by Mick Harford, who was born in Sunderland.

> *You're 19 and you're a lot older than a lot of people younger than yourself.*
>
> **MIKE GRAY**

Serial own-goalers

Sam Torrans of Ireland was the first player to score two own goals in international matches (1894) and the first to score three (1895), a feat matched by Swiss full-back Severino Minelli in 1938 – but the latter had to play 80 times (a world record at the time) to achieve that distinction. Torrans won 26 caps – and missed a penalty against England in 1892! His own goal cost Ireland the match against Scotland in 1894.

John McTavish of Manchester City scored an own goal in each of three successive matches in November 1959.

With friends like these... (2)

In the red corner: Graeme Le Saux

In the blue corner: David Batty.

The European Cup match in Moscow in November 1995 had been in play only a few minutes when Blackburn Rovers left-back Graeme Le Saux began laying into his own team-mate David Batty out on the touchline, then turned his attentions on his captain Tim Sherwood when he tried to break it up. Le Saux and Batty were fined by the club and banned for two European matches by UEFA.

Colin Hendry's last-minute sending-off sealed an embarrassing night for Blackburn, whose 3–0 defeat left them firmly at the foot of the Champions League table (one point from five matches) and ended their last slim chance of qualifying for the quarter-finals.

When the Spartak coach Oleg Romantsev had recovered from his surprise, he said he'd expected to be facing a team which would come out fighting for ninety minutes, 'but not with each other'.

Tom Mann, who ran a Spurs souvenir shop near White Hart Lane, once owned a club handbook which he refused to sell. It was very old (1905) and very valuable. One day, while he was on holiday, his father, who was looking after the shop, sold it to a Tottenham fan from Norway – for 20p. 'He's dead now, my dad, God rest his soul.'

David Fairclough's knack of scoring after coming on for Liverpool made him one of the original Supersubs, scorer of a vital goal against St Étienne in the 1976–77 European Cup. On one occasion, manager Bob Paisley was in too much of a hurry to make the switch: referee Peter Willis (the only one to send a player off in an FA Cup final) booked Fairclough for coming on without permission. It was his only booking in English football!

England did well to draw against Scotland at Hampden in 1968, a result that sent them through to the European Championship quarter-finals, given that they went into the game with a centre-half, Brian Labone, who had stitches over one eye.

These were necessary despite all of Alf Ramsey's care and attention to detail. He made sure the team took things easy on a frosty practice pitch before the game – but couldn't do much about Labone's collision with Martin Peters in the bath! The mind's eye boggles. Peters made amends by scoring England's goal.

The principal operator of Oxford FC's surveillance system was a policeman whose surname was Cockhead and who probably never forgave his parents for christening him Dick.

Who needs friends...when you can undo it yourself?

Rajko Mitic was one of the best players in Yugoslavia's splendid team of the early 1950s, a skilful inside-forward who scored 32 goals in 59 internationals, including the only one of the match against England in 1954.

He scored another in the 1950 World Cup finals, in which Yugoslavia won their first two games 3–0 and 4–1 to set up the deciding group match against the hosts in Rio. Brazil had some brilliant players (Zizinho, Jair, Ademir, Bauer) but Yugoslavia almost matched them in that department (Bobek, Zlatko Cajkovski, Mitic himself), and needed only a draw to qualify at Brazil's expense.

The giant Maracaná stadium was still unfinished. In the changing room before the match, Mitic stood up without looking where he was going – and banged his head on a protruding girder. When the rest of the team filed out for the kick-off, he stayed behind to have his head bandaged. By the time he took the field, Yugoslavia were a goal down on their way to losing 2–0.

Another Yugoslav, Milan Rapaic of Hajduk Split, missed the start of the 1995–96 season after injuring himself at the airport, sticking his plastic boarding-pass in his eye.

> *With the very last kick of the game, Bobby McDonald scored with a header.*
>
> **ALAN PARRY**

Paraguayan club Olimpia lost the 1991 Libertadores Cup final without scoring a goal in either match – but might have done better if their leading striker Adriano Samaniego hadn't accidentally shot himself in the heel (don't ask).

He missed the, er, second leg.

Keegan. Shilton. Robson. McDermott. Latchford. Those perms. And the Waddle two-haircuts-in one. Say no more.

Pride cometh...

We have nothing to fear from Costa Rica. ANDY ROXBURGH

Kevin Keegan's transfer to Hamburg and the more technical environs of the Bundesliga had a lot to do with his selection as European Footballer of the Year for 1978 and 1979 – but he had trouble settling in during his first season with the club, partly because the man who signed him, business manager Peter Krohn, insisted on building him up to the press, which did little for KK's relationship with the rest of the team.

For example, before the first match of the season, one of the hardest on the calendar, Krohn proclaimed that 'With God and Kevin Keegan, we shall win in Duisburg.' Hamburg lost 5–2.

Milan approached the 1994 European Cup final as clear underdogs. Stuttering in Serie A, struggling to score goals, they went into the match without their established central defensive partnership of Alessandro Costacurta and the great Franco Baresi – this against the two best strikers in the world, Romário de Souza Fária and Christo Stoichkov, backed by Ronald Koeman's long-range gun, a package which encouraged Stoichkov, with his usual modesty, to announce that Barcelona would win the match 1–0, with no need to ask who the scorer was going to be.

In the event, Paolo Maldini moved across from left back, Stoichkov didn't get a kick, and Milan equalled the widest margin of victory in any European Cup final by winning 4–0.

Still, another mistake brought Stoichkov a little compensation: he was voted European Footballer of the Year despite being outplayed by Maldini in this and the subsequent World Cup semi-final.

Two seasons later, Stoichkov was at it again. Bulgaria and Germany had both reached the 1996 European Championship finals, so the second match between the two, in Berlin, would only decide who topped the qualifying group. Because the visitors had beaten Germany in the 1994 World Cup after being a goal down, then in the first European qualifier after being two behind, Stoichkov announced that they would win again, even if they let in the first three goals.

Bulgaria lost 3–1 in Berlin – after Stoichkov had put them ahead!

Eraldo Pecci was such a gifted player in his youth that he was moved to announce that 'The only difference between Pelé and me is that Pelé is black.' His final totals for Italy: six caps, no goals.

Despite Liverpool's 5–1 defeat against Ajax in the 1966–67 European Cup, manager Bill Shankly was unbowed – 'I still thought we could get through at Anfield' – and announced that Liverpool would win 6–0, which even by the Shanks' standards was stretching it a bit.

After a 19-year-old called Johan Cruyff had scored both Ajax goals in a 2–2 draw, the *Daily Express* quoted an advertising slogan of the time: 'Now we know for sure – Ajax does kill 99% of all germs!' Liverpool never won the European Cup under Shankly.

Before the 1968–69 season, Celtic full-back Tommy Gemmell looked down the entries for the European Cup and decided that although Milan were former winners, 'I cannot see them as a threat to us since, being Italians, their strength is sure to lie in a tight defence. I think our style of play will always overcome this kind of team.'

Milan went on to win the Cup after their tight defence hadn't conceded a goal in the quarter-final against Celtic.

A narrow 2–1 defeat away from home gave Nottingham Forest hope of beating Bayern Munich in the 1996 UEFA Cup quarter-final, especially if they could keep a clean sheet in the home leg, which keeper Mark Crossley was confident they could. He said so on air – then fumbled in Bayern's first goal. Forest lost 5–1, 7–2 on aggregate.

A Tottenham supporter at the 1948 FA Cup semi-final against Blackpool carried a placard saying 'In fond remembrance of Blackpool, who passed out at Villa Park on March 13th. Funeral arrangements by Burgess [Ron, the Spurs captain] & Co.'

Tottenham lost 3–1 and didn't reach the final again till 1961.

That marvellous header of a ball Tommy Lawton won his first England cap in 1938, scoring from a penalty against Wales. The day after hearing the news of his call-up, he strutted into the Everton changing room and behaved as any confident 19-year-old might do. He never did it again. 'Sit down, Lawton,' said Dixie Dean. 'Stand up all the internationals.' Fourteen players got to their feet.

The famous plaque at Liverpool FC, which says simply 'This is Anfield', was put there to intimidate opposing teams, and seems to

It's all gone quiet over there: Supermac at the Cup Final in 1974

have worked pretty well for many years. Some players aren't bothered by it, though – or say they aren't. The story goes that in his first match there for Newcastle, Malcolm Macdonald, who used to say quite a lot in his time, greeted the sign with something flip along the lines of 'Well at least we're in the right place,' which was overheard by Liverpool's abrasive manager Bill Shankly: 'You'll soon bloody find out you're in the right ground, son.' Newcastle lost 5–0.

Macdonald also had his usual say before the 1974 FA Cup final, letting us all know what his pace was about to do to Liverpool's central defensive partnership of Phil Thompson and Emlyn Hughes. According to Ian Callaghan, Liverpool were 'happy to let Malcolm do all the talking'. He didn't get in a shot until the last twelve minutes and put another way over the bar. Newcastle lost 3–0, and before the end the Liverpool fans were singing 'Supermac, superstar, how many goals have you got so far?'

Dundee, surprise package of the 1962–63 European Cup, beat Cologne 8–1 and Sporting Lisbon 4–1 at home, but it was their 4–1 win at Anderlecht that finally convinced them their forward line of Smith-Penman-Cousin-Gilzean-Robertson could beat anyone anywhere, a belief that was to cost them dear.

At half-time in the first leg of the semi-final, Dundee were holding Milan to a 1–1 draw in the San Siro, with Ian Ure and Alex Hamilton in such command at the back that the team and manager Bob Shankly (Bill's brother) decided to go for the win instead of holding out for the draw they looked perfectly capable of achieving.

A real attack of hubris. Dundee's sudden expansive policy gave Gianni Rivera and Dino Sani room in midfield to ping high balls to the far post, where all their second-half goals were scored. Dundee lost 5–1, went out 5–2 on aggregate, and have never taken part in the European Cup again.

> *I'm not going to make it a target but it's something to aim for.*
>
> **STEVE COPPELL**

After his Manchester City team had won the 1967–68 League title, Malcolm Allison proclaimed that its attacking style (Lee, Summerbee, Bell) was about to take the Champions Cup by storm, to 'take football to the moon' and 'frighten the cowards of Europe'.

Most of the continent didn't have time to tremble at the knees. City went out in the first round, without winning either match, to a Fenerbahçe team so unfancied that Allison didn't bother to have them watched. It was City's only appearance in the European Cup.

Five years later, Big Mal still hadn't learned. When he took over as manager of

Crystal Palace, newly relegated from the First Division, he crowed, 'We will walk this division.' They did, but not in the direction he meant. They were relegated again in his first season.

In 1939 England fully expected to beat Yugoslavia in the first match between the two countries. The opposition hadn't won any of their last seven matches and had no-one to compare with Stanley Matthews, Stan Cullis, Tommy Lawton or the England captain Eddie Hapgood, who was as confident as anyone. A little too much so, as he later admitted.

Asked to say a few words on Belgrade radio just before the match, 'I am afraid it all sounded rather superior when I said: "Good evening. We have brought a strong team and I am sure you will enjoy the football."'

No doubt they did. Yugoslavia won 2–1 and Hapgood didn't win another official cap.

In the third round of the 1956–57 FA Cup, Newcastle United held the holders Manchester City to a draw then won the replay 5–4 after being 3–0 down, which inspired manager Stan Seymour to believe that the club's name was on the silverware – especially when they were drawn against Third Division Millwall in the next round. 'Now we've got as good a chance as we've ever had,' he said. 'It's a piece of cake.'

Newcastle lost 2–1 and haven't won the Cup since 1955.

Wales were so depleted by injuries and club commitments in 1930 that they arrived in Glasgow with ten new caps, some from non-League clubs – which encouraged one local poster to wonder if Scotland would stop after scoring 24 goals! Wales drew 1–1.

After Celtic beat MTK 3–0 in the first leg of the 1964 Cup-Winners Cup semi-final, the club chartered a plane to take the players and their wives to the final in Brussels. They lost 4–0 in the second leg.

Brian Clough's success with Derby County doesn't need repeating here, but it took a year or two to start happening. Before his first full season in charge, the modest one predicted that the club would finish higher than they had the previous year – which shouldn't have been difficult: Derby were 17th in 1966–67. In 1967–68 they were 18th!

Mansfield won the Third Division championship in 1976–77. Earlier that season, at home to non-League Matlock Town in the second round of the FA Cup, they twice fell behind, only to equalise for the second time after an hour, surely enough to dispirit the underdogs. Certainly their players seemed to think so; Matlock's Peter Scott remembers one of them running back to the centre circle waving his fist and shouting, 'Come on, we can beat this load of *@!#§•s.'

Within two minutes, Matlock had taken the lead yet again, on their way to a 5–2 shock, their only win against League opposition in the FA Cup.

Italy's first match after winning the 1934 World Cup was at Highbury later that year. They travelled with the bulk of the team who'd played in the final, but there was a change in goal, where Carlo Ceresoli took over from Gianpiero Combi, who'd retired after the tournament.

Actually Ceresoli, a brilliant shot-stopper, would have been in the World Cup team if he hadn't broken an arm in training, allowing the veteran Combi to come in and not only pick up a winner's medal but captain the team. The match against England would be only Ceresoli's second international.

He began it in sensational fashion. After less than two minutes, England were awarded a penalty, taken by Eric Brook, a winger with one of the hardest shots in the game. He proved that again here – only for Ceresoli to bring off a marvellous save. So far, so good; proof of just how lucky Combi had been.

Two minutes later Brook was invited to try again, from longer range. England won a free kick – and Ceresoli, intoxicated by his earlier success, waved away the wall, whereupon the affronted Brook hit the free kick even harder than the penalty and put England 1–0 up. Ceresoli barely saw it. It's said that one of his defenders repeatedly kicked the ball back into the net in his fury, whereupon Ceresoli picked it up and sat on it.

It was a crucial goal. Italy were reduced to ten men after five minutes, fell 3–0 behind after fifteen, and lost 3–2. Ceresoli had effectively cost his team the match, and Eric Brook had his revenge – but it wasn't complete: that famous penalty save not only made him the only player to miss a spot-kick in the first minute of an England match, it deprived him of what would have been his only international hat-trick.

> *That's a priceless goal worth millions of pounds.*
>
> **ALAN PARRY**

Hard to imagine a more gross example of the great sin than when it was displayed by the governor of Rio de Janeiro state just before the deciding match of the 1950 World Cup. And what a come-uppance.

Brazil were the hosts and heavy favourites, especially as they needed only a draw to take the title. Their inside-forward trio of Jair-Ademir-Zizinho had done some wonderful things in the mini-league which would decide the tournament. Whereas their final opponents Uruguay had been drawing 2–2 with Spain and bruising their way to a 3–2 win over Sweden, Brazil had beaten the same two sides 6–1 and 7–1.

All this went to the head of the governor, whose speech of the eve of the last match apparently went something like this. It probably hasn't lost much in translation.

You Brazilians, whom I consider victors of the tournament, who in less than a few hours will be acclaimed champions by millions of your countrymen, you who have no equals...'

There was more where this came from. Brazil lost 2–1.

Just before the 1979 League Cup final, Southampton captain Alan Ball wrote in a newspaper that his team would win and the opposition boss wasn't all that good a manager. If this put Brian Clough's back up, he didn't show it – even when Ball ran to the touchline to gesticulate to the two benches when Southampton went a goal up. They were still 1–0 ahead at half-time, but Ballie was considerably quieter after the final whistle: Forest won 3–2.

Tommy Docherty was Manchester United's manager when they won the 1977 FA Cup final, presumably after learning a lesson from the previous year's final. Before that match, against underdogs Southampton, he was even more confident than usual:

'We haven't watched Southampton and we won't talk about them. They're a lovely club full of good people, but this final is about an exciting performance by Manchester United.'

United lost an unexciting final 1–0.

Alan Ball leaves Wembley with something to wash down his humble pie

When Carlisle United from the Third Division North held First Division Arsenal to a goalless draw at Highbury in the 1950–51 FA Cup, the whole town made itself ready for victory in the replay. It's said that the Carlisle manager Bill Shankly (yes, that one) 'thought the result a foregone conclusion'. The local magistrates ordered an extension of the licensing hours to celebrate the win. Carlisle lost 4–1.

As soon as England went 2–0 up in the 1970 World Cup quarter-final, some of the English press stood up, gestured to their German counterparts in the stand, and shouted 'Auf Wiedersehen'. Fair comment, but not in the way they thought. West Germany of course recovered to win 3–2 and England didn't play in the finals again till 1982.

Towards the end of 1970–71, Liverpool striker John Toshack said he agreed Arsenal had had a great season so far. 'I like them. And it's very sad that they're not going to win the FA Cup.' Arsenal beat Liverpool in the final to complete the Double.

If you've got it, don't flaunt it

The final of the 1992 UEFA Cup was a success for Ajax – it made them only the second club to have won all three European competitions – but not an unqualified one for Stefan Pettersson.

Their Swedish striker had scored from the penalty spot in the first leg. Now, in the last minute of the second, with Ajax trying to preserve the goalless draw that would win them the Cup, he took the ball down to the corner flag to waste some time. Now, no-one condones the subsequent foul by Torino's Roberto Policano, but it's possible that some might see it as just desserts. Pettersson suffered a broken arm.

> *I'm not a believer in luck, but I do believe you need it.*
>
> **ALAN BALL**

Back in 1964, much the same thing had happened – with even greater repercussions – to Jim Baxter.

Having won the first leg only 1–0 at home, Rangers were apprehensive about visiting Rapid Vienna in the 1964–65 European Cup. In the event, Baxter was so masterful that they came away with a 2–0 win.

Unfortunately, the temptation to rub it in was never very far under Slim Jim's surface (witness his performance against England in 1967). In the last minute, with the tie well won, he took the ball back from the Rapid penalty box into his own half, then kept it as he made his way along the left wing. Finally, Walter Skocik put an end to the show by tackling him from behind.

The broken leg kept Baxter out of the next round, in which Rangers lost to Inter, and overshadowed the rest of his career: he was never quite the same player again (see CHEQUEBOOK CHARLIES). Skocik's tackle seems to have been rash at best, but Baxter knew he'd contributed to his own downfall. His own succinct verdict: 'I overdid it.'

Very little grey cells

Slips of the mind (on the pitch)

In February 1996, Beppe Signori converted a very late penalty to beat Roma in the local derby, then ran off the field to celebrate with the Lazio fans, which earned him a booking, his second of the match. He joined that exclusive club of players sent off immediately after scoring the winner!

Near the end of the last Manchester derby in 1995–96, City captain Keith Curle shepherded United's Ryan Giggs out to the left-hand edge of the penalty area, then indicated the City goal with an outstretched arm, apparently daring Giggs to shoot.

This Giggs did, hitting the top corner to win the match 3–2 and secure three vital points in United's charge to the domestic Double, which compounded City's despair at the end of the season: they were relegated on goal difference.

For the first hour of the 1970 World Cup quarter-final against West Germany, Gordon Banks' absence made no difference to England, who played their best football of the tournament to lead 2–0.

When Alf Ramsey substituted Bobby Charlton almost immediately after Franz Beckenbauer had pulled a goal back, pundits made knee-jerk noises about panic and error – but Charlton's replacement Colin Bell almost settled the match within minutes of coming on, first with a shot that Sepp Maier had to save, then a run and cross from the right.

Geoff Hurst had been making these near-post balls his speciality for years. It had taken all his persuasion to get Francis Lee to send the ball into space there and not to the crowded far post. When the penny dropped, against Uruguay the previous year, Hurst had arrived late to bury Lee's centre with a thumping match-winning volley. Here another Man City player provided the same kind of centre, and Hurst got in front of Maier and Willi Schulz for a diving header of courage and great timing, glancing the ball to the far post, where Lee was waiting.

All he had to do was step in and push it home. Instead he waited, expecting the ball to either go in or come back off the post. It bobbled wide.

Instead of leading 3–1 and striding into the semi-final, England lost in extra-time and didn't qualify again until 1982. Lee never scored a World Cup goal.

In 1939 Willington, playing in their first FA Amateur Cup final, were out-and-out outsiders but held Bishop Auckland, playing in their eleventh, goalless for ninety minutes.

In extra-time, one of the Willington players, expecting the referee to blow for a foul, picked the ball up instead of playing to the whistle. Bishop Auckland scored from the free kick, and won the seventh of their record ten Amateur Cups by three goals (all by inside-right Wensley) to nil. Willington had to wait till 1950 to win the cup for the first and only time.

Roberto Rivelino, Brazil's explosive mid-fielder in the World Cups of 1970–74–78, didn't take long to make his mark for Corinthians in a match against Rio Preto.

Just a few seconds, in fact, enough for his famous left foot to blast the ball into the opposing net straight from the kick-off.

At this point, goalkeeper Irandir Isidore looked up. He was still on his knees, not out of fear of Rivelino's well-known shooting prowess but because he was still saying his pre-match prayer.

The implications of not playing to the whistle were never better demonstrated than in the Republic of Ireland's match in Switzerland in 1935. For an hour their injury-stricken team held out comfortably enough, then a cross from Lauro Amadó found Leopold Kielholz, who hesitated, thinking he was offside – which prompted Irish new cap Leo Dunne to pick the ball up inside the penalty area. Swiss captain Walter Weiler's penalty was the only goal of the game. Three days later, Dunne's foul on Ernst Lehner gave Germany their equaliser on the way to a 3–1 win. He didn't play for Ireland again.

Of course, if you do play to the whistle, it had better be the right one. In the decisive qualifying match for the 1950 World Cup finals, at home to Sweden, the Irish defenders stopped and stood still when they heard a whistle as Kalle Palmér ran through. It had been blown by someone in the crowd, and Palmér scored his second goal on the way to the first hat-trick ever scored against the Republic, who didn't reach the finals till 1990.

When Billy Wright won the toss for England against Sweden in 1949, he chose to play facing the sun in the first half, which he wouldn't have if he or the England officials had done their homework. The sun sets very quickly at the Rasunda stadium, and Sweden didn't have to face it in the second half. In the first, they dazzled the opposition 3–0, holding on to win 3–1, their first ever win over England.

Before leaving football to become a Jehovah's Witness [BLUNDERS VOL.1], Peter Knowles was a skilful forward with Wolves. When he headed a goal at Fratton Park in 1967, he celebrated by kicking the ball out of the ground – and later paid the bill which Portsmouth sent him for the cost of a replacement.

When James J Lang joined Sheffield Wednesday in 1876, he was probably the first Scottish player to be signed by an English club. He almost certainly came south for the money (which wasn't officially being paid yet) – but perhaps he was still miffed at the way things had gone for him in Glasgow.

Early in the first ever Scottish Cup final (1874), he scored a goal for Clydesdale. Fine so far, even though the referee, James McIntyre, thought it offside. In those days, officials could only disallow a goal if the opposition appealed. Queen's Park didn't appeal – and McIntyre didn't appeal to the Clydesdale players by muttering under his breath that the opposition should have said something. When one of the Queen's Park players heard this, he said something pronto and McIntyre disallowed the goal. Clydesdale lost 2–0 and never reached the final again. If Lang's goal had stood, it would have been the first scored against Queen's Park in the first seven years of their existence!

There were only four minutes to go to the end of the traumatic England–Poland World Cup qualifier in 1973 when Alf Ramsey belatedly accepted the need for a substitute. From the England front bench, he called over his shoulder for Kevin to get stripped, whereupon Keegan began removing his tracksuit, a task he was helped in by Ray Clemence, who tugged so hard at his trousers that he pulled his shorts down with them.

It was the only flash of Keegan magic that night. Ramsey had been calling to Kevin Hector.

If ever anyone's name seemed to be written on the FA Cup, it had to be Nottingham Forest's in 1991. A man sent off against them in the semi-final, another (PJ Gascoigne, who else?) carried off in the final, a goal up, a Tottenham penalty missed, a Tottenham goal wrongly disallowed. Then it

began to go wrong, Paul Stewart equalising early in the second half, Tottenham bossing things against Forest's youngsters.

Brian Clough could see it happening but seemed to do nothing about it, most glaringly in the rest period before extra-time. While Terry Venables came onto the pitch to pass on instructions, Clough stayed on the bench, saying afterwards that 'Once they're out on the pitch, you can't do any more,' something Alf Ramsey, among others, would probably argue with.

Perhaps he thought that by typically doing the unexpected, he might affect things precisely by not doing anything. Perhaps he

The last time Brian Clough was on the Wembley pitch with his players that afternoon – Stuart Pearce introduces HRH to BHC before the 1991 FA Cup final

didn't think at all. Either way, it didn't work. Forest lost 2–1 and Clough never won the FA Cup either as player or manager.

Mind you, his record and personality gave him a stature others didn't have. It's convincingly told, for instance, that another League club manager once stood up when he spoke to him – on the phone!

By his own admission, Kevin Keegan's main strength as a player was the desire and ability to cover every blade of grass during a match. He was being modest and there

was more to his game than that, but the point's been made: work rate was the thing.

It helped Liverpool and Hamburg win all those trophies, as well as being a main ingredient in England's impressive run through the 1978–80 European qualifiers (in which Keegan scored seven goals, more than any other player in the competition). Unfortunately, in the finals, in a single move, it undid all the good work.

After being unfortunate not to win their opening match, the 1–1 draw with Belgium, England needed at least a draw against the hosts Italy to maintain their interest in the competition. Again they had no luck, this time when Ray Kennedy hit a post, and were level at 0–0 until ten minutes from the end. Then Francesco Graziani brushed Phil Neal aside on his way to the goal line, and put in a low cross from the left.

Throughout the match, Keegan had been shadowed by Marco Tardelli, the very talented and very ruthless Juventus man-marker. As play worked its way into the England half, Keegan had obeyed his instinct to follow the ball, which in this case led him into trouble. He was back in his penalty area trying to help out, which meant that Tardelli, as sure as night follows day, was in there with him. When the ball didn't reach Kev, it reached Marco, who scored the only goal of the game from a position he wouldn't have been in if the England captain hadn't taken him there! It was the nearest England came to the European Championship final till 1996.

With their team 2–0 down to Clyde with only six minutes of the 1910 Scottish Cup final to go, hundreds of Dundee supporters streamed out of Ibrox. It wasn't until some of them reached Glasgow city centre that they were told the match had ended in a draw. They'd missed the most famous fightback in their club's history. Presumably they stayed all the way through both replays, which Dundee drew 0–0 then won 2–1 to take the Cup for the first and only time.

Very little grey cells (2)

Slips of the mind...off the pitch

Having already turfed Garry Birtles off the team coach before the start of a trip to the Middle East, the Nottingham Forest manager, one BH Clough, lived up to his reputation for decisive if unorthodox action by clipping the ear of a passenger who was failing to control his offspring on the plane.

Fine. All adding to the Clough legend and no great harm done. Just one thing. His victim wasn't the children's father. Cloughie had hit the wrong man.

When the organisers of the 1994 World Cup finals advertised for security staff, they required applicants to send in their thumb prints as well as their CVs. Fifty-seven of them were arrested on outstanding criminal charges!

> *And with just four minutes gone, the score is already nil-nil.*
>
> **IAN DARKE**

Kenny Dalglish once agreed to talk to Sky TV's Richard Keys, but only if the interview took place on the golf course. The stake: £5. Canny Kenny won it with virtually the first shot.

Keys, who went first, was complimented on the length of his opening drive. But, said his opponent, his second shot would have to be even longer. Dalglish then turned 180 degrees and hit his ball down the fairway. Keys had teed off in completely the wrong direction.

In 1967 Malcolm Macdonald was playing for Tonbridge when they reached the final of the Kent FA Cup. After arranging to join the team bus for the second leg in Folkestone, he arrived, got on the waiting coach, which was empty, watched the time tick by, then began to worry when thirty strangers boarded it at the last minute. He was on the wrong coach.

He missed the match and didn't play in another cup final till Newcastle United lost at Wembley in 1974.

Before the Rangers–Marseille European Cup match in 1992, Dougie McDonald of Radio Clyde managed to arrange an exclusive interview with the French club's German striker Rüdi Völler, then left the tape with producer David Tanner.

It wasn't until anchorman Archie McPherson asked for the first question and answer to be played that Tanner realised the tape was no use to them. To make Völler feel more at home, McDonald had conducted the entire interview in German.

Before the match against England in 1967, Brian Morgan, a young photographer with the *Glasgow Daily Record*, was sent down to take pictures of the Scotland team on the Wembley pitch. It was a big assignment for him and he wore his best suit for the occasion.

One of his favourite techniques was to take photographs at an angle. Here he went down on one knee and was about to start shooting when Jim Baxter, the famous Rangers wing-half, suggested he move back a little. Morgan didn't think this was necessary but decided not to take the risk of offending anyone and missing the picture, so he went back. No no, said Baxter, further than that.

Eventually, after much shuffling backwards, the star midfielder pronounced himself ready, whereupon Morgan took his pictures. When he stood up, he realised this was Baxter the inveterate prankster he'd been listening to: Slim Jim had moved him back onto the touch-line, which left a big white stripe across the knee of Morgan's trousers.

Before the Keegans' marriage, the course of true love hadn't always run smooth, for instance when they arranged to meet at a restaurant called the Golden Egg – and Kevin went to the Golden Egg in Liverpool, Jean to the Golden Egg in Manchester.

Tommy Gemmell and Jim Craig were Celtic's full-backs in the 1967 European Cup final – and very good friends. But big Tommy should have known better than to allow Craig, a trainee dentist, to fill one of his teeth. Assorted injections were applied to the offending molar to not much avail, time went by, pain was suffered – only for a passing surgeon to come in and tell Gemmell that the tooth would have to come out. All of Craig's work had been a waste of time.

So why do it? fumed the patient. Well, explained a red-faced defensive partner, the hospital awards more marks for a filling than an extraction.

Ramalho, a Brazilian playing for Real Murcia, once suffered a bad stomach upset which

confined him to bed for three days after taking something which had been prescribed for a dental infection, explaining afterwards that he'd never seen this kind of medicine before. He'd swallowed a suppository!

What were Bukta thinking of when they designed a jersey, modelled by a Manchester United player, called 'Munich'?

The secretary of Oxbarn Social Club could have done more to check the standard of the club they arranged to play in a friendly in West Germany – but so could the secretary of SVW Mainz. They were in the Bundesliga, Oxbarn in the Wolverhampton Sunday League. Apparently the hosts had been expecting to entertain Wolves.

According to the Oxbarn secretary, the Mainz crowd behaved very well: 'Whenever we got the ball, they gave a prolonged cheer.' Oxbarn lost 21–0.

> *I don't blame individuals, Elton, I blame myself.*
>
> **JOE ROYLE**

FA secretary Stanley Rous once wrote to reporter Ivan Sharpe informing him that he'd been reported for entering the referee's changing room before an important match, in contravention of the rules. The referee had referred to Sharpe's 'air of contemptuousness'.

Rous said that the FA now considered the affair closed, to which Sharpe replied that it had never really been open. On the afternoon of the match, 'I was finishing a fishing holiday in North Wales!'

Liverpool speeding to yet another title? Old Bill at Old Trafford

Bill Shankly once stormed into the Liverpool changing room muttering darkly about the sneaky tricks used by the boys in blue (the police, not Everton) to catch him speeding.

'I saw the policeman with the radar, so I slowed down. Once I was past him, I picked up speed again – but there was another of the crafty *@!#§• waiting up ahead and he stopped me.'

He hadn't realised that in every speed trap one police car used the radar while another further along flagged drivers down! It's a true story because Emlyn Hughes says so.

In many ways, Hugo Meisl was the father of Austrian football, the manager who put together the famous *Wunderteam*, the best national team on the continent in the very early '30s. A real magpie, he borrowed his tactics from the old Scottish short-passing school, imported Jimmy Hogan as coach, and generally used a variety of methods he'd picked up over the years – including one that did Austria no harm before the 1936 match with England.

On the morning of the match, Meisl called at the visitors' hotel and offered to show them the sights. Eddie Hapgood and the boys 'jumped at the chance, and set off on what became the longest tour I have made of any city – on foot.'

Meisl walked them for miles – then, when they paused for breath, insisted on showing them the birthplace of Johann Strauss 'just round the corner'. It wasn't until the 'corner' had gone on for another two miles that Hapgood & Co twigged and called off the trek. 'Otherwise we might still be wandering around Vienna.'

That afternoon a tired team conceded two goals in the first seventeen minutes and lost 2–1, England's first ever defeat by Austria.

Towards the end of the 1927–28 season, Tottenham seemed to have gained enough points to avoid relegation from Division 1 –

so they arranged to complete their fixtures before anyone else, and took the final three matches relatively easily, drawing one and losing the last two.

It went horribly, freakishly wrong. Results fell in such a way that seven clubs finished with 29 points, Tottenham were relegated with 28 and didn't come back up for another five years.

When David Pleat arrived at Tottenham as manager in 1986, he introduced a system of code words for certain moves during a match. 'Fred', for instance, was a back heel, 'Sid' meant take the ball over, 'Jack' told you to let it run. If it sounds iffy on paper, you should have been there on the pitch. Players found themselves losing the ball while trying to remember who Jack and Sid were – and even when they'd memorised all this for the start of the new season, they ran into trouble when they played Pleat's former club Luton Town, who were still using the system, but with different names: their Fred was a Sid, their Sid a Jack. Confusion reigned, here and against Norwich City, whose players were asking the Spurs boys, 'You don't use those daft names as well, do you?' After abandoning the system, Tottenham reached the FA Cup final.

The Nottingham Forest team coach on the way to the 1979 European Cup final in Munich was a quiet, nervous place. For once, all of Clough and Taylor's efforts weren't enough to dispel the butterflies. Then, outside on the pavement, as some of the players watched, a young German spectator played his part in Forest's success.

Once his companion had pointed out the English players travelling alongside them, our hero was so engrossed in identifying the likes of Shilton, Trevor Francis and Clough himself that he walked smack into a lamp post. It's a true story. Ask Frank Clark or any

of them. The laughter broke the tension, the team won the Cup.

Elisha Scott was Liverpool's famous Irish goalkeeper of the 1920s and '30s; Dixie Dean's heading power we all know about. The two met in any number of Merseyside derbies. On one such occasion, Dean only had to move his head for Scott to throw himself full length to make the save.

Not a good idea. There was nothing to save. Dean had merely been nodding hello across the street after a match. Scott had dived, instinctively, into the gutter!

It's a very old tale, and it just can't have happened. But if fiction really is the best way to tell a truth...

Gordon Strachan, not the tallest of footballers, was 'always on the lookout for someone who might possibly be smaller.' When he met Lesley Scott in a disco, he thought she fitted the bill and approached her – only to discover that she'd been dancing with her shoes off. When they were back on, she was as tall as he was in his platform soles. They married anyway.

Talking of Strachan, when he scored the third goal in the 1982 Scottish Cup final, he did a somersault – which an Aberdeen fan, watching on TV in his living room, decided to emulate. He landed in his stone fireplace and broke his leg. Strachan visited him in hospital.

No-one ever did his personal reputation among the fans more harm than Graeme Souness in 1992. While in hospital recovering from a heart operation, he allowed himself to be photographed kissing his girlfriend – by the *Sun*, which had alienated Liverpool supporters with its reporting of the Hillsborough disaster

(Merseyside boycotts of the paper costing it £10 million a year). The picture was enough to undo all the goodwill Souness had built up as a player with Liverpool. They won the FA Cup a few weeks later, but his days there were now numbered.

When Mo Johnston and Ally McCoist crept into the hotel room of team-mate Scott Nisbet one night, their intention was probably to wake him up none too gently (this passed for humour among the jolly jesters at Rangers). The cunning plan was for Johnston to jump onto Nisbet's bed and...well, that's it really: to jump on his bed. It probably loses something in the writing.

Unfortunately for Johnston, but all well and good for Nisbet, the intended victim had decided to put his mattress on the floor that night. Johnston landed on the bedsprings, bruising his face so badly that journalists interpreted it as the result of an altercation with manager Graeme Souness – who had, it's true, been so furious that he ordered Johnston to 'sort yourself out or leave' – whereupon Johnston misunderstood and flew home!

He'd committed a graver *faux pas* than that before coming to the club. Before the 1989–90 season, Johnston was so confident he knew which club he was about to rejoin that he allowed himself to be photographed wearing a Celtic shirt, a picture he regretted for a long time to come (especially after being fined £3,000 by the Scottish FA). He signed for Rangers the following month!

It's not far from Tottenham to Chelsea, but obviously enough of a trek through uncharted territory for the driver of the Spurs team coach to find an illegal parking spot for their lunchtime break in late 1990. When he returned, he found that the vehicle (with all the players' kit inside) had been towed away. Tottenham lost 3–2.

In 1996 the *Western Mail* ran a spot-the-ball photo which showed an item you don't normally expect to see in this kind of competition. The ball.

Bad memories

In September 1995, William Hill quoted Luton Town as 125–1 to win the League Cup – scarcely generous odds for a club which had already been knocked out!

Kevin Keegan's book *Against The World* is an excellent, revealing piece of work (yes, honestly), so it can be forgiven the occasional lapse of memory, especially about England's heady 5–1 win over Scotland in 1975 – 'I scored one myself' (he didn't) and the fifth was put in by 'either Kevin Beattie or Colin Bell' (it was David Johnson) – and the dismal World Cup defeat by Italy in 1976: a picture shows Trevor Brooking being tackled, 'but the ball is slipped to Dave Watson' (who didn't play).

After Poland's famous 1–1 draw in the World Cup qualifier at Wembley in 1973, England's left-back that night, Emlyn Hughes, wrote that goalkeeper Jan Tomaszewski 'had all the luck in the world and I will never know how he kept out a shot from Kevin Keegan right at the end.' Nor will Tomaszewski, or anyone else. Keegan wasn't in the team.

Pelé's autobiography mentions the first match of the 1962 World Cup finals, in which he scored the first goal of a 2–1 win [It was actually 2–0]; then Brazil's 3–1 win over Zaire in 1974 [It was 3–0]; Brazil's quarter-final and semi in that tournament [There were no quarters or semis that year]; the goal he scored against Czechoslovakia in the 1970 finals, volleying the ball before it touched the ground [He didn't]; Djalma and Nilton Santos playing in the World Cup aged 38 [They didn't]; and how well Jack Charlton played against Brazil in 1970 [He wasn't in the team]!

Ronnie Clayton, who won his first cap in 1955, recalled that there were 'five newcomers to the England team that day...the goalkeeper Ron Baynham, Bedford Jezzard at centre-forward, left-winger Bill Perry, inside-forward Johnny Haynes; and I completed the nap-hand of new boys.'

Which must have been news to Baynham, Jezzard and Haynes, who'd all been capped before.

Jack Charlton's memory for names and faces is legendary ('The boy – what's his name? I signed him last week'). On an ITV programme just before Euro 96, he praised the managerial skills of Gunnar Nielsen, referring to him twice by name ('He's a good man, Gunnar') – this after watching an interview with Denmark's coach Richard Møller Nielsen.

Bob Wilson didn't correct him on that one but felt he had to say something when Big Jack went on to mention the Portuguese players Rui Sosa and Paola. You mean Rui Costa and Paulo Sousa? Aye, that's right, said Jack, quality players.

Emlyn Hughes is a big Princess Anne fan. When she presented him with the FA Cup at the 1974 final, he thought it 'lovely

Before the 1974 FA Cup final, Emlyn Hughes meets two well-known horse riders: Mark Phillips and John Reid

meeting Princess Anne'. When he met her again at Aintree racecourse, a small comment of hers 'only added to my view that Princess Anne is a tremendous person.' She once sat next to him on *A Question of Sport*.

How is it then that when he was shown a photograph of her on another edition of the show, he famously identified her as jockey John Reid?!

Why did the gifted Tony Currie win only 17 England caps scattered over eight seasons? Something to do with his knowledge of the international scene, perhaps? On one *A Question Of Sport*, asked to name the teams taking part in a televised derby match, he was shown a clip featuring Berti Vogts, Gerd Müller & Co playing against East Germany.

'Got it,' he said. 'No problems. Norwich City v Ipswich Town.'

For all we know, the single-minded dedication that made Alf Ramsey a successful player and manager may have had repercussions at home. It's said that on the first Saturday after his marriage he passed a young woman in the corridor at White Hart Lane and was about to leave the ground when someone called out, 'Hey, Alf. You've forgotten your wife!'

Prophets and their losses

After a goalless first half in the 1982 World Cup match between Poland and Peru, TV pundit Mick Channon was asked how he thought the game might go. 'I think Peru will win,' he said (and he said it more confidently than it sounds). Peru lost 5–1 and haven't played in the finals since.

After their first match of the same tournament, the Brazilians made a big impression on everyone, none more so than Denis Law, who announced that 'Brazil will win the World Cup – that's certain.' They didn't reach the semi-finals.

Colin Wood was the Liverpool football correspondent of the *Daily Mail*'s northern edition throughout the 1970s. At the start of the decade, he wrote that 'This team will dominate the seventies...nothing can stop it becoming one of the greatest club teams of all time.' Since Liverpool won four European trophies in the next ten years, as well as the League four times and the FA Cup in 1974, these sound like prophetic words.

'Er, not really,' said Wood. 'I wrote them about Everton.'

Shortly before being sacked as Arsenal manager, George Graham recited the mantra of so many in his position: 'I know I have the backing of the board.'

Just before the 1946 FA Cup final between Derby and Charlton, match referee Ernest Smith announced on the radio that the chances of the ball bursting were a million to one. It did burst – in that match, in the League match between the same two clubs only five days later, and in the final the following year!

During 1989–90 a witch doctor assured the players of the Tongogara club in Zimbabwe that they would win matches if they urinated on the pitch. Four of them tried it and were banned for life. [I'm taking this one on trust, you understand.]

'I think our fans know how to behave. I don't believe there will be any problems. Those days are behind us now.' Reg Burr, Millwall chairman, just before the riot at the play-off match with Derby in 1994.

In a newspaper column in October 1993, Jimmy Greaves wrote that Manchester United 'were full value for their place in the second round [of the European Cup] and they'll beat the Turks easily enough.'

United lost to Galatasaray on away goals. Greaves had been replying to someone he called Geek Of The Week.

At the start of 1995–96, Ian Stirrup wrote in the *Daily Star* that 'If Manchester United finish above Liverpool, my backside will be on display in Trafalgar Square in June.'

Any anticipation was probably restricted to the pigeons.

After the Arsenal prophecy, Big Ron puts his finger on the problem

When Arsenal fell 3–2 behind on aggregate against Sampdoria in the 1995 European Cup-Winners Cup semi-final, Ron Atkinson was asked if he thought they had any chance. 'No, they're out,' he said firmly. Arsenal equalised almost immediately and went through to the final on penalties.

Ivan Sharpe, Olympic football gold medallist and journalistic class act, recalled how in 1923 several newspapers were asked when Bolton Wanderers had won the FA Cup. 'Never,' was the written reply. 'And they never will.'

Maybe they just needed a move to Wembley. That year, in the first final played there, they won the Cup, and did it again in 1926, 1929, 1958...

Jimmy Howie, who scored both Scotland's goals in their win over England in 1906, was sometimes less successful as a pundit. In April 1934 he went on record as saying that Rangers had no chance of winning that year's Scottish Cup. They won 5–0 in the final.

After João Saldanha was sacked as Brazil's manager just before the 1970 World Cup, the job was offered to Dino Sani, who'd played in the 1958 finals, then to Otto Glória, manager of Portugal in the 1966 tournament. Both turned it down, believing that Brazil hadn't had the right preparation for success. Penny for their thoughts when Brazil won every match on the way to the title.

Aston Villa were drawn against Arsenal in the third round of the 1953–54 FA Cup. A week before the match, the teams met in a League fixture at Highbury, where Arsenal scored three times in the first ten minutes before fog caused the game to be abandoned. The day before the Cup match, Villa trainer Jimmy Easson ended his pep talk with, 'At least there's one thing: they won't score three goals in ten minutes this time.'

In fact, they went one better, winning 5–1 after being three up in nine minutes.

Peter Harris was a fast and tricky right-winger who scored more League goals for Portsmouth than anyone else (194) and helped them win the First Division in 1949 and 1950, which prompted one scribe to opine that, 'Round about 1952 the name of Peter Harris will appear in England teams with the same joyful frequency as Stanley Matthews. That's a safe prediction.'

Harris won a grand total of two caps, against the Republic of Ireland in 1949 and Hungary in 1954. The first match was England's first home defeat by a country from outside the Home Championship, the second was England's biggest ever defeat!

After Nottingham Forest had beaten the holders Liverpool 2–0 at home in the first round of the 1978–79 European Cup, the other First Division managers were asked if they thought Brian Clough's team could hold on to their lead at Anfield. Only three of the twenty said yes – which infuriated Peter Taylor: 'I ask you, with our record they still doubted us. It made Brian and I absolutely determined to get it right for the second leg.'

They did. After the 0–0 draw, Clough wondered if 'perhaps now you people will realise that we are quite a good side.' Forest went on to win the Cup that season and the next.

When George Raynor, the English coach who built three fine Swedish national teams, led them to the 1958 World Cup final at home, he hoped for an early goal. 'When the Brazilians are a goal down, they panic all over the show.' Brazil conceded a goal after only four minutes – and won 5–2.

Brazil took a psychologist with them to those 1958 finals, an unshaven gent called João Carvalhaes who wandered around the training camp in a grey sweater, preferring not to address the players in a group because it couldn't accomplish anything – but not talking to them individually as this simply made them nervous. What to do, then? Get them to draw pictures of a man, that's what to do. The most sophisticated would draw detailed figures, the least sophisticated childlike stick figures. The two different types would make good combinations on the wing.

Hard to know whether the Brazilian manager Vicente Feola took much notice of this, but he certainly didn't when Dr Carvalhaes was asked for his opinion about two players who were challenging for a place in the third group match against the USSR.

About one, a right-winger, he said that his lack of sophistication was so complete that it went beyond the limits of his theory; including him in the team would be a disaster.

The winger was Garrincha, who ran the Soviets ragged, went on to make two goals in the final, and dominated the finals four years later. And the other player?

'Obviously infantile,' said the good doctor. 'Lacks the necessary fighting spirit. Too young to feel the aggressions and respond with the proper force to make a good forward. Does not have the feeling of responsibility so necessary for team play. Should definitely not play.'

He definitely did. Like Garrincha, he hit the bar against the USSR. Then he scored the only goal of the game in the quarter-finals, a hat-trick in the semi, and twice in the final. Pelé had arrived. The psychologist departed.

> *I have other irons in the fire, but I'm keeping them close to my chest.*
>
> **JOHN BOND**

Before the 1970 World Cup finals, a number of English pundits were scathing about Brazil's chances. Eric Batty, for instance, the opinionated *World Soccer* columnist, wrote that unlike 'more gullible' observers, he'd noticed serious weaknesses in Carlos Alberto at right-back and Gérson and Rivelino in midfield.

Other, more expert witnesses thought much the same. Although England had lost 2–1 in the Maracaná in 1969, Francis Lee thought that, 'Defeated though we were, I think this game showed us one thing, that Brazil would not be a problem to us, and my immediate reaction was that I wished I could stand all the bets laid on Brazil to win the World Cup...with their suspect temperament they were not a team that deserved to carry a ha'penny of anybody's money in the World Cup.'

Later, before the finals themselves, Alan Ball seemed to be of much the same mind, though he was less long-winded about it: 'We'll beat these.'

Brazil beat England on the way to winning the World Cup. Rivelino scored three fulminating goals in the finals, Gérson and Carlos Alberto both scored in the final itself.

> ## Everything in our favour was against us.
>
> **DANNY BLANCHFLOWER**.

When Terry Venables' bright young Crystal Palace side won the Second Division title in 1979, they were rather predictably hailed by many (in print, too) as the Team of the Eighties.

That first season back in the top flight, they finished 13th. When they lost nine of their first ten matches the following year, Venables left for QPR. Palace returned to the Second Division at the end of the season and didn't come back up till 1989. They reached the FA Cup final for the first time in their history in 1990. Nobody called them the Team of the Nineties.

Frederick Wall was FA secretary for 39 years. Too many. Praised for his organisation skills, he was nevertheless surely an anachronism, the man chiefly responsible for banning two great players, Charlie Roberts and Billy Meredith, for their union activities. Wall, who belonged to a different, amateur era, was behind the times in any number of ways. Take this, from 1935:

'I cannot easily predict an era when the sorcerers of science may easily turn night into day as they now talk to a man on the other side of the world.'

To translate: he was saying that most clubs would never install floodlights.

After joining Arsenal, the great Alex James became almost exclusively a midfield provider rather than a goalscorer. In 1934–35, for instance, he managed only five all season. But three of those came in the 4–1 home win over Sheffield Wednesday, whose manager Billy Walker had told his team to forget about James the goalscorer and mark the men he was inevitably going to pass to. It was his only hat-trick in first-class football.

At the beginning of 1981–82, Stoke City manager Richie Barker told his unsettled forward Adrian Heath that 'If you want another job it will be outside football.'

Within six months, Heath had moved to Everton, with whom he won the FA Cup and League title.

When QPR manager Tommy Docherty signed David McCreery for £200,000 in 1979, he was sure that 'At today's prices I have the bargain of the century.' McCreery played 57 league games for Rangers, scoring four goals, before moving to the USA.

Before the England–Germany semi-final in Euro 96, the *Daily Mirror* ran a front page featuring photographs of two England players superimposed on helmets, with the headline: 'Achtung! Surrender! For you, Fritz, ze Euro 96 is over.'

England's defeat sent Fritz into his fifth European Championship final, while Tommy has yet to appear in one.

Foot in mouth

Slips of the tongue and famous last words

After Ipswich lost 9–0 at Old Trafford in March 1995, Alan Shearer jokingly informed the TV millions that there were no more easy matches 'except perhaps Ipswich Town at home' – words which came back with a vengeance the following season when Blackburn (Shearer included) lost 1–0 at home to Ipswich in the FA Cup.

The prospect of facing Ipswich at home has Alan Shearer heading for a fall

FA chairman Bert Millichip once asked a journalist who 'that big chap standing over there' could be. It was the England captain Tony Adams. In January 1994, Millichip said that Terry Venables had 'a funny reputation' and would be appointed England manager 'over my dead body'. Well, he was 79 at the time...

Ronnie Allen, who was 53, said the same thing in October 1981 about Bryan Robson's rumoured move to Manchester United. 'Over my dead body,' swore the West Brom manager – a sentiment echoed by his chairman, none other than B Millichip, who announced that Robson was 'the one player who is not for sale at any price'.

Robson joined United that very month.

When Howard Kendall was made manager of Notts County in January 1995, chairman Derek Pavis went on television to say that no County supporter could possibly find fault with the appointment. 'I might just have done it this time.'

He certainly had. Kendall lasted ten weeks before being fired 'because of the way the club was being run'. They finished bottom and were relegated to the Second Division.

When Steve McMahon became Swindon Town's player-manager in November 1994, he decided the team's attitude on the pitch needed some of the attributes he'd always shown as a player. 'No more nicey nicey stuff...I'm looking for a team which fights...I don't mind if we pick up a few yellow cards.

McMahon gathered a few himself. Two in his first match, in fact, which led to his sending off. He was sent off again in April, a month before Swindon were relegated for the second year in a row.

Trevor Francis wins the 1979 European Cup in the gran manner

Despite the Italian surname and London birthplace, Terry Mancini was one of the earliest players picked for the Republic of Ireland because his father was born there. It's said that as he lined up for his first international, in 1973, he turned to Paddy Mulligan and ventured something along the lines of 'This bleedin' Polish anthem goes on a bit, doesn't it?' Hush, said the Irish captain. It's our anthem they're playing.

Just before the 1979 European Cup final, Brian Clough was derisory about Trevor Francis' ability in the air: 'My granny heads the ball better than Trevor.' Francis scored the only goal of the final. With his head.

The following year, Clough was at it again. Before the FA Cup final, he aired the view that Trevor Brooking 'floats like a butterfly, and stings like one.' Brooking (stung into

Ferruccio Valcareggi was Italy's manager when they won the 1968 European Championship and reached the World Cup final two years later – which redeemed his reputation somewhat.

As assistant manager in the 1966 finals in England, sent to watch Italy's next opponents North Korea, he described them on his return as *una squadra di Ridolini*, a team of clowns.

The Koreans' famous 1–0 win knocked Italy out of the tournament.

An exchange between two Labour MPs as transcribed for Hansard:

Bruce Grocott: Who could forget the 1953 Stanley Matthews cup final...?
Dennis Skinner: What was the score?
Bruce Grocott: Three-two.

[Blackpool beat Bolton 4–3.]

Don Revie once invited John Robertson for a get-together with about eighty other England possibles – even though Robertson was a Scot. Much the same happened to Newcastle United manager Gordon Lee, who wanted to recommend Aidan McCaffrey for the Republic of Ireland squad, only to be told that McCaffrey wasn't Irish.

What? frowned Lee. How dare he have a name like McCaffrey and not be Irish?

Well boss, said his chief striker, my name's Malcolm Macdonald and I'm not Scottish.

Well, you shouldn't be allowed to play for England with a name like that.

Excuse me boss, ventured another player, but are you Chinese?

When he was at Charlton Athletic, Malcolm Allison was drafted in to mark England

action?) scored the only goal of the game, again with a header.

Just before travelling to an FA Cup match in 1971, Coventry City manager Noel Cantwell stirred things a little by asking, 'Where *is* Rochdale?'

He found out soon enough: his First Division team lost 2–1 to the Third Division side.

centre-forward Roy Bentley – and did such a good job that manager Jimmy Seed told him he was the centre-half they'd been looking for all this time.

Allison had been with the club for five years.

Just before selling Gazza to Lazio, Tottenham manager Terry Venables spelled out exactly how he saw the future of things: 'One of the further conditions...is that a key player, P Gascoigne Esq, will not be transferred.'

> *In a European tie both legs are equally important, if not more important than each other.*
>
> **COLIN CALDER**

Arthur Ellis, one of the leading referees of his time (1952 FA Cup final, 1956 European Cup final), had little regard for the way papers like the *News Chronicle* awarded points to each player in League matches. 'I cannot believe that one reporter...can judge accurately the performances of 22 players and the referee.'

Taking the *News Chronicle*'s football writer John Camkin to task over this in a radio interview, he said bluntly that journalists didn't know what they were talking about. About time some of them took the referees' exam.

'I have,' said Camkin.

On the BBC's comedy sports quiz programme *They Think It's All Over*, actor Rory McGrath, trying to elicit the answer John Daly from his team captain Gary Lineker, gave him the clue 'Golfer. Happens every day.' Lineker's response: 'Weekly.'

The Sun, which hounded Bobby Robson through much of his time as England manager (they offered badges urging 'Robson Out Clough In'), were unequivocal after England's first match of the 1990 World Cup finals: 'The Sun speaks its mind: Bring them home.'

After the win over Belgium which ensured a place in the quarter-finals, the tone had changed somewhat: 'We never seriously doubted England's chances of clawing their way through the World Cup field.'

By the end of the tournament, the U-turn was complete: 'Around Gazza and his young gang we can build a team to win the world. Four years on, remember you read it here first.'

Let's see what those badges say now. England didn't qualify for the finals in 1994.

After scoring on his England debut, against Ireland in 1913, Charlie Buchan overheard one of the linesmen making uncomplimentary observations about his performance. 'So, with the hot-headedness of youth, I told him just what I thought about him.'

The linesman turned out to be a member of the England selection committee, and Buchan had to wait seven years for his next cap.

When goalkeeper Pat Jennings received the Footballer of the Year award in 1973, he tried to use his acceptance speech to thank the Tottenham defenders. We think.

'How could I avoid being player of the year playing behind our defence?'

After the goalless draw at Anfield in the European Cup semi-final of 1981, Bayern Munich's famous midfielder Paul Breitner accused Liverpool of having played 'unintelligent football', adding that English football was unimaginative and predictable – with the inference that Bayern were now sure to reach the final.

Not the smartest remark he ever passed. Kenny Dalglish, for one, was sure that 'no-one should start shouting the odds in the game of football. It has a habit of rebounding on you.'

In the second leg, Liverpool took the lead, went through on the away goal, and won the Cup for the third time. Bayern haven't won it since 1974.

Seven years later, Breitner was at it again. Before the match with Spain in the 1988 European Championship finals, he was scathing about team selection up front: 'West Germany might as well choose the stadium janitor rather than Völler.'

Rüdi Völler scored both goals in the 2–0 win that sent the Germans through to the semi-finals at Spain's expense.

Before the fifth round of the FA Cup in 1971, Colchester United manager Dick Graham was pessimistic about the visit of the mighty Leeds. If his Fourth Division outsiders somehow contrived one of the biggest upsets in Cup history, he said, he'd climb the walls of Colchester castle. They did, and watched while he did.

Norman Burtenshaw, FA Cup final referee in 1971, felt that many professional players had a very limited grasp of the rules of the game. When he gave a goal kick in one First Division match, two international players shouted to a team-mate to move up because he was offside. He reminded them that you can't be offside at a goal kick.

In 1972–73 he sent off Mel Blyth of Crystal Palace for elbowing Everton's Alan Whittle after a free-kick had been awarded. 'How about a penalty?' demanded Everton captain Howard Kendall. Burtenshaw explained that he couldn't give a penalty when the ball was dead.

He had an equally low opinion of those who thought they could read a referee's mind from the commentary box. Kenneth Wolstenholme: 'There's referee Norman Burtenshaw giving Bremner a wigging.' Burtenshaw: 'In fact I never said a word.'

> *But football's not about facts,*
> *it's about what happens.*
>
> **DAVE BASSETT**

At half-time during the home defeat by Bolton in April 1995, Swindon's PA announcer Pete Lewis gave the crowd the benefit of his opinions on the refereeing they'd seen so far – which earned him a warning from a senior policeman and the sack from the club.

After Ian St John had headed the winner in the 1965 FA Cup final, BBC radio announced that the goal had been scored by Sinjun! Oh, and during the 1966 FA Cup final, Kenneth Wolstenholme famously insisted on pronouncing the name of Everton goalscorer Mike Trebilcock as 'Trebilco'.

During the 1966 World Cup finals, the England squad were taken on a tour of Pinewood Studios, after which manager Alf Ramsey gave a small speech of thanks. Unfortunately, in front of the team and assorted movie personnel, he referred to the star of the film *You Only Live Twice* as Seen Connery. As befits Bond, the latter kept a commendably straight face, a feat beyond any of the England players. Indeed, Jimmy Greaves said it was the funniest thing he'd ever shawn or heard.

England had had a bellyful of the USSR by the end of the 1957–58 season. The three matches against them resulted in two draws followed by the 1–0 defeat that knocked them out of the World Cup finals.

So when the Soviets came to Wembley early the following season, the scent of vengeance was in the air – but not if the same players were retained. Or so the BBC seemed to think.

Just before the match, their *Sportsview* crew (Ronnie Noble, Paul Fox, Kenneth Wolstenholme) broadcast their idea of an England team – which didn't include England's playmaker in the World Cup, Johnny Haynes. They went so far as cutting a film of Haynes 'to show that I was not really much of a player.'

The *Sportsview* pundits appeared in sackcloth and ashes (yes, literally) after Haynes had scored the first three goals in a 5–0 win.

> *The drought which has plagued Manchester United all season seems to have evaporated.*
>
> **JAMES REEVE**

At the end of 1995–96, after David Beckham (aged 21), Nicky Butt (21), Paul Scholes (21), the Neville brothers (19 & 21) and the venerable Ryan Giggs had helped make Manchester United the first club to win the domestic Double twice, Alan Hansen was reminded on *Match of the Day* of his prediction at the start of the season: 'You win nothing with kids.'

Asa Hartford had a long and successful career, including exactly 50 Scotland caps,

for a man diagnosed as having a hole in his heart. During the 1978 World Cup, David Coleman famously described him as 'a genuine whole-hearted player'.

Oh, and Roy Small once said that 'One of Asa's qualities is not scoring goals.'

When Brian Clough was a player with Middlesbrough, the club didn't realise that it had one of the most ruthless goalscorers in League history on its books – and would have let him go very cheaply if any kind of offer had come along.

Peter Taylor, later his right-hand man in management, then a team-mate at Boro, pressed Clough's case with Harry Storer, once an England international, now the manager at Derby County – and one of the shrewdest football brains in the country.

Well, usually. Even though Taylor protested (at length) that Clough could be bought for a nominal sum, Storer turned him down with 'Sorry, but I haven't a bean' – words that came back to haunt him when Clough scored the fastest 200 goals in League history and helped Sunderland into the First Division while Derby stayed locked in the Second.

After trying for some time to persuade the Scotland international Frank Shaw to join them, Accrington finally offered the amateur a salary of £120 a year (a good living wage in those days). Shaw's reply: 'Dear Sir, on my return from a fortnight's cruise on my yacht...' Instead of joining Accrington, he sailed for India in 1885.

In 1987–88 a young striker scored twice in France's 2–2 draw at Highbury which took them through to the European Under-21 Championship final at England's expense. However, he didn't play in the decider, in which France beat Greece 3–0 on aggregate, after coming to some singular, and now famous, conclusions about national team manager Henri Michel:

'I would like it to be known that I think he is one of the most incompetent managers in world football. I am not far from thinking that he is a shitbag.'

In no uncertain terms, Eric Cantona had arrived.

As Cantona prepared to take a penalty in the 1994 FA Cup final, he says Chelsea captain Dennis Wise tried to put him off by betting him £100 he'd miss. He didn't, with this or another penalty five minutes later. United won 4–0.

After scoring from a long-range free-kick in the 1987 FA Cup quarter-final, Glenn Hoddle went on record as saying that 'I just went up and twatted the ball' – which made fellow *Top Of The Pops* star Chris Waddle wince: 'The word has a totally different meaning in the North-east.'

Before the 1994–95 season, a leading yearbook wrote of a foreign striker that 'His only weakness is a rather tame right foot,' which came as a surprise once the player in question started dominating BBC's Goal of the Month. It was written about Tony Yeboah.

Stefan Effenberg was just about the least popular footballer in Bundesliga history, heckled even when he was playing for Germany. Hardly surprising, given his penchant for utterances like 'Bayern will win the championship [in 1990–91] because the others are too stupid.' Kaiserslautern won the title.

Effenberg was dropped from the national team for making gestures to the crowd during the 1994 World Cup finals.

> *The Brazilians aren't as good as they used to be, or as they are now.*
>
> **KENNY DALGLISH**

When Jim Smith became the new manager at Birmingham City, the first thing he was asked by one of the players, Archie Styles, was would bonuses still be paid to injured players like himself? He wasn't at the club long enough to get an answer!

During the early 1960s, there was a spate of thieving from the Manchester United changing room. Matt Busby took personal charge of unmasking the culprit – then, when the affair had been satisfactorily concluded, mentioned at a staff meeting that it was good riddance to 'the nigger in the woodpile' – a reference which can't have gone down well with Denis Walker, a black player on the United books.

Writing wrongs

Did Kenny Dalglish move 'upstairs' at Blackburn because football had fallen way down his list of interests? *Ceefax* in September 1995: 'Dalglish missed Saturday's defeat by Liverpool – their fourth in six League matches – to attend a weeding.'

In February 1995 a *Times of Zambia* headline declared 'Charlton disowns Cantona' above two photos. The one captioned Charlton was a picture of Cantona, the one captioned Cantona a mugshot of Bobby Moore!

The 1973–74 edition of *Rothmans Football Yearbook* announced the appointment of 'Leslie Lawrie, the former West Ham goalkeeper' as Millwall's trainer-coach. He was probably used to this versa vice by now; his name's Lawrie Leslie.

Kevin Keegan's been married to Jean and only Jean since 1974. Or has he? The Newcastle Christmas *Football Pink* in 1994: 'Newcastle United manager Kevin Keegan will take his players, wives, girlfriends and kids to the chairman's Christmas party.'

West Ham were relegated from the top flight in 1991–92 – and no wonder. The *Malta Times* reported that when they played Chelsea they 'lost 32–1 to make relegation little more than a formality.'

Hands up if you're getting enough – Tony Gale holds it aloft

Tony Gale had his own explanation for the Hammers' poor form. His column, Galey's Gossip, in the *Ilford Recorder:* 'Since that brief good run in November we have not been having it off, collectively or individually.'

Gary Lineker's reputation as a goalscorer isn't in much doubt. The only player to become First Division leading marksman with three different clubs, scorer of 48 goals for England, including ten in World Cup finals, etc etc.

Not that you'd know it by reading the *TV Times* in September 1995: 'His seventeen years in the game spanned five clubs, three countries, two World Cups, and 30 goals in 655 games.'

'The home side were perilously close to an equaliser in the 75th minute when Benjamin sent an overhead kick against the food on Pears' right-hand post.' *Middlesbrough Evening Gazette*.

'It'll take me a week to read the new-look bumper Mirror Sport.' *Mark Lawrenson*.

Under the headline Fatima Retires, a 1992 edition of the *Norwich Evening News* announced the retirement of javelin thrower Fatima Whitbread – and printed a picture of Norwich manager Dave Stringer.

'Hartlepool extended their winning run to six games with this draw.' *The Sunday Post*.

'Once I am settled in, I will get better and the fans will really see my fly.' *Ricky Otto*.

The *Colchester Evening Gazette*: 'Tony English poked home an inch-perfect Chris Fry for number two.'

During the 1877 FA Cup final, Wanderers keeper Arthur Kinnaird stepped back over the line after catching the ball. Referee SH Wright rightly awarded Oxford University the

goal, extra time was played, and the Wanderers won 2–1.

Nothing unusual in all that – but after the game Kinnaird, who was on the FA committee, succeeded in having his own goal deleted from the books. Indeed, for more than a century the result appeared as 2–0 in FA records, even though extra time wouldn't have been played if Kinnaird's goal hadn't been scored!

> *And I honestly believe we can go all the way to Wembley unless somebody knocks us out.*
>
> **DAVE BASSETT**

This wasn't by any means the only omission from early record books. A number of players, for instance, were left out of lists of international caps. Some of them are still missing.

The leading modern yearbooks took a while to restore the names of Welshmen like Phil Griffiths, Jack Edwards and Ralph Jones – and while they can be excused for still excluding one of the Robert Robertses (there were four!), it's time something was done about the most neglected of them all, the unfortunate Willie Gordon.

A strong rugged full-back typical of the time, he won six caps for Ireland from 1891 to 1893. There are no doubts about this: he's mentioned by christian name in several newspapers of the period and was actually captain against England in 1892.

Unfortunately for his place in posterity, Willie G had two brothers who also played for Ireland: Tom, who was a goalkeeper and therefore not a problem – and Hugh, who was a decided pest.

The latter, capped from 1895 to 1896, was a full-back like his brother – and statisticians of the time added Willie's caps to his total. A full century later, even though Willie was 'rediscovered' several years ago, the two players are still rolled into one in yearbooks and almanacs. Let's hear it at last: Free Willie.

This kind of error has dogged reference books since they were first written, too many to list here – so we'll confine ourselves to one more.

When Howard Kendall (1964) and Paul Allen (1980) played in the FA Cup final, they were fêted as the youngest players ever to appear in the famous showpiece. Neither ever was.

Kendall was 17 years 345 days, Allen 17 years 256 days. But James Frederick McLeod Prinsep was 17 years 245 days when he played for Clapham Rovers in the 1879 final – and only a week older when he played against Scotland the same year, the youngest player (not Duncan Edwards) to win a senior England cap.

> *Sadly the immortal Jackie Milburn died recently.*
>
> **CLIFF MORGAN**

When looking for a translator for their official report on the 1950 World Cup final, the Brazilians unfortunately found someone with little understanding of English idiom. Here's the description, word for word, of the USA's shock winner against England:

'At the 38th minute, Edward Souza gives a violent shoot, Williams succeeds on the defence, but is overthrown by John Souza, who was following the move, and probably not resisting the impact, he loses the equilibrium and falls down surpassing the goal line. The goal of the United States side was scored.'

What actually happened was that Walter Bahr (not Ed Souza) crossed, and Joe Gaetjens (not John Souza) headed past Bert

Williams – but why let facts spoil such a vivid scene?

Because Liverpool had beaten Crystal Palace 9–0 in September 1989, when the two clubs met in the FA Cup semi-final later that season the *Sunday Correspondent* felt it safe to include, in its TV listings: '3pm. Match of the Day, the Road to Wembley, highlights (i.e. the Liverpool goals).'

Liverpool did indeed score goals, three of them – but a season's a long time in football, and Palace were much improved. They won 4–3 to reach the final for the only time in their history. Liverpool won the League, leaving captain Alan Hansen to reflect ruefully that 'We're forever blowing Doubles.' Meanwhile the *Correspondent* soon went out of circulation.

An *Independent* press release once advertised a video promising more than 300 goals, including BBC Premier League goals of the month and others by 'a wealth of world class players' including Cantona, Baggio, Giggs, Yeboah – and some interesting misspellings: Klinsman, Stoichkof, Dimitresku and (most indecipherable of all) Hontleg.

Al Ahram in February 1991 mentioned the Liverpool goalkeeper Joe Webler – which must be the most impenetrable spelling of Grobbelaar so far.

In September 1991 the Bolton Wanderers manager announced that three of his players had recovered from or were still suffering from injuries: Michael Brown (groin), Mark Winstanley (back) and Tony Kelly (keen). Whether the latter ever recovered from the bout of eagerness was never explained.

Is this where Eric Cantona got his reference to seagulls and sardines? The *Independent* in February 1991: 'Overwhelmingly the biggest sport in South Africa, football is in the vanguard of change and a coelacanth, that species of fish presumed extinct but which abruptly got netted off the coast.'

'There are no easy games and if you take liberties with any opposition they will pull your trousers down.' *West Ham v Oxford United programme.*

'The chairman has been absolutely magnificent...all along I have had nothing other than 10 percent support.' *Everton v Leeds United programme.*

'Brentford Reserves were involved in a nine-goal thriller when they beat Orient 4–3 on Wednesday.' *Ealing Gazette.*

'Harry McNally has recently been in hospital and I hope today's game does not help to improve his health.' *Bury v Chester City programme.*

'Phil Alexander and Derek Cottrell are still battling against full fitness.' *Wokingham Town programme.*

FUNNY MONEY (1). 'The Main Stand is finally to come down. In its place, a new £5.35 complex is to be erected.' *Leicester City v Bristol City programme.*

FUNNY MONEY (2). 'Welsh international midfield player Pembridge cost £1.25 from Luton Town.' *Derby Evening Telegraph.*

'Police made six arrests – two for coin-throwing, two more for racial abuse aimed at the Gunners' black strikers Ian Wright and Kevin Campbell, a drug-pusher and a drunk.' *Yorkshire Post.*

'Patrick Kluivert faces a charge of causing death by wreckless driving.' *World Soccer*

In December 1988, *Post Sport* announced that Burnley had lost to Futcher [*sic*] 46–5 in the FA Cup (half-time 78–2) and that one of Burnley's goals was scored by Scunthorpe.

When Doncaster Rovers sacked Joe Kinnear after only three months in 1989, *Football Monthly* gave the club its Black Mark for August – then referred to him as Roy Kinnear, who was not only a comic actor but had been dead for some time.

The *Malay Mail* once printed their choice of the three best Liverpool teams, with the managers they played under: Shankly, Paisley and Dalglish, who were all pictured. Unfortunately, instead of Bob Paisley they showed a photo of the Reverend Ian.

When Tottenham beat Newcastle United 2–0 at White Hart Lane in 1988, the head-line in the *Sunday Post* announced, rather mysteriously, Woodley Sinks His Old Mates. The match details showed Woodley scoring

Looking the part? The Arsenal Tony Adams adopts a theatrical pose

in the 31st minute, and the main copy mentioned 'ex-Newcastle player Chris Woodley'. Could this be who we thought it was? Ah yes, just about: 'Brilliant Chris Waddell created the chance for a third goal.' Meanwhile the Newcastle sub was listed as Liam O'Brady.

In 1993 the *Peterborough Evening Telegraph* announced that Tony Adams would be helping raise funds for a charity appeal. Not Tony Adams the Arsenal captain but Tony Adams who played Adam Chance in *Crossroads*. They printed a picture next to the article – of the Arsenal Tony Adams not the Adam Chance Tony Adams.

In March 1989, above the caption 'Gordon Strachan puts his name on the dotted line as a delighted Leeds manager Howard Wilkinson looks on', *Today* showed a picture of Frank McAvennie playing for Celtic, with Wilko nowhere to be seen.

ALL FOREIGNERS LOOK ALIKE TO ME (1): The *Daily Mirror* once marked the appointment of Carlos Alberto as Brazil's manager by printing a photo captioned 'Alberto: New boss' – but showed a smiling Carlos Alberto Torres, the 1970 World Cup winning captain, instead of Carlos Alberto Parreira, the 1994 World Cup winning coach. CA Torres is black, CA Parreira isn't and has a moustache.

ALL FOREIGNERS LOOK ALIKE TO ME (2) *[a.k.a. Wish I Hadn't Said That (1)]*: This from Barry Davies, who watched the 1966 North Koreans in training and 'they all looked the same – short and yellow.'

ALL FOREIGNERS SOUND ALIKE TO ME (3) *[a.k.a. Wish I Hadn't Said That (2)]*: George Best on the 1966 World Cup finals: 'We had the great Italians being beaten by some unknown team that read like a convention of Chinese launderers.'

The Hammer, October 1988: 'Steve Bould came back into the side at Hull City – his second appearance since his £39,000,000 transfer from Stoke.'

Small wonder Colin Addison and Ron Atkinson didn't last any longer than the other managers who suffered Jesús Gil's presidency at Atlético Madrid – the language barrier stretched as far as Colombia, where the *Diario del Caribe* called them Collin Adrison and – intoxicating, this – Rum Kinkoson.

In one of its Golden Goof features, *Match* magazine showed a photo which had appeared in one of the national dailies: 'Here's today's Golden Goof. It's a Glynn Snodin picture with a Derek Mountfield caption, spotted in 'Today.'

A slip by *Today* – but a positive pratfall by *Match*. It was a shot of *Ian* Snodin.

'Lamptey also notched a last-minute Villa equaliser, beating several defenders in a great run only to put his shot just wide of the post.' *Birmingham Evening Mail*.

In April 1989 the *Bournemouth Evening Echo* rushed three quotes into print. 'Goals change games,' pronounced Leeds United manager Howard Wilkinson. Who could disagree? Certainly not Bournemouth manager Harry Redknapp: 'Goals change matches' or his midfield hard man Tony Pulis: 'Goals change matches.'

Some guys have all the luck. *The FA Cup Non-League Giant-Killers Annual*: 'Chris Kelly...jinxed his way through to equalise.'

'The Somerset side enjoyed the better of this goalless draw and with more adventure they might have grabbed all six points.' *Bristol Evening Post*.

'It wasn't until ninety minutes from the final whistle that we definitely smashed the Hampden bogey.' *Stanley Matthews*

> *This top of the table clash between Chelsea in second place and Manchester United in ninth.*
>
> **ALAN GREEN**

To celebrate Euro 96 being held in England, the Royal Mail brought out a set of stamps honouring famous British footballers. The 19p stamp features Dixie Dean, the 25p Bobby Moore, the 41p Billy Wright, and the 60p Danny Blanchflower.

But the 35p, while using Duncan Edwards' name on the caption, shows an illustration of Bobby Charlton. A youthful Charlton, with a full head of hair, but definitely him and not Edwards. Sir Bobby thus becomes the first living person, monarchs apart, to be commemorated on a British stamp. Footballing royalty alright – and a genuine collectors' item.

After the death of the legendary Herbert Chapman in 1934, Arsenal received more than two hundred applications for the manager's job, including one which made intriguing reading, from a trainer who claimed to be fitter than any of his players. The club might just have been interested if the letter hadn't ended with the boast that he could run a mile in three and a half minutes!

> *Peter Ward has become a new man. Just like his old self.*
>
> **JIM ROSENTHAL**

For years it was taken as read that the fastest goal ever scored in British first-class football was by Jim Fryatt of Bradford Park Avenue against Tranmere Rovers in 1964: a mere four seconds according to referee RJ Simons' watch.

Now, four seconds is just about feasible – if one player taps the ball to another from the kick-off and the second man hits it more or less straight away. However, it transpires that this didn't quite happen in Fryatt's match. It was he who kicked off – and by the time he shot past the keeper, he'd run nearly forty yards and the ball had been touched by four of his team-mates!

Those four seconds have been quietly forgotten, and the 'official' record is now a whopping six seconds. For the time being.

Just before Daniel Amokachi joined Everton in 1994, *The Guardian* wrote that he was only 5ft 6in, which would have surprised a few of the defenders who've had to mark him, in the Premiership or the last World Cup. He's 5ft 10in and over 13 stone.

George Best in 1968: 'I cannot picture myself getting old. The more I think about old age the more I find an uneasy desire to die peacefully in my sleep around the forty mark. Old age? Ugh!'

George Best is 50.

Index

Acknowledgments for Illustrations

Allsport UK Ltd
Shaun Botterill 17, 82, 148 (left)
David Cannon 96, 117
Chris Cole 7, 124
Mike Hewitt 29, 171
Steve Morton 68
Mark Pain 116
Ben Radford 148 (right)
Billy Stickland 79
Anton Want 70, 93

Colorsport pp 14, 24, 34, 42, 60, 72, 100, 106, 121, 130-1, 151

Hulton-Getty Library 67

Popperfoto pp 19, 36, 37, 38, 41, 49, 50-1, 57, 76, 81, 88-9, 95, 105, 113, 118, 134-5, 138-9, 142, 154, 158-9, 162, 166, 168, 172-3, 178, 182